Routledge Revivals

Social Dance

Originally published in 1963 and authored by the then Editor of the *Dancing Times*, this was a pioneer work discussing not only the origins and development of many social dance forms from early times, but also relating these forms to their environment. As well as its role in social history, the book analyses the role of dance as a prime creative power in Renaissance spectacles which depicted and celebrated diplomatic, military and regal occasions. After a wide-ranging introductory chapter on the origins of dancing, the book takes the reader through the centuries, discussing in turn the Basse Danse and the Moresco of the Middle Ages the Pavane, Galliard and Courante of the 16th Century, the Minuet of the 17th & 18th, the Allemande, the Waltz and the Polka as well as Jazz, the Cha Cha Cha, the Jive and Twist.

Social Dance
A Short History

A.H.Franks

First published in 1963
by Routledge & Kegan Paul

This edition first published in 2021 by Routledge
2 Park Square, Milton Park, Abingdon, Oxon, OX14 4RN
and by Routledge
605 Third Avenue, New York, NY 10158

Routledge is an imprint of the Taylor & Francis Group, an informa business

© 1963 A.H. Franks

All rights reserved. No part of this book may be reprinted or reproduced or utilised in any form or by any electronic, mechanical, or other means, now known or hereafter invented, including photocopying and recording, or in any information storage or retrieval system, without permission in writing from the publishers.

Publisher's Note
The publisher has gone to great lengths to ensure the quality of this reprint but points out that some imperfections in the original copies may be apparent.

Disclaimer
The publisher has made every effort to trace copyright holders and welcomes correspondence from those they have been unable to contact.
A Library of Congress record exists at LCCN:65000715

ISBN 13: 978-1-032-01262-9 (hbk)
ISBN 13: 978-1-003-17796-8 (ebk)
ISBN 13: 978-1-032-01341-1 (pbk)

DOI: 10.4324/9781003177968

SOCIAL DANCE

A Short History

by

A. H. FRANKS

Routledge and Kegan Paul
LONDON

*First published 1963
by Routledge & Kegan Paul Limited
Broadway House, 68–74 Carter Lane
London, E.C.4
Printed in Great Britain
by Western Printing Services Ltd
Bristol*

© *A. H. Franks 1963*

*No part of this book may be reproduced
in any form without permission from
the publisher, except for the quotation
of brief passages in criticism*

For
Those members of the Official Board of Ballroom Dancing who have voluntarily, behind the scenes, accomplished endless work for the development of ballroom dancing in Britain; and for those members of the International Council of Ballroom Dancing who have worked unceasingly for the promotion of the social dance throughout the world.

Acknowledgements

IN the preparation of a book of this kind debts of gratitude are inevitably owed by the author to a number of people who so gladly devote time, energy and specialized knowledge in helping to track down various kinds of information. Firstly, however, I must express my thanks generally to a number of friends in the small enclosed world of dancing who have encouraged and stimulated me with questions, discussion and sometimes with downright disagreement.

More specifically I am indebted to Mr. Ivor Guest for lending me invaluable material concerning the nineteenth century. Others who have also lent me material are Mrs. Rachel Dickson, Mrs. Olive Ripman, Miss Belinda Quirey and Miss Natalie René. For some research in Paris I am indebted to Madame Lily d'Erlimont. I am also extremely grateful to Miss Beryl Poole for all her practical secretarial help, in the process of which she retyped much of the manuscript a number of times and made a number of invaluable suggestions.

I owe much to all those authors from whose works I have quoted, some of them liberally. In particular I am greatly indebted to Mr. Joseph E. Marks III, whose *America Learns to Dance* was indispensable to my references on the dance across the Atlantic.

Perhaps some readers will be surprised at the absence of footnotes in a book of this kind. The reason is partly that I have developed a prejudice against them by virtue of the fact that a number of dance books endow themselves with a false impression of scholarship through too many footnotes; and partly that I believe references can usually with advantage be shown in parentheses in the text itself.

Contents

	ACKNOWLEDGEMENTS	*page* vii
I	INTRODUCTION Sources and Beginnings	1
II	THE FIFTEENTH CENTURY The Development of Technique and Some Early Dance Literature	26
III	THE SIXTEENTH CENTURY The Teachings of Arbeau and Others	53
IV	THE SEVENTEENTH CENTURY The Minuet and a Variety of Forms	73
V	THE EIGHTEENTH CENTURY The Growing Technique	101
VI	THE NINETEENTH CENTURY Revolutions and Scandals—and the Birth of a New Style	123
VII	THE TWENTIETH CENTURY Jazz and After	159
	APPENDICES	196
	INDEX	227

Plates

(Between pages 68 and 69)

1. Most of our scanty knowledge of the dances of classical Greece derives from low reliefs and paintings on vases
2. Roman Pantomimes caught by the sculptor in dancing pose
3. Botticelli's famous painting of the Nativity
4. Reproduction from one of the drawings from the Roman de la Rose
5. An engraving from a painting by Israel van Meckenham
6. Queen Elizabeth dancing La Volta with the Earl of Leicester
7. A painting by Giulio Romano
8. A contemporary artist's impression of the Duc de Joyeuse' Ball in 1581
9. Two reproductions from *Nuove Inventione di Balli* by Cesare Negri
10. Two reproductions from illustrations in Antonio Cornazano's Treatise
11. David Teniers' *The Village Wedding*
12. King Charles II dancing with his sister, Mary Princess of Orange (*Reproduced by gracious permission of Her Majesty the Queen*)
13. Antoine Wattau's *The Pleasures of the Ball*
14. From an engraving in Kellom Tamlinson's book *The Art of Dancing*
15. A painting by William Hogarth inspired by the Wanstead Assembly
16. An engraving from Hogarth's *The Analysis of Beauty*

(Between pages 132 and 133)

17. Le Bal Paré, Paris 1773
18. Francis Heyman's *Dance of the Milkmaids*
19. Twelve figures from the Allemande reproduced in a book by Simon Guillaume
20. An impression of the Cotillon by a contemporary artist
21. A ball dress featured in the *Illustrated London News* in 1844
22. This is how the Polka was first featured in the *Illustrated London News*

PLATES

23. Three pictures of the Polka from the *Illustrated London News* of May 11th, 1844
24. A contemporary artist's impression of the Pytchley Hunt Ball, Northampton in 1844
25. The Caledonian Ball of 1844 at the Hanover Square Rooms
26. Le Bal de l'Opéra à quatres Heures du Matin, from a drawing by Gustave Dor
27. Le Bal du Château des Fleurs from a drawing by Gustave Doré
28. Another Paris dance hall of the late eighteenth century, le Prado d'Hiver
29. A Paris dance scene in the open air from *Views of Paris*
30. A contemporary artist's impression of one of the figures from the Contredanse
31. Reproduction from an aquatint by Isaac Roberts and George Cruikshank, showing a set of Lancers
32. A Ball in progress at the Argylle Rooms, from an engraving by Robert Cruikshank

(Between pages 164 and 165)

33–35. Reproductions from Laborde's book on the Cotillon
36. Three reproductions from Edward Scott's book *Dancing as an Art and Pastime*
37–38. Reproductions from *The Tango and How to Dance It* by Gladys Beattie Crozier
39. The actual 'hesitation' in the Hesitation Waltz
40. A figure in the one step
41. The Tango. Note that Castle actually has his hand in his pocket
42–43. These two pictures show clearly the diversity of holds
44. The Castle Walk
45. The final of the International Professional Championship
46. Sonny Binick and Sally Brock
47. A formation team at the end of its performance
48. At the Winter Gardens Blackpool every year the most important championships, known as the British, are held

CHAPTER I

Introduction

SOURCES AND BEGINNINGS

The dance is godlike in itself. It is a gift from heaven.
PLATO

PRIMITIVE man is frequently attributed with any number of instincts and attributes which he may or may not have possessed. As far as his dance is concerned everything written about it is a matter for little more than mere conjecture. We have no knowledge whatever of the precise nature of the dance of any period or of any people before the fifteenth century; and even then a great deal of that knowledge is at the outset far from certain. All that we can assume is that every age since the birth of man has been characterized and symbolized by some kind of dance. In fact the whole development of dance depends upon the constantly changing points of view which have affected man's ideals and emotions rather than a mere description of the steps and techniques of the forms of dance in each period. Academic historians have ignored the dance in their researches presumably because of the impossibility of obtaining knowledge as accurate as in other forms of past human activity, for although there have been many efforts to record human movement, even in primitive times, none of them has been comprehensive and few successful, even within their own limitations, until the twentieth century.

Before we proceed further perhaps a definition of our subject is needed. In all its ramifications dance can be defined as rhythmic human movement performed as an outlet for or an expression of ideas or emotions. But rhythmic human movement covers a wide field and our immediate conception of it will vary according to our own outlook and in what part of the world we were born. In parts of the West, for example, our movements are largely governed by our legs with the arms and head, generally speaking, playing a more or less subordinate role. In parts of the East, on the other hand, the arms and body have for centuries been the dominating factor, with the feet providing no more than the support and perhaps the underlying rhythm. The range of movement, then, is enormous; so are the various causes of dance. One of the most primitive causes, a cause which grows weaker in proportion to the civilization of any people, are those powerful emotional reactions which result among primitive people to spontaneous muscular activity. Far removed from this, one of the most sophisticated causes is the constant demand of advanced cultures for forms of expression created by one mind for others to enjoy; this results in combinations of movements being imposed on the performers for the pleasure of spectators. This in turn leads to meticulously trained performers who execute movements imposed upon them in the execution of which they themselves do not necessarily experience any emotional response. Between these two extremes are many different degrees of personal and vicarious participation.

In spite of our limited knowledge of his activities there is little doubt that for primitive man the dance served the vital function of expressing every conceivable kind of emotion; his reaction to the birth of an heir could be framed in movement just as forcefully as his excitement at the prospect of war with a rival tribe, his exultation at his wedding or at his fearful propitiation of the gods. But he employed the dance for other reasons than the outlet or expression of his emotions; he also sought deliberately by means of dance to identify himself with the objects, both animate and inanimate, of his love, his fear, his admiration, and by this identification either assimilate himself into them or gain absolute power over them. The hunter, for example, danced round the effigy of his prey, and even at times donned the fur of the animal, and by thus impersonating it, mastered it. Many of these primitive forms of dancing, in common with those of certain religious sects today, induced a state of hypnosis or ecstasy, this state itself leading to a further development of spontaneous dance. While dancing round this effigy the hunter would imitate the movements of the animal he wished to conquer, for the mind of the primitive sees everything as a spirit and seeks to subject this spirit to his purposes by means of assimilation. Here surely is the origin of his magic, of the grotesque mask and the primitive costume. In the high artificiality of our own cultures we cannot today appreciate fully the intensity and completeness with which the savage is able to enter into the creations of his own imagination. It is not so difficult to realize, however, that these two distinct forms of dance, that used for the expression of emotion and that for the imitating and assimilating of animals and spirits, running parallel one with the other through history, eventually fused to emerge as a form of theatrical art. At the same time the two distinct forms remained potent in their own right, losing the intensity of their power only with the growth of unbelief and sophistication.

The more cultured a people become the more definite the objects and functions of their activities; whereas primitive peoples are more or less unconsciously motivated, especially in their dances, only some small initial stimulus being necessary to obtain the emotional reaction which in turn begets a muscular response. Following this a chain reaction is set up, each movement creating another without any call upon the will. Indeed, on the contrary, the will is deadened and soon automatism sets up. Dependent upon the excitement of the dancer the speed of movements grows, reducing still further the extent of conscious activity. Taken a stage further the movements become yet more and more repetitive, remaining equal in rhythm, creating the state of hypnosis or ecstasy (often the same thing) to which I have already referred. There can be no doubt whatever that primitive races, whether of the past or of those few remaining in but not of our present civilization, seek to induce this state in themselves by deliberate intention, for it creates a pleasure in them the intensity of which can only be vaguely guessed at by those who have undergone the inhibitions of our advanced civilization.

But of course this expression of the emotions through the dance did not remain for long the prerogative of primitive man. The Athenians of classic Greece certainly could not be regarded as primitive, yet Plato included the dance among the essential accomplishments for the people of his ideal republic, seeing in the pursuit of dance a desirable method 'for the acquisition of noble, harmonious and graceful attitudes'. Socrates recommended the dance to his students and Lycurgus regarded it as highly important in the education of youth. Socrates appears to have put his precept into practice, for he is said to have danced around the trophies after the battle of Salamis. It would be hard today to imagine Lord Russell dancing around the hydrogen bomb.

We know what Socrates said—at least what Plato said he said. If only we knew what and how he danced! It is however safe to assume that the earliest expressive acts of man were random, unorganized movements and equally random, unorganized sounds, although which came first, if either, must remain a question comparable to that of the chicken and the egg. But although his movements and sounds were unorganized they were doubtless made on some basis of rhythm, for all the functions of the human body depend upon a very definite rhythm. Among numerous primitive races today the sounds and movements they make remain inseparable one from the other. As the feet, body and arms move in the dance so the larynx is also set in motion, and frequently the hands clap and the feet stamp to accompany the movement with a different kind of rhythmic sound. This clapping and stamping are undoubtedly the ancestors of the drum and other percussion intruments.

We find therefore that early human movement, other than that of a purely functional kind in the performance of work or play, was either an expression of emotion or some kind of imitation. From his single state man soon developed into groups with the result that individual desires and impulses grew into group activity, widening the range of dance in the process. Although man still continued to express his love, fear, hate, anger in the dance, and to identify himself with creatures he wished to subdue or kill, all this kind of activity now became governed by his identity with a group of like-minded people. Man found that he could relieve his pent up feelings more completely within the activities of a group than he could on his own. This kind of expression took on mostly an exultant nature, as with children; indeed, many of the movement habits of a child can be compared in some details with those of primitive man, for a child, before it acquires self-restraint, will express its joy or anger far more vividly by jumping about and yelling incoherently than by the use of mere words. Taking the comparison further, primitive man possesses the same love of make-believe as the child and by means of the imitative dance identification with that which is imitated is the more readily induced.

As he grew up man developed a sense of discrimination and a deeper power of thought. With these developments in his mental and emotional nature he naturally found other means for the communication of his thoughts and feelings. Music and poetry became the chief instruments for this kind of communication with dance remaining a powerful medium to communicate the unintelligible, the mystic and the religious emotion. But dance led to another development, the emergence of religious drama, which in itself was to lead later into the masque and the secular drama. With the growth of his intelligence man's emotions did not diminish, but his control over them became more effective. Art took over from spontaneous reaction. But still the dance, and other art forms for that matter, had to have some kind of functional value; otherwise they would have disappeared, for nothing survives unless it has this kind of value, no matter how deeply hidden.

Egyptian carvings of 6,000 years ago show that dance at that time played an important part in religious ritual. Doubtless this form of dance was imported into Greece, for Plato came to the conclusion that certain kinds of Egyptian dance symbolized the movements of the stars. As eminent astronomers and astrologers the Egyptians would naturally have been extremely likely to bring this kind of symbolism into their religious observances. Taking Plato's discovery further, later historians formed the theory that in those observances the central altar must have represented the sun and the dancers revolving around the altar the stars.

But it is not possible to take these researches very far, for all that we can trace of ceremonies of that time which included dance or symbolic movement of any kind exists in the few carvings that remain. It is to say the least scanty evidence.

In contrast to the Egyptians, who believed that life on earth was simply a preparation for life in heaven, the Athenians maintained that life in this world was all important, and that in consequence it should be lived fully and abundantly. In this civilization, which has exerted such a profound effect on the intellectual development of the whole christian world, there was, strangely, no fear of god in any christian sense, although there were of course many divinities who had to be placated. The Athenians adulated the beauty of the human form and expressed this adulation in their dance as much as in their sculpture. Alas, while one form of this adulation is kept alive today for all to admire, again the dance historian is completely frustrated, for nothing concrete remains. However, although we do not possess any accurate knowledge of the movements of the dance, it has been possible to gain some conception of them by means of careful study of the Greek vases and freizes which, incidentally, in the opinion of some remain today the finest examples of the expression of movement in the plastic arts. What we are unable to guess with any certainty is where social dance left off and theatrical dance began; not until the seventeenth century in fact, does any clear-cut dichotomy develop between the dance floor and the stage.

The history of the Greek people begins in the isle of Crete and extends from about 3000 years B.C. to about 1200 B.C. The whole of this long period is known as the Minoan age, although the height of its culture lasted a little less that 300 years from 1600 B.C. Ceramics played a vital part in the art life of the people and it is by this means that we obtain most of our sketchy ideas of what their dance forms were like. Frescoes found in the great palace of Knossos, the capital of Crete, include many which show women dancing before the king and his

INTRODUCTION

court. One excavator discovered what he called the dance ground of the princess Ariadne. There was a great deal of Egyptian influence in Crete and one Cretan dance which stemmed from Egypt was the Labyrinth. In it movements of the stars and constellations were demonstrated, probably in almost exactly the same form in which the movements had been executed in Egypt itself. It is however believed that after a while the dance began to change its character in order to conform to the different religious beliefs of the Cretans, who put no credulity in a future life and who worshipped a bull known as Minotaur. What more likely than that the sinuous passages of dance from Egypt should be modified in character to represent the labyrinth which was believed to lead to the sanctuary of the Minotaur?

When Knossos was burnt to the ground by the Greeks the burial dances of the Cretans were firmly established in Greek ritual, taking the form of complicated processional movements and revolutions around an altar. Following this, between 1200 and 1000 B.C., the Greek mainland suffered an invasion from central Europe. The invaders were of an entirely different physique and character from the Greeks, being tall and slender, whereas the natives were short and dark. Their cultures too were quite different; as they settled in the various cities they had conquered they plastered over the wall paintings and replaced them with far more crude drawings of their own. As a fighting race they were infinitely superior, introducing armour in place of the Minoans' costume which consisted of little but a loin cloth. In spite of the inferiority of their plastic art, however, they were lovers of music, and they introduced the lyre into Greece. Homer describes certain dances of this period, some of them being of a gentle nature to be enjoyed by members of both sexes. But the Achaeans also introduced the war dance into Greece as well as a new kind of religion which recognized the gods and goddesses of the celestial sphere. With the blend of the northern people, warlike and athletic, and the people of the south, emotional and superstitious, came the birth of Greek poetry and a form of dance to match the outlook. In the Dorian period, during which this outlook developed its highest culture, came the marriage of great sculpture and architecture, and probably painting, with the pursuit of the physical ideal. The handsome Apollo, in addition to this ideal of physical beauty, also represented law and order as well as music and poetry. Physical culture became a vital feature of education both for children and adults, and naturally the dance played its part in this kind of education. Apollo himself, speaking through the mouths of his priestesses, is said to have laid down some of the rules of the dance.

Plato, less than a century after the Dorian era, included the dance among the requisites for his ideal republic, proclaiming its godlike, gracious and harmonious qualities. Socrates too urged his students to dance and physicians were of the opinion that rhythmic physical movement was a cure for certain physical ailments. Lycurgus placed it in his physical training curriculum, and important and distinguished citizens took much pride in their dance skill.

I have already referred to Socrates dancing around the trophies, and he is also said to have danced among his friends after dinner. Both Aeschylus and Aristophanes danced in several performances of their own plays. Professional dancers were as acceptable in society as they are in Russia today, Philip II of Maceda having taken one to wife. The mother of Nicomedes, who became king of Bithynia, was also a dancer of some repute. Through this period in fact the dance was practised by every strata of society, rich and poor, wise and stupid alike. As Ruby Ginner writes in *Gateway to the Dance:*

'The Dorian ideal gave a kind of sanctity to athletics, and to the discipline of the body through physical training. But this was not all, for to the Dorian people the body was capable of expressing not only physical powers, but could through rhythmic movement, give expression to man's mind and spirit, and it was from this idea that the dance took a high place in religious ceremonies. The conception of proportion, balance and restraint which is to be seen in all Dorian art, and the ideal of the human body as the finest work of creation were the contribution of the Dorian era to the culture of Greece. It was this period that paved the way to the ultimate fulfilment of Greek art and life and laid down the foundations of the *Hellenic age* which contained the fifty years known as the golden age of Hellas.'

As far as dance is concerned these conceptions of proportion, balance and restraint, together with the ideal of the human body, led to a division into three classes: sacred, military and profane.

These classes in turn were divided into further groups. The sacred group for example was split into four. The first of these was known as Emmeleia. Some of the dances in this group were grave and noble in character, and were danced for the invocation of the gods. Others in the same group were heroic, stressing the majesty and strength of the people. In this group there was no chorus and no song, a rare omission, for most performances at this time depended on combinations of various forms of expression. Not until much later in western civilization were the arts to be divided into so many separate pigeon holes.

INTRODUCTION

Another group in the religious dances was known as Hyporchema. These did have a choral accompaniment, sometimes song and sometimes poetry. Dignified in nature, they were performed by groups of men and women, chiefly for the purpose of personifying poetic metaphor.

In extreme contrast, but in the same group, were the Gymnopoedia, the dances dedicated to Apollo and especially cultivated in Arcadia. This form was practised chiefly by nude youths who sought by pantomime and movement to represent combat.

The Endymatia consisted of a mixture of sacred and profane. The dances themselves were of a vigorous nature and professionals appeared in them with amateurs. Bright, flowing costumes were worn and from what it is possible to gather today it seems that the form of these dances was of a nature to entertain onlookers as much as for the benefit and pleasure of participants.

Unlike any of these groups was the Pyrrhic dance, which sprang from the need of fighting men to express the heat, fury and excitement of battle. According to Plutarch this form of dance provided ' . . . an indefinable stimulus which inflamed courage and gave strength to persevere in the paths of honour and valour'. Greek law in fact prescribed this form of dance for the soldier, which he was required to practise in full armour. Probably the first form of this kind of war dance was the dance of the Kuretes, which celebrated among other things the birthday of Zeus. In their very fine work *Of Pantomime*, H. W. and F. G. Fowler quoted Lucian on this form of dance:

'The dancing was performed in full armour, sword clashed against shield, and inspired heels beat martial time upon the ground. The art was presently taken up by the leading men in Crete, who by dint of practice became admirable dancers; and this applies not only to private persons, but to men of the first eminence and of royal blood.'

The title Pyrrhic is usually believed to have stemmed from Pyrrhus, son of Schilles, who is claimed to be the originator of this form of dance. A number of contemporary writers, including Homer, refer frequently to it. A soldier by the name of Meriones is said by Homer to have gained such agility through his pursuit of the Pyrrhic dance that he was able to skip out of the way quite easily from spears flung at him in battle.

It is sometimes stated that the Pyrrhic dance emanated in Sparta. Although that claim is not true, the dance certainly established itself firmly in that militant state, becoming an essential feature of the training of the youth and young soldiers. In one form it was danced in honour of the gods and goddesses who were supposed to have brought victory in a particular battle. Surprisingly, in view of its combative nature, another form was danced by Greek maidens; and with the decline of Hellenic ideals round about the end of the fourth century the dance lost its significance, deteriorating into a form which was a fitting accompaniment to the orgies so symptomatic of the decadence into which the great nation had fallen.

Strongly akin to the Pyrrhic dance was the Memphitic dance, the division indeed now being almost completely indefinable. The origin of the Memphitic group is believed to have sprung from Minerva, the legend being that she created this kind of dance for the celebration of the defeat of the Titans. A sword or spear was carried in this dance, together with a shield, and the movements were based on those of actual fighting; cutting and thrusting, parrying and dodging. The dance was probably as realistic as a duel scene in a Shakespeare play when the actors have been coached by a fencing master. The Memphitic dance, however, was a little less concerned with the fighting element than the pyrrhic, and its accompaniment was played by the flute in melodies of considerable tranquillity. This style was in fact more frequently practised by the Greek maidens than the Pyrrhic dance, and a number of young ladies gained high distinction for themselves by virtue of their skill.

But chiefly these dances were practised by boys and young men. It is ironic today when one considers the contumely heaped by the unknowing upon men whose profession is the dance, for the Greeks looked upon it as one of the means by which to obtain the sternest discipline and even to harden their bodies to endure hardship and pain. From about seven years old boys were taught to dance. The movements they learned were mimetic of armed combat, but performed in a rhythmic and stylized manner, so that the movements, musically accompanied, were actually transformed into dance. At first they practised without weapons, but as soon as their bodies had acquired sufficient strength and resilience they were accoutred in full armour.

Of an entirely different character, and in time through their orgiastic nature the most notorious of all ancient dances, were those associated with the name of Dionysus. Also known more familiarly in the west today as Bacchus, he is believed originally to have been a Thraican fertility god who, in the form of a bull, was worshipped by means of orgiastic rites. When he found his way into Greece is not known with any certainty, but his popularity there became widespread (he was

INTRODUCTION

particularly popular with women it seems). Although in classical myths he is the son of Zeus and Semele, he does not appear in Homer as one of the great divinities. He is there however described as the god who teaches the preparation of wine, which would seem in ancient Greece, as much as in twentieth-century Europe, to qualify him for greatness. With these associations Dionysus became the god around which the wine festivals grew gradually more wild and licentious. In most Greek art he is represented in a form which endows his masculine body with an element of feminine softness and roundness. His companions were satyrs and centaurs, and other like creatures, and his followers were mostly women, represented in art and literature by women suffering from an excess of enthusiasm, their heads thrown back, their hair dishevelled and carrying a thyrsus.

It will then be readily believed that the ancient dances concerned with Dionysus or Bacchus were of a wild and passionate nature. According to Ruby Ginner, the origin of these dances lies in:

'The primitive festivals of spring and autumn around the figure of a god who was regarded as the life force of all growth in nature. In those early ages he was represented by a pillar made of a roughly hewn tree, which was decorated with sprays of ivy, bunches of grapes and honeycombs. On the top of this was placed the likeness of a human head. This can have been none other than a tree god, the power of the sap which brings life to the tree in spring, and which, sinking back to the ground in the autumn, leaves the tree lifeless. In the spring season his worshippers danced around him as the giver of life, in the autumn they mourned his death.'

Some dressed themselves up as satyrs, smearing their faces with the lees of wine; others favoured chitons and the skins of animals. In this costume they danced in couples, sometimes facing each other, sometimes in a circle and sometimes in a chain. But in whatever pattern they danced the form of the movement itself was unceasingly ecstatic and at times this movement became so wild that the performers dropped, insensible to the ground. In autumn the dances took the form of pressing the wine, with stamping on the ground in simulation of the act of wine pressing. But the wildest of all the Dionysian festivals was the Thiasus, a form in which only women participated. Taking place at night in the spring, it began with a procession which was accompanied by tambours, pipes and cymbals. Arrived at a suitable clearing the women then began a wild dance, beating upon the earth in order to shake nature from its slumber and then swinging themselves into an

SOURCES AND BEGINNINGS

ecstasy, making up their own figures as they grew more and more frenzied.

This form of dance originated from the desire to achieve spiritual exaltation, but in their search for ecstasy the dancers in time lost the spiritual purpose, with the result that the ecstasy remained only as a means to stir up orgiastic practices.

From the fragments of Greek art left today it is still possible to gain some idea of the form of the movements from the wonderful postures of the performers which contemporary artists froze into their sculptures and freizes. One or two true enthusiasts, notable among them being Ruby Ginner, have made a lifetime study of these fragments and from them have reconstructed a large number of dances. Their problem has largely consisted of how to work out the kind of movement which was made between one posture and the next. In order to do this Miss Ginner and her followers steeped themselves in the lore, history and literature of ancient Greece. They do not claim authenticity for their results, but they have undoubtedly built up fascinating series of dances and a theory of movement which provides thousands of students with an insight into one of the earliest dance forms. These forms undoubtedly influenced the great classical sculptures and set up in the human mind certain ideas about movement patterns in relation to music and rhythm which have influenced the dance through history to the present day.

Just as they copied so much else that they admired in the Greeks, the Romans also emulated their dances. But whereas it is plain that the Greeks created their dances out of their life, and in consequence actually lived in and through the dance, the Romans merely copied the outer form, as they did with Greek scuplture. In the early days of the city, in the time of Romulus, the Romans appear to have danced very little, there being records of only one dance. This was a solemn ritual dance performed by twelve priests known as Salii, the dance thus gaining the title of Salian. Probably all the dances which followed originated in this form, although of course the Greek forms were brought in to vary and renew it. The Romans possessed but little original talent of their own and adopted all the gods and goddesses of Greece, altering only their name into the language of Rome.

The dance of the Salii was in a rhythm of three beats and was in choral form, with a leader whose movements were either copied or 'answered' by others as the groups proceeded in a circle to the beating of shields. Evidently the dance did not suffer from undue complexity.

With the advent of Greek influence, however, round about 200 B.C.

INTRODUCTION

the next period of Roman dance history opens. In fact the arrangements of steps and patterns of the dance itself were influenced by the Etruscans as well as the Greeks, and the dance began to play an ever increasing part in secular—indeed in social—life. Cicero could rail against the dance as much as he liked—he once proclaimed that 'no sober person dances'—but the people found growing fascination in it. In Greece, no matter how secular various forms had become, and how much they were enjoyed at certain festivals, the dance had always had some underlying purpose beyond the pleasure of its participants and observers. Now in Rome, possibly for the first time, the dance became a social activity, pure and simple, without further aims and ideals. At the same time, however various forms retained their original functions of propitiating the gods, inducing fertility or preparing the mind and body of the soldier for combat. But the power of that original function had faded to such an extent that in many cases it was forgotten altogether.

In the reign of Augustus (27 B.C. to A.D. 14) the dance in Rome reached its highest pitch, although in order to reach such a state a number of 'visiting artists' were necessary. At this time there were said to be about three thousand foreign women dancers in the city. At the same time, too, the dance was introduced into the theatre, although there it was more usually in the form of pantomimic dance than pure movement. This pantomimic dance consisted of rhythmical movements of the head, hands and body, and according to contemporary writers the human passions were so eloquently depicted by this means that spectators were frequently moved to tears. It must however be remembered that the auditorium was vast and open and that gesture could therefore often mean a great deal more than speech, which could not be heard.

This kind of mime led gradually to the growth of the Commedia dell'Arte, a combination of mime and dance which was later to be practised throughout Europe by strolling players. On a basis of a few plots these players improvised in mime, movement and song a limitless number of plays in the towns and villages of every country. Although quite distinct from the social dance, and in fact perhaps little to do with dance at all, the highly stylized movements developed by the Commedia undoubtedly played their part in the growth of the balli—the mimetic social dances practised by the patricians of the fourteenth and fifteenth centuries.

Social forms of dance were however highly favoured in Roman society and a dance teacher was included on the staff of most patrician families. Among young girls the dance was considered as desirable an accomplishment as it is today. They were taught both music and dancing, the practice of the latter calling especially for the development of a noble carriage of the body and graceful motion of the arms and hands. The Greek dances, on the other hand, were now danced for the entertainment of onlookers, being performed by slaves or hired men and women. Gradually this form of entertainment grew licentious. Cato as well as Cicero condemned it, considering it immoral for a man to twist his limbs so horribly as was apparently required in this kind of entertainment.

Although no detailed literary records of the dances of either the Greeks or the Romans have come down to us (in spite of many vague if colourful references in contemporary literature) it is possible to state with reasonable confidence that in the mixed dances there was no actual physical contact between men and women. It seems that they often danced quite separately from one another; and at other times, in couple and round dances, simply faced each other without so much as holding hands. Hands were linked, however, as can be seen in a great deal of Greek art, in the chain dances which played an important part of the social terpsichorean scene. A form which we should probably regard today as old-time dance was extremely popular. In the *Iliad* such a dance is described; boys and girls held one another by the wrists and advanced in lines towards one another before retreating; sometimes they were on tip toe and at others not. The *Iliad* here speaks of a large crowd of onlookers and a bard singing and playing his lyre. Apparently two tumblers led the dance, twirling vigorously around.

Undoubtedly too the Greeks and Romans enjoyed the kind of chain dance which we now refer to as the Farandole. A Syrian named Lucian, after spending a number of years in Athens, wrote a book on the Athenian dances. He describes one of these chain dances as follows:

'It is performed by men and girls together, dancing alternately, so as to suggest the alternating beads of a necklace. A youth leads off the dance: his active steps are such as will hereafter be of use to him on the field of battle. A maiden follows with the modest movements that befit her sex; manly vigour, maidenly reserve—these are the beads of the necklace.'

Another dance, this time described in the Homeric Hymn, bears a marked resemblance to that above:

'Also with great skill he made a dancing floor, like that which Deadolos had done in breoad Knossos for blonde Ariadne. These youths and maidens worth many oxen were dancing, holding each other hands by the wrist. Of these some wore delicate linen dresses, and others golden swords hanging from silver belts. At one time they moved rapidly in a circle with cunning feet, reight easily, just as when a potter, seated, tries the wheel fitted to the hand to see whether it runs; at another time they moved rapidly in file. And a great crowd stood round the charming dance, enjoying the spectacle; and among them a divine bard sang to the cithara; and two tumblers, when he began his song, whistled a bout in the middle.'

A number of social dances both in Greece and Rome were inspired by work; others by play and yet others to celebrate the harvest. Some of these dances probably took the form of games, in the same way that the nineteenth-century Cotillon developed, or deteriorated, dependent upon the point of view, into a parlour game.

We need not suppose that the Latin character was less disposed to dramatic mime and gesticulation than it is today. We can therefore reasonably assume that wherever it was possible the Romans either increased the mimetic element in the dances they took from Greece, or even that in some cases they added mime and drama where hitherto these elements were absent. For of all the Mediterranean peoples the Latins remain by far the most demonstrative, their beautiful language still seeming inadequate to express their thoughts and, more important, their emotions.

Although they were concerned with the theatre rather than dance two great Romans so strongly influenced the course of mime that there can be no doubt that they were also indirectly responsible for the form of mime taken by the Commedia and subsequently by the mimetic social dances of the early renaissance. These two, about whom many apocryphal stories are told, were Bathylus and Pylades. So great was the interest in these two, who must be regarded more as actors than dancers, that one writer could say:

'The rivalries of Pylades and Bathyllus occupied the Romans as much as much as the gravest affairs of state. Every Roman was a Bathyllian or a Pyladian.'

It is said that many who went to the Coliseum were so partisan that they used to fight in the streets around the great amphitheatre.

From the dance and mimetic gestures of these two, Pylades apparently being the greater dancer and Bathylus the better mime, stemmed the development of the mimetic and stylistic elements in the social dance, and the conventional mime which finally established itself in the classical ballet.

But the Romans became obsessed by the idea of material power and luxury. Gradually the ideals with which the dance had been invested by the Greeks were lost in the decadence which inevitably attended this material philosophy. There must have been many degrees through which these dances passed, but eventually they were corrupted to such an extent as to remain no more than, at best, a display of physical energy, and at worst exhibitions of obscenity. The sex urge, its expression in dance forms and its symbolism, has always been a powerful factor in the development of many forms of dance, as it has in all other kinds of art. As such it is to be admired and cultivated, not despised and furtively practised, but time after time in history, during decadent periods, one finds that the incompetent practitioner can gain easy fame and wealth by means of an obscene exploitation of forms which talented artists employ to more imaginative, more worthy ends.

Thus in Rome the dance became closely associated with disreputability and salaciousness. So much so in fact that in Roman society dance participation became increasingly more rare. The thousands of imported dancers were now augmented by others. They came from Spain, from Greece and from Syria. For some centuries these 'guests', very often little more than slaves, entertained their masters at feasts and festivals. Although not all of these affairs reached the depths of some of Nero's orgies there can be no doubt whatever that these 'dancers' were no credit to the art they pursued. This meant that to be skilled at the dance was likely to bring disgrace, and more than once, according to contemporary writers, ladies were attacked for having acquired a skill beyond the level of that expected from a virtuous woman.

The dance was associated in Rome with the public games and these reached such a state of disgusting savagery that anybody who participated in them acquired something of their evil reputation. Augustine and other members of the church condemned them in the strongest possible terms of righteous horror, and in doing so attacked the dance in similar terms, for dancing played a part in the games. Lincoln Kirstein in *Dance: a short history of classical theatrical dancing*, in which he traces the growth of the western theatre from the earliest forms, sums up the situation as follows:

'For Rome was falling and falling fast, and still the arenas were full and churches were not. Hell's mouth yawned. The late Romans drugged themselves with games. Three thousand dancing girls were allowed to remain in the starving city, while scholars were driven away. Although invaders infested the once invincible town, its people flocked to the games. And Augustine, with that insight which would make his monument an encyclopedia for the Dark Ages, and the one philosophy of history the Middle Ages knew, concentrated all his energy on denunciations of the shows. It was not as a Puritan that he had felt in his youth the attractions of the theatre.'

In A.D. 300 the Church Council at Elvira prohibited the baptism of any person connected with the circus or with pantomime, which included the theatre, and a hundred years later a similar council at Carthage passed a law whereby anyone attending the theatre on holy day would be excommunicated. It seems clear, however, that this law was not put very firmly into effect. At the same time the church, in order to compete with the theatre on its own ground, developed its own form of miracle and mystery plays. In this way religious themes were dramatized by the priests themselves, and there are accounts of such famous incidents in religious history as the crucifixion being represented by means of mime and dance. But far from reconciling the theatre and the church, this development parted the two more firmly from each other. As late as A.D. 971 a priest wrote to a friend:

'The man who brings actors and mimes and dancers to his house knows not what a bevy of unclean spirits follow them.'

As always the theatre and the dance faithfully represented the morals and climate of the time, forecasting for those with the ability to interpret the signs the final corruption and downfall of the Roman Empire. After this downfall the whole of Europe was for many years the scene of warring tribes and nomadic groups. This led inevitably to a conflict of religions and an intermingling of cultures. For a while however the cultures of Greece and Rome were disregarded and a number of centres of learning put to the fire. The philosophy of the Greeks during this medieval period made little or no impact on the peoples of Europe, but instead Christianity now began to make an ever growing appeal. Times were hard, life perilous, and man sought security no longer in life on earth but in the life of the spirit after death. Religion became the one dominating emotion throughout Europe.

With religion came cruelty and oppression—and subservience to authority. Man's one unreasoning desire was to save his soul. The dance, simply because it connoted physical pleasure, suffered suppression, for the soul could be purified and uplifted to heaven only if the body were robbed of its pleasure and importance. One wonders who does most harm: those who lead excesses into sensual corruption, or those who suppress and seek to deny the good inherent in physical pleasure. Certainly the only form of dance to survive to any extent during this period was that of a religious nature; and even that was from time to time suspect. This means that the forms of dance that were no longer practised at all could after a few years no longer be revived, for unlike the written word, music or the plastic arts, dance, as we have already seen has never possessed a widely accepted form of notation. It is believed by some that the Egyptians employed some kind of notation of movement, but no evidence remains to substantiate such a belief. Not until recent times has there come into existence a form of notation which can be reliably used to recreate dances of group movements, in fact human movement of any kind, thus ridding us of the necessity to hand down dances and ballets by word of mouth and personal example alone. It is surprising that those concerned with the use of human body as an expressive medium have not interested themselves more in this development. But that is of course another story.

In one of his books St. Augustine included a chapter on the profane songs and loud stamping dances practised in the church in which a saint lay buried. First he quotes Matthew xi,17:

'We have piped unto you, and ye have not danced; we have mourned unto you, and ye have not lamented.'

He continues:

'May anybody dance in this place even though psalms be sung? Once upon a time, not many years ago, impudent dancers intruded into similar places. As many of our Elders can remember, they brought their uncleanness and their insolence even into the holy place where the body of the Martyr lies. During the whole of the night they sang their shameless songs to the accompaniment of dancing. When the Lord commanded holy vigils from our holy brother, your Bishop (Cypreian) then his pestilence added some little lustre to the festival, but later this custom fell out of use because of stricter care and from shame from the teachings of wisdom. Here we celebrate the holiness and the festival of the martyrs—here there shall be no dancing. And in spite of the fact that there was no dancing, yet we read in the Gospel: We have sung for you and ye have not danced. Those who have not danced are blamed, reproached, accused, banished. Though vanished until now this insolence begins to reappear: listen rather to what

INTRODUCTION

wisdom proclaims. *Let him who strikes up, sing: let him who dances, dance.* For what is the meaning of dancing if it is not to harmonize the bodily movements with song. What sort of song, my brethren? Let us listen to the song; let us hear the dancers. Be ye harmonious yourselves in your habits as are the dancers in the movements of their limbs. Take ye care in your inner selves that ye harmonize in virtuous deeds John.'

St. Chrysostom, who lived between about 345 and 407, is also referred to as an opponent of the dance. In his comment on the Gospel of St. Matthew he says:

'For where there is a dance, there also is the Devil. For God has not given us our feet to use in a shameful way but in order that we may walk in decency, not that we should dance like camels (for even dancing camels make an unpleasant spectacle, much more than women), but in order to dance ring-dances with the angels. For if it is shameful for the body to behave thus, the more so is it for the spirit to do so. Thus dance the demons and thus dance the servants of the demons.'

But this same St. Chrysostom, has a quite different opinion of the dance employed for spiritual ends. In a lecture on Lasarus he discusses the celebration of the Whitsun festival:

'You have passed the greater part of the day together in transports of moderation, in the performance of ring dances in the Spirit of St. Paul. By this your merits have increased doubly, in the first place because you have refrained from the indecent dances of the drunken, and in second place because you have danced those spiritual dances which are most pleasing and most modest... and while others performed dances for the devil, you circled instead of this place and used musical instruments of the spirit, revealing your souls as do the musical instruments on which the Holy Ghost plays when he instils grace into your hearts.'

But even the forms of dances practised as part of religious ceremonies were not free from censure. Again and again one finds the condemnation of this kind of dancing when it has seemingly been practised to excess. As late as the seventh century a Church Council published a decree with special clauses condemning 'public or objectionable dances of women and festivities in honour of false gods'.

The clergy fostered the belief that the devil was a special patron of the dance—some of them going so far as to assert that he was its originator. In sermons and elsewhere they declared that the dance had been evil and accursed ever since Salome had through the dance seduced the Tetrarch to gratify her mother's fearful desire.

In this long period of suppression and the denigration of life on earth to the glorification of the soul it is not surprising that in various parts of Europe people broke out into extraordinary exhibitions. In his *Ecclesiastical History*, Mosheim refers to a kind of dancing madness, in about 1374, in which men and women, both old and young, publicly and in private, suddenly began to dance. Holding each other by the hand they threw themselves about with such sustained violence that after a while they dropped exhausted. These 'dancers' claimed to be possessed of wonderful visions, and were obviously in fact not dancing in the sense that dancing consists of co-ordinated, disciplined movements in a definite rhythm, but suffering from some kind of mass hysteria which manifested itself in a paroxysm of movement. Records of the time refer to numberless outbreaks of this kind, although this particular one was probably more intense in its character and endemic over a wider geographical area than any other before or since. Some of these outbreaks were the result of the suppression of earthly pleasures, a kind of safety valve in which masses of people gave way to paroxysms of movement, thus either consciously or unconsciously exorcising some mythical ill or evil. Other outbreaks were artificially stimulated as a deliberate invocation of specific saints, and in this form continued until well into the eighteenth century, part of their efficacy lying in their practice by groups rather than individuals. It may well be argued that these various forms have very little relationship with the social dance forms of my study, but there is no doubt that they did have some influence on the country dances practised on the village green on feast days, for even these distinctly secular occasions were linked strongly to religious and mystical beliefs. Not until well into the sixteenth century was the dance, with a few exceptions such as those of the acrobatic dancers and tumblers, to be divided into various forms. The court dances of the fourteenth and fifteenth centuries were, it is true, quite distinct from the dances of the people of the same time, but each from time to time strengthened the other. The very definite pigeon-holing was not to develop until much later, coming to an absurd climax in the twentieth century, when various groups of teachers developed about ten or more separate divisions of the dance. As we shall see, it was the social dance of the fifteenth and sixteenth century which formed the kind of theatrical entertainment which came to be known as ballet. At first there was no difference in the steps as they were performed on the ballroom floor and those for the ballet. But of course,

INTRODUCTION

when ballet elevated itself to the stage, and when the dancers became professional, then there had to be virtuosity. As a result the theatrical dance grew rapidly further and further away from social dance. Students of dance history should however never forget that the ballet has its roots deep in the social dance forms, having even taken its turned out position of the legs from the early court dances.

In his magnificent *Dance* Lincoln Kirstein classifies the inspiration and functions of dance into the seasons of man's life, the seasons of the year and tribal development. He continues:

'Within these grand divisions two convenient subsections suggest themselves—those dances which originate in social aims, and those which have a magic or religious purpose. There are birth dances of family and tribal congratulation, initiation dances which instruct new tribal members into occult secrets and sexual information, marriage dances of sexual selection and property endowment, war dances of welcome to strangers, or testimony of good fellowship. No hard or fast separation from magic-religious rites can be asserted, but there is an obvious difference between such functions, and those which involve dance worship of the tribe's deity, Sun, Moon, Fire or River, Snake or Lion which gave the tribe its seed. Definitely utilitarian dances involving mimicry and magic are more dramatic, more concentrated than the others. Food, fish or game are desired. Or rain is needed. Or floods must be dried up. Then dance for it. A warrior is sick. Dance the demons out of him. A man dies. Dance to lay his ghost and protect his survivors from possible threats of his wandering shade.'

In various forms of invocative dance it is the monotonous pounding of feet and the rhythmic movement of a number of bodies in unison which creates the power of this innovation—or more likely sets up a state of semi-self-hypnosis. It is a far cry from those dances to the sequence of the Edwardians, but even in the revivals of those dances to be seen today there is a certain hypnotic fascination, however diluted, in the performance of the same rhythmic movement to music by hundreds, sometimes thousands, of dancers. There can be no doubt whatever of their common ancestry. In primitive times the warrior often relived his successes in battle by means of mimetic dance; he also copied the animals in order to possess power over them, and he danced to bring down the rain and when he was unsuccessful the priests blamed his faulty performance. These rituals grew into feast days of celebrations and ceremony, which surely accounts in part for the importance of the social dance in the celebration of feast days at the present time.

But today, of course, the purpose of the feast day is usually forgotten while the dance survives.

With the emergence of the middle ages man slowly came to renew his interest in this world as well as the next. This was the time of the growth of the universities as great seats of learning as well as the age of the Crusades. A lay culture arose which, although it remained closely wedded to the church, was nevertheless accepted as pleasure-giving in a secular sense. Even so the conditions of life remained more or less barbaric and it did not need a Chaucer to stress the tremendous contrast between the ideals of knightly chivalry and the actual mode of life of the people.

Sacred music continued to remain completely free of sensuous rhythms, while the dances of the people, as always, sometimes became robust to the point of indecency. Besides, there was still a tremendous fear of death, for its horrors were stressed by the church, so that people might at least save their souls by putting them at the mercy of the priesthood. With this mass tension dance manias, as well as other forms of mass unbalance, swept through Europe, with the result that again and again, in spite of a certain amount of enlightenment, the dance itself, regardless of its nature, was from time to time the object of attack and suppression.

But yet the dance flourished. The chivalrous knight had to be well versed in the courtly arts as well as those of the field. Great balls were held frequently in his castles and mansions, with masquerades and morality plays to enrich them. For these affairs there can be no doubt that the form of the dances stemmed from the dances of the people, but subjected to such refinement as eventually to make them unidentifiable with their originals. At the same time the dances of the village, although practised on the green rather than on the floors of the castles, also took back from the court dances some of this refinement and polish, for the people, given the chance, will always imitate those above them in station. Thus there existed a constant two-way traffic.

As the Middle Ages emerge into the Renaissance, the time in which the story of the development of social dance can at last be traced in some detail, culture begins to grow independent of religion. Secular music and secular painting now enjoy a life of their own, although continuing to maintain strong associations with the church. The thread of development from the Greeks and Romans to the great artists of the Renaissance can still be traced without difficulty and without undue speculation. But dance, as far as the historian is concerned, must make virtually a new start, for not until the fifteenth century is well into its

INTRODUCTION

stride does there appear any form of contemporary description which now remains extant. Before that we can but surmise from attempts in the visual arts to express the stylized movement forms of their time. Obviously the history of the dance cannot properly commence without reasonably detailed contemporary records. Thanks to three Italians of the next century, and to one in particular, the history of the dance from that time becomes a matter for far less conjecture, although still demanding judicious interpretation.

Through both the fourteenth and the fifteenth centuries the tendency grew for Court entertainment to became more and more unified. At the beginning of this period the Court had ample leisure and stability, a fitting environment for the development of entertainment. What developed at Court would also be embraced in the great houses, both secular and ecclesiastic. Mostly nocturnal recreation consisted of amateur participation in singing and dancing, with a stiffening of professionals. These professionals were generally the minstrels of the time, sometimes maintained by a great household as a resident troupe; as such they were often hired by neighbours; and other performers who were essentially itinerant. These were the troupes who disseminated new customs and new styles in entertainment, and there can be little doubt that as they went about their travels they frequently introduced new and interesting ways of performing the various dance figures of the time. Who can tell the extent of their exaggerations? Doubtless many a fine lady was taught this or that figure by itinerants who claimed to have acquired it from the king's entertainers. Today, when communication of such things is virtually simultaneous throughout the world, it would not be easy to indulge a similar practice, but at that time it sometimes took months for a new fabric design or fashion to be introduced from one part of Britain to another.

During the fourteenth century the secular tournament and the religious miracle cycles had become increasingly popular, with the result that both these outdoor entertainments formed the sources of inspiration for the indoor entertainments of the evening. The prize-giving for the tournament was frequently deferred until the evening and the pageants for the miracle plays gradually found themselves, with modifications, taken indoors. At the end of the fourteenth century there came a tendency to amalgamate the various forms of entertainment into a co-ordinated whole. This gave greater opportunity for speaking actors rather than mummers, for obviously it was easier to achieve audibility indoors than outdoors. This facilitated the adaptation of the miracle plays for more specifically dramatic purposes, and soon the herald was borrowed from the tournament to introduce the characters and explain any obscurities.

What place has the social dance in this kind of entertainment? Towards the end of the fourteenth century, from extant records, it is clear that the participants in the entertainment, at its close, took part in the dancing which followed, but remained segregated from the host and his assembly, whereas by the end of the fifteenth century the mummers, disguisers, or actors, call them what you will, were taking their partners from among the audience. At first this innovation was known as a Disguising for the actors were still at this time masqued. The custom of mixing entertainers and audience, however, in common with so many other features of European entertainment, appears to have stemmed from Italy; from Italy too came the special masques and visors designed for this particular custom. From this Italian word *maschere*, we derive the word Masque or Mask under which this custom came to be known for many years.

There are many contemporary reports of this kind of entertainment. Although as usual none of them contains any detailed reference to the style of the dancing, much less its steps and figurations, we can get a general view of the scene. When, for example, the eldest son of Henry VII, Prince Arthur, married Katherine of Aragon, lavish disguisings (this was before the Italian Mask had been developed) were held at Westminster Hall and the Palace of Richmond. At Westminster, when the King and Queen had taken their seats, a magnificent entertainment, called by the chronicler a 'disguysing', began, the first scene, a pageant consisting of 'a castell set upon whelys, and drawn into the seid hall' by 'beasts' each made up of two men. In the castle were eight 'goodly and fresshe ladies', all of them disguised. Now another pageant in the form of a ship appeared, from which descended two ambassadors from the 'Mownte of Love' to seek the favours of the ladies in the castle. The ladies spurned them, at which came another pageant in the form of a hill, carrying knights who descended and laid siege to the castle. The ladies at last yielded, after which they and the knights 'dauncyd togyders dyvers and many goodly dances'.

The chronicler records that the pageants were removed from the floor of the hall to make room for the dance, and that after the knights and their ladies had completed their own rounds, the audience then took the floor, led by the newlyweds, in a series of dances. The occasion must not be regarded as one of sustained formality for the chronicler tells us that a certain noble dancer, finding himself too encumbered to dance with desirable freedom, cast off some of his garments and

INTRODUCTION

'dauncyd in his jaket'. Only because of a tragedy the best known of all the late fourteenth-century affairs of this kind is usually referred to as the 'Dance of Savages' in 1393 (see Appendix IX). This kind of 'extravaganza' was frequent during the fourteenth century.

On another occasion the king and several of his companions are recorded as having left the dancing in order to put on different clothes and masks in a Venetian style, with vizors and beards of gold.

'... then with minstrels is these viii noble personages entred and daunsed long with the ladies, and whn they had daunced there fill, then the quene plucked of the kynges visar, and so did the ladies of the other lordes, and then all were knowen.'

It seems probable that the mobility of the pageants was required chiefly to allow room for the dancing which followed the set presentation.

Most of my information concerning these early entertainments has been taken from Glynne Wickham's *Early English Stages 1300 to 1660*. He sums up their nature as follows:

'They were truly secular in that they were designed to accompany feasting as an enjoyable social recreation. This enjoyment, however, was never far removed from ceremonial rituals. The simple, allegoric compliment latent in this and similar entertainments and its obvious affinities with the *Pas d'Armes* and Heraldry testify to that. The formality of the one is softened to permit the informality of the other, and the whole consequently forms a basis for the mixing of professional and amateur talent in pleasing harmony. Minstrels, gentlemen and ladies could meet on an equal footing, as the pages of Hall's Chronicle bear eloquent witness throughout the reign of Henry VIII, while tailors carpenters and painters laboured to give to their sophisticated revels "a local habitation and a name". Presiding over them all, by virtue of his authority in the Hall or Great Chamber respectively, was the Steward of the Household or the Lord Chamberlain.'

It is clear that from this composite form of entertainment came the separate forms which were to develop during the sixteenth century. At times the spectacle was little more than an excuse for dressing up and dancing; then with the development of one or the other elements, one gained ascendancy over the others. Later, during the reign of Queen Elizabeth, the growth of drama naturally put more stress on the words and minimized the spectacle. Besides, Elizabeth was not keen to spend large sums of money on such affairs. In addition she herself loved to dance, and doubtless found irksome the long periods of boredom which the spectacle must have brought to one of her intellectual inclination. During her reign the theatre was to be firmly established as an entity in its own right and the dance to be enjoyed quite separately, on a different intellectual and emotional level.

CHAPTER II

The Fifteenth Century

THE DEVELOPMENT OF TECHNIQUE AND SOME EARLY DANCE LITERATURE

Under the stress of joy, man makes words. The words are not enough; he prolongs them. The prolonged words are not enough; he modulates them. The modulated words are not enough, and without even perceiving it, his hands make gestures and his feet begin to move.

(From a Chinese philosopher)

IN the fourteenth century, generally speaking, there existed a great deal of intellectual unrest, with new outlooks developing as the result of a certain amount of discovery. Now came a period of consolidation, especially in England, where the waging of war was considered to be the right and proper business of every true native. Throughout the century there is little doubt the feeling existed that one Englishman was the equal of three foreigners. Indeed, this myth lived far beyond the century. Even so, England was during this time driven back across the English Channel, losing its tenuous hold upon France; further, the country's social ills and gross inequality were as bad as they ever had been.

These factors had certain effects upon our culture, and can easily be traced in our dancing. Among the aristocracy the dances of France were readily adopted by the English who invested the movements with a pride and hauteur even greater than that of the French. Unfortunately we know little of the nature of the dances of the peasants, but there is little doubt that the hard life most of them led, the long hours and monotonous diet, caused them to play with great vigour and lack of restraint during their several holidays and saints' days in order to forget awhile their toil and poverty.

Movement, as we have already established, is the most ephemeral of all human activities. Painters and sculptors throughout the ages have attempted to create an illusion of movement, just as they have created

DOI: 10.4324/9781003177968-2

an illusion of the third dimension. But movement demands an entirely different kind of illusion from that of perspective. The third dimension deceives the eye by means of natural laws—laws that were built up by fourteenth-century Italians, and which have been handed down to their successors. The illusion of movement depends upon no natural laws at all. Botticelli sought to suggest movement by means of flowing draperies. Poussin showed men and women frozen midway through a movement as though he had possessed a modern camera with a 1/1000 second shutter. Not one of his creatures could ever have moved a fraction of an inch. Rodin in his sculpture employed a more profound method, seeking to express the muscular energy, the interior motivation of movement, rather than a surface deception of the eye. Today, probably because of the ubiquity of the fast camera, fewer and fewer painters even experiment with the illusion of movement at all.

Whether we hope to learn something of the dance styles of the Greeks or the early Renaissance Italians, we possess as evidence only such things as the sculpture of the posed human body, the urns which inspired Keats and a few paintings. But none of these works of art really demonstrates the human body in movement; what the artists of those periods did was to define the body and limbs at the climax of a movement.

The first time, as far as we know, that any definite pattern was written down must be credited to the early fourteenth century. In 1313 a Rabbi named Hacen be Salomo taught some round dances to the parishioners of Saragossa, the steps having first been written down. Later in the century there are records of great court entertainments in which dancing played an important part. In 1377 for example, Charles V of France presented an entertainment in honour of Charles IV of Germany. Contemporary writers tell us that two heavily armed wagons were employed, one depicting Jerusalem and filled with men dressed as Saracens, and another with soldiers of Godrey of Bouillon. At given times in the long entertainment which followed the entry of these wagons or 'pageants', various groups of warriors danced after the manner of their time, finally mixing with the nobility who formed their audience in a great ball.

Gradually this kind of dancing and entertainment grew more complex and extravagant until finally it was taken from the floor and put on to the stage, thus leading to the birth of ballet, although some centuries yet had to pass before the spectacle at first known as ballet became anything like the theatrical entertainment of today.

Doubtless in the fourteenth century dancing grew into an art as well as a social pastime, but if the masters of that time did commit to paper any of its figures and technique, nothing remains of such records. The earliest manuscript from which we can cull any real knowledge of the actual form of the dances of the time, as distinct from vague if colourful descriptions of great balls and occasions, was dated 1416, and even that remains to us only in transcript form. The author of this manuscript was Domenico de Piacenza, whom we can therefore claim to be one of the earliest of professional dancing masters.

Domenico first set out to defend the dance, discussing its natural beauty and stressing the necessity for an intellectual grasp of the scientific principles underlying the practice of the dances of the time. He also urged that the student of dance must possess agility and bodily grace, that all the movements must be temperately performed and that they should on no account suffer from exaggeration. In this connexion he used a delightful image, describing the undulating movements of a gondola on wavelets. How urgently teachers in the twentieth century seek to obtain that same undulating movement from their advanced pupils! I have not, however, heard of any them employ quite such a colourful exhortation and example. After dwelling at some length on the theory of movement and gesture, Domenico then proceeds to outline the twelve fundamental movements which form every kind of dance, dividing them into nine natural and three 'accidental' movements. These fundamental, or basic, movements, as they are frequently known, provided the key to the structure of dancing for well over two hundred years. Domenico included in the 'natural' group all the movements based on normal physical behaviour; whereas in his 'accidental' classification he included 'flourishes' and ornamental steps, gliding steps and pirouettes. He said that he put them in this category as they were not necessary according to nature.

After some discussion on timing and measure Domenico next differentiates four different kinds of dance, as follows:

1. Bassa Danza, slower than the other dances, with music in major imperfect time. This really means duple time in modern terminology.

2. Quadernaria, in minor imperfect time. This was slightly faster than the Bassa Danza.

3. Saltarello, in major imperfect time. This again was slightly faster than the Quadernaria.

4. Piva in minor perfect time—very slightly slower than the Saltarello.

After a short dissertation on the shortcomings of those musicians who unwittingly accelerate their tempi during a dance (dance band musicians too, it is clear, retain their characteristics during the centuries) and explaining certain fundamental differences in the movements, Domenico next devotes himself to a discussion on the correct modification of tempo and how the dancer may rightly adapt his style so that he shall not appear maladroit in the quick dances and not shed his natural dignity in the slow ones. The manuscript then concludes with descriptions of various set dances, giving fifteen balli and five bassa danze.

Before proceeding any further it is obviously desirable to define these words *bassa* and *balli*. The first of them has been the cause of some controversy, certain authorities maintaining that the word (which means low) referred to the lowly origin of the dance, although it has never been clearly established that it did in fact have such an origin; and others that the name referred to the style of the dance, in which the feet are kept low, never being lifted off the floor. Today most writers are advocates of the latter theory. *Balli* was the generic title for all the pantomimic dances which in the succeeding century were to develop into a kind of spectacle which was in its own turn to lead to ballet. There were countless dances of this kind, the steps themselves being quite simple, usually the easiest basic steps of the bassa danze. Upon this framework was built up an element of mime developed from an easily followed theme or story. One such dance, for example, was La Mercantina, who was a lady who would readily listen to the love entreaties of any man. The lady who was to perform this dance would stand side by side with one man, another man immediately behind her. The minute description of the dance specified eleven measures of the Saltarello, a stop, the gentleman behind the lady performing six riprises, the lady turning and the other gentleman advancing. Next the first partner rejoins the lady and the sequence is repeated.

Whatever can be said about the origin of the basse danse itself, there is a great deal of evidence to suggest that these balli stemmed from the people.

In the *Musical Quarterly* of July 1941 appeared a most interesting article on the difference between the basse danse and the ballo.

'... in contrast to the basse danse the ballo is pantomimic in form. It consists of a number of separate parts, each of them called misura. During the dance itself the tempo is changed several times. The basse danse retains the same time throughout .The ballo has a melody in the treble which is often taken from a song and is not only slightly altered. In the basse danse the melody is a "tenor" which is expanded or shortened as the choreography of the dance requires it; while the melodies used in the ballo are called "canti", the basse danse melodies have the title "tenori". Therefore it is easy to understand that the favourite orchestra of the fifteenth century consisted of two or three shalms and a slide trumpet. There is no other combination of instruments that better answers the requirements of a polyphonic bassandaza. The slide trumpet obviously sounded the theme, the single tones of which were clearly audible, since the steps of the dance had to correspond to them. The rich figuration of the counterparts could not have been better performed than by the shalms which were able to play rapid passages and had a peculiar nasal timbre that contrasted sharply with the sound of the trumpet, so full of sonore dignity.'

Even with this information about the actual structure of the two forms, basse danse and ballo, however, and at least some conception of the kind of sound which prompted the dancers, we still cannot build up any kind of mental picture of the spectacle the dancers presented unless we know the nature of their dress. Throughout the century, whether in Italy, Spain, Germany, France or England, the women appear without exception, no matter for what occassion, in long, concealing garments, which undoubtedly restricted their movements, and which would in any case completely have hidden any fancy footwork. On the other hand, the men of the court quite frequently wore doublet and hose and would thus have been able to indulge in a great variety of intricate and arduous figures. Doubtless many of them did, especially in certain periods, when they wanted to show off their prowess in front of their womenfolk. This is what led them away from the dignity of the textbook version and the strictures of their dancing masters, prompting the latter to intersperse their writings with regret at such bad taste.

Before the first dancing master appeared dancing had been taught and circulated by the buffoons and jesters, who naturally enlivened the social life of the courts with some of the lusty customs and habits of the people. Gradually these jesters became dancing masters to the exclusion of their other functions. In time they wormed their way further into society as highly trusted and privileged servants, the arbiters of etiquette and essential both for the social instruction of the younger members of the household, and to keep the older members adequately up to date in social etiquette and behaviour.

All our scanty dance literature of this time is naturally concerned only with the dances of the gentry. The 'lower classes' are completely ignored, and our only information about their dancing comes from contemporary pictures. From these it is clear that the movements of the dances of the peasants were in marked contrast to those of their betters. Although it would be unwise to jump to many conclusions from this kind of pictorial evidence, for painters and sculptors sought a no more perceptive view of movement than those of today, one can safely declare that the movements of the peasant dances were much freer in scope than those of the court. Peasants are depicted in a number of works, both in Northern Italy and in other parts of Europe, jumping and skipping, cavorting and frolicking, often in the midst of a crowd by now too drunk to dance themselves.

Hours of work for the peasants were long, their standard of living lower than the twentieth-century mind can easily imagine. But they kept their holidays and feasts days with jollity, in a highly communal spirit and, as far as contemporary literary and pictorial evidence can testify, with much dancing.

Doubtless the younger people of the upper classes occasionally joined in the carousels with the peasants; doubtless, too, the uninhibited figures and movements of the lower class dances excited the envy and emulation of the young bloods, with the result that at certain times the dignified court dances must have been reinvigorated by new and daring figures taken from the village green.

But of such developments as this in the fifteenth century there is no definite evidence. One can only draw conclusions from fairly safe assumptions. Four hundred years later the 'kitchen' lancers were to corrupt or enliven, according to one's point of view, the more restrained original versions of that ubiquitous nineteenth-century dance; and there are several other equally powerful examples of this intermingling of above and below stairs in various phases of dance history. We can have no reason to suppose that the situation was different in the fifteenth century.

In order to realize yet further the inadequacy of our conception of the social dance of the time, it is necessary to remember that Domenico, from whom we have derived all our textual information so far, was active in Italy, and as far as we know he did not come into any kind of contact with the dance of Northern Europe. We can however be equally certain that Northern Europe was to a very large extent influenced by the style and fashion of Italy. The great renaissance was already working its way upwards through Europe. Dress and manners, as well as music and the plastic arts, were in all the countries in this geographical group already coming powerfully under its influence. Germany alone appears to have been at this time impervious to the influence from the South, although we have even less reliable information from that country than from the others. In the first place, however, the absence of such influence can be accounted for by the fact that in Germany there were few, if any, really dominant courts in which such an influence could germinate. Instead there were numerous small courts, most of which were in close touch with the people. Further, the German folk-dance was throughout the century very much alive and full of vigour. In consequence it was able the more successfully to resist the influence of a more refined southern dance element, just as it resisted other elements of the renaisaance

Generally speaking, it seems, the dance customs of the German courts were practised by means of a quiet introductory dance and a lively one to follow. This lively dance became in all probability the Allemande of the next century. A processional dance with couples one behind the other, turning at the end with regular exchanges of partners, was also much in fashion.

It is to Germany that Europe owes much of the turning figures which developed during the next two centuries. Indeed, the turning figure appears in practically all German couple dances, especially those which stem from southern Germany. Apart from this exciting figure, the dances consisted, as far as can be established, of rather dull steps, which were moreover performed without the grace and dignity of those from Italy and Spain. But all the while the turning element grew in importance. Contemporary writers speak of this feature in a variety of ways, many of them expressing the moral indignation of the church and even of the civic authorities. In Nurenburg, for example, the turning became so prolonged, so furious, that women were taken out of the dance dizzy and fainting, and the police actually forbade this particular kind of dance.

An example of a peasant dance embraced enthusiastically by the aristocracy is the Piva. Danced originally to the music of a bagpipe the Piva (which means that instrument) was a vigorous dance demanding an ability to leap and skip in rapid time. According to one contemporary authority the music was in a three-beat measure played twice as fast as the music for the basse danse. Naturally the aristocracy tamed the dance considerably before they took it into their halls, but it still seems to have retained its essential characteristics. Even so, like most exaggerated novelties, when it was taken from its proper habitat it soon became obsolete and does not appear to have featured as a social dance after 1450. Musically the Piva lasted longer, however, for it appeared in certain books of lute music as late as 1508.

Following Domenico came three other famous fifteenth-century dancing masters. In fact there were doubtless many others, but we know about these three because they were responsible for technical manuscripts on the dance which have been preserved. They were Guglielmo Ebreo (William the Jew) Antonio Cornazano and Giovanni Ambrosius. All of them based their work on that of Domenico whose manuscript can be dated as *circa* 1416. Today the study of all three technicians can best be carried out through the remarkable work of Doctor Otto Kinkeldy, whose book, *A Jewish Dancing Master of the Renaissance*, was published in 1927.

A study of this small body of work shows that in the first half of the fifteenth century the Italians had already departed from the classic model for which they were in the first place mostly responsible and which was then in vogue in France and England. But this departure is only one of variation and decoration, for the basic pattern and style remained the same.

We are able to make this comparison chiefly by means of the manuscripts I have already mentioned and the famous 'Golden Manuscript'. This, to give it its full title is *Le Manuscrit des basses danses de la Bibliothèque de Bourgogne*. The date of this manuscript has not been definitely established, but the first reference to it found so far is in an inventory of the library of the Regent of the Netherlands, Marguerite of Austria (1480–1532) in the year 1523. Derra de Moroda, writing in *The Dancing Times* of December 1937, says:

'Most probably she inherited it from her mother, Marie of Burgundy, who may have inherited it from her father, Charles the Bold. True, it does not figure in any other inventory before that date, but it may not have been very precise or it may have belonged to someone else at court.'

There is little doubt that the manuscript itself was written during the first third of the fifteenth century. The original is in the Royal Library of Brussels (MS 9085). It is in oblong format, consisting of twenty-five pages of mat black paper ruled in gold. Pages 1 to 6 give the theory of the steps and the rules of the basse danse. Pages 7 to 23 give the music and notation of fifty-nine basse danses. In 1912 Ernest Closson published a facsimile edition of the 'Golden Manuscript' for the Société des Bibliophiles et Inconophiles de Belgique, tracing in the preface the history of the manuscript and discussing the details of the dances, but mainly from the musical point of view. Following the publication of this facsimile there came a spate of articles by the most famous historians working up to a controversy which is still occasionally resuscitated today. Only 250 copies of the facsimile were printed, with the result that it has become extremely rare. There is however a copy in the magnificent library of dance literature belonging to P. J. S. Richardson.

The first printed book did not appear until about 1450 and in England the first printing press did not come into operation until 1476. Until then all dance literature including descriptions and music notation, was naturally in the form of manuscript. Even with the advent of printing dance descriptions remained for the most part rather vague and sketchy, for they were never written for those who did not dance, but chiefly for those who had at least some experience in the art who now wanted either a reminder of certain steps or instruction in a figure that was strange to them. This point is perhaps best illustrated by means of a modern example.

If I say to three people who have never danced and never seen any dancing: 'step forward on the right foot,' each of them is almost bound to set about this operation in a different way. One will gingerly glide his foot obliquely forward, keeping his weight back; another will pick his foot up and place it down; and the third will simply take a normal walking pace forward. Now, apart from general stylistic discussions, these early manuscripts contain no definite instructions as to the manner in which each step shall be performed, so that today we have to interpret those instructions, bearing in mind the style of the period, its costume, and with due regard for any pictorial record. Much of the reconstruction inevitably takes the form of an inspired guess, but it is remarkable that various practising teachers of what we now call historical dances come to the same conclusions in an exceedingly large section of their researches. The remainder of their work is a rich and constant source of often heated controversy, but this very heat often blinds us as to the large measure of agreement.

The first printed book on the social dance—at least the first so far discovered—was published some time in the last decade of the fifteenth century. Entitled *L'art et instruction de bien danser*, this work opens with five pages of music and the notation of forty-nine basses dances. These instructions are almost identical with those given in the 'Golden Manuscript' and forty-three of the forty-nine dances are the same in each. It seems that we can therefore safely draw the conclusion that during the larger part of the century there were few if any fundamental changes in the manner of social dancing, the main differences being those concerning the greater decoration given to the Basses Danses by the French as distinct from the Italians.

It certainly was the century of the Basse Danse. In England, however, no definitive litetature appears to confirm our addiction to this form of the dance until 1521, when Robert Copelande's *Manner of dancynge of bace daunces after the use of Fraunce* was published, and even then this work was very brief, consisting of two pages at the end of a book on French grammar and pronunciation, probably for the use of English visitors to France (a treaty of peace and alliance between the two countries had been signed in 1514). Although the instructions are reasonably clear as far as they go, some important matters are omitted, most noticeably the branle step itself, on which there is no reference whatever. The reference is also treated but slightly, and there is little allusion to style. This does not however mean that in England these details were not regarded as of prime importance. These two pages added to a book of this kind were doubtless for reference purposes, and were probably added as an afterthought. The main point to be taken today from the Copelande instructions is that to all intents and purposes the Basse Danse in England did not differ in its essential details from that of the continent.

The Basse Danse is probably of Italian origin, although strangely enough the first reference to it found so far is in the Spanish poem *La Danze de la Muerte*. The date of this poem has not been determined with any precision, but it must have been either towards the end of the fourteenth century or the beginning of the fifteenth. There can then be no doubt that the dance was known at the beginning of the fifteenth century. Cornazano calls it the queen of dances, and sums up its special quality by stating that it is slow and stately, but at the same time courtly, with small gliding steps and a rising on the toes.

Throughout the fifteenth century the Basse Danse remained tremendously popular in most European countries, surviving until well into the next century, and then gradually disappearing, although still danced occasionally in Spain and Italy until early in the seventeenth century.

During this long life the dance naturally underwent a number of technical and stylistic changes, but in the fifteenth century there was no longer any regular arrangement of steps, the figures now consisting of bows, simple and double steps, sidling and backward movements being amalgamated in whatever order the man determined. Incidentally, the fashion of describing only the man's steps in technical literature, except when those of the woman are markedly different, is often criticized today, but it started with those early writers, for all the books of this period describe only the man's steps.

In spite of this wide choice of amalgamations, there were it seems, in northern Europe at any rate, certain accepted patterns, for the Golden Manuscript recognizes seven definite groups of steps, each group being known as a measure, but this by no means exhausts the possibilities, and many other combinations of the steps were employed, Copelande himself giving a number of groups. Again referring to the 'Golden Manuscript' we find that at no time should there be more than two consecutive single steps.

For many years the Basse Danse was invariably followed by the Saltarello (known in France at this time as the Tourdion). This provided an ideal contrast, for it was in character a gay and even joyful dance. Its tempo was fast and skilled dancers included in it a special leaping movement. A striking feature of the dance was a movement of the feet in which the left foot was struck sharply against the right foot and then immediately thrown out backwards. Another feature was a hopping movement.

Cornazano stated that the speed of the Saltarello was faster than that of the Basse Danse in the proportion of eight to five. He also laid down that the Saltarello was in triple rhythm, beginning with an upbeat, although there are extant examples of music beginning on the downbeat. Gradually the two dances, Basse Danse and Saltarello, merged into a well-nigh inseparable unity in which, to quote Curt Sachs, in his *World History of The Dance*:

'all the nuances in the human mind in the spirit of a dignified festival found expression: ceremonial grandeur and impish exuberance, restraint and wantonness, gravity and license.'

Sachs adds that this unity became so strong that the Saltarello rarely had a melody of its own, but only a rhythmic abbreviation of the Basse Danse. Normally Saltarello music was not even notated, the players having to read it from Basse Danse music and transcribe it into the correct rhythm.

This close association of two or more dances was to continue and even develop in successive periods, gradually leading to the growth of the musical suite. Conversely, as musical development strengthened, this form of the dance itself, from which the idea stemmed, gradually dropped the set sequence of dances tied to a musical pattern, programmes eventually being bound by no more than the expedient of juxtaposing the gay and lively dance with the solemn and slow dance, three-four time with common time, and similar contrasts.

Looking at pictures of fifteenth-century dancers today, it is strange to see only one couple on the floor, with onlookers all around them. But this is in fact what actually took place. One couple would dance first and then their place be taken by another couple. Following which, perhaps a number of couples would take the floor together. Undoubtedly this led in later times to the 'leading off' of a dance by an honoured guest or exalted personage, before all the dancers followed them on to the floor.

As there was no order of steps the dancer had considerable choice as to how to arrange his own sequences. On a special occasion, however, a dancing master arranged a number of set sequences in order to fit them into the space available and to the music which would have been written specifically for the occasion.

Sometimes the musician was called upon to modify an existing composition for the requirements of the dance. In this case he normally took an established melody and adjusted it to the necessary length. An examination of the 'Golden Manuscript' shows that the melodies are written in plainsong notation, not in mensural form. The reason for this is that the plainsong form did not lay down any definite rhythmic values, so that these could easily be adjusted to fit the dances.

As each couple took the floor for the Basse Danse they proceeded round the room. This formed the first part of the dance. Then followed the Saltarello without a break. The scene presented can I think be well imagined. Let us assume it was a ball in celebration of some important event. Perhaps our best picture comes from France right at the end of the fourteenth century. At this time the court of the Valois under King Charles VI and his bride Isabella of Bavaria, was pleasure loving in the extreme, with masquerades, jousts, fetes and balls following one another in rapid succession. Paris was then the centre of Europe, so that the nobility and aristocracy of many countries crowded into society. In addition, to fan the flames of youthful high spirits and mad capers, the Latin-Quarter was already well established. Noblemen and the king vied one with the other to produce the most daring, the most outragous and the most original ideas in the way of pranks and fancies. The most famous, or as it turned out, infamous, of these great occasions, took place on January 29th, 1393, as part of the nuptials between a knight of Vermandois and one of the Queen's ladies-in-waiting. The king himself entered with zest into the spirit of the occasion and decided to take part in the masquerades. The bride had been twice a widow, and it was by no means uncommon for the celebrations of marriages of widows to be wild and licentious. The king lent his own residence for the celebrations. This was the Hotel de Saint-Pol of which now nothing remains but written descriptions. It appears that the edifice was a vast network of virtually unplanned rooms and galleries, with all the latest innovations for the court. Twelve galleries connected the separate buildings which contained great halls.

The organizer of the king's amusements was a Norman knight named Hugonin de Guisay, apparently a man of gross cruelty who sometimes turned his servants into human trestles for his dining table, digging his spurs into them at the slightest movement. The king, it is said, admired his talents for original entertainment, and there is little doubt that the idea for the special masquerade at this wedding celebration came from this knight.

The king and five of his noblemen set about disguising themselves as satyrs. Costumes specially prepared for them had first been steeped in resin and then covered with flax, so that they resembled human hair. Incidentally the costumes were of such a nature that our revellers had to be sewn into them. The utmost secrecy had been secured for the adventure, so that none might know that the king was a participant. Already, for several hours, the dance had been in progress, starting with the formal dances but gradually growing more exuberant as the wine and the spirit of the occasion made their impact. Imagine all the jugglers and acrobats and the clowns who added to the chaos of the scene. Remember too that at this period Parisian fashion had reached its most frivolous and extravagant style. Tonight the ladies wore enormous headdresses, many of them sporting fantastic horns, together with long trains of rich and heavy material. While their draperies reached nearly to the floor, their decolletage would have scared even Jayne Mansfield. The men too wore extravagant costumes with fantastic devices woven on to their doubtlets; astronomical charts, botanical motifs, musical notation and even obscene jokes were emblazoned about them, both fore and aft.

Midway through the ball a banquet of thirty courses was served to the revellers. This does not mean that even these gourmands enjoyed every one of them but they simply picked their way through all that took their special fancy. Then back to the dance. By midnight the older people had probably retired, leaving the field open to the uninhibited wildness of youth. And this was the time when the king and his co-conspirators in the masquerade retired to change. Before their metamorphosed return the torch bearers around the hall were ordered not to move away from the walls, for somebody had realized that one tiny spark on one of the costumes would cause a deadly conflagration. This retirement of the torch bearers into the recesses must have caused the light to dim before the disguised king and his friends returned frolicking into the hall. Hand in hand they came, gambolling round the ladies and putting them to fright. Everybody was by now of course wondering who the wild jokers could be and doubtless there was some annoyance among the men when these satyrs romped with the women, the ladies who fled in fright being chased, ridiculed and embraced by these hairy creatures.

The Duc d'Orleans, according to Froissart, who has recorded this 'Dance of Savages' was determined to find out who the creatures were; taking a torch from one of the torch bearers he held it so close to a masquer that 'the heat of the fire entered into the flax (wherein if fire take there is no remedy) and suddenly was on a bright flame, and so each of them set fire to the other'.

So intense was the heat that some of the men who attempted to go to the aid of the agonized victims were themselves burnt. The blazing satyrs writhed and yelled; the dancers must have rushed in all directions. Yet it is said that the musicians, playing in the gallery aloft, mistook the cries and the frenzied activity for signs of increased gaity, and that in consequence they played louder and with renewed vigour. At last one of the blazing victims remembered having seen a great water butt in the buttery; racing to it he threw himself in. The others were however by this time past aid and died a hideous death. The queen, fearing that the king was among them, fainted, but fortunately when the torch began its fatal work he was elsewhere, sporting with one of the ladies of the court. (See Appendix II.)

For a while, so great was the effect on the court and the people, balls of this kind (this one becoming known as *Le Bal des Ardents*) became rare, but not for long, for soon Catherine de Medici, perhaps the greatest female schemer of all time, revived them with greater splendour than ever, as a breeding ground and cloak for her vast and complex diplomatic intrigues.

A great and historic ball with a happier ending, and one which has been well recorded, was presented in Milan in 1490. This is how a minor court poet of the period wrote about it:

'Signor Ludovico il Moro had it done in praise of the Duchess of Milan, and it was called Paradise because there was made for it, with great ingenuity and art by Master Leonardo Vinc of Florentine, the paradise with all the seven planets which revolved, and the planets were represented by men, in the style and costumes which the poets have described, the which planets all spoke in praise of the perfect Duchess Isabella.'

This same poet, Bellincioni, had been commissioned to write the words to be spoken by the planets. The host of the celebration, the Duke of Milan, is said by a contemporary chronicler to have

'... invited about a hundred ladies and young maidens from among the most beautiful and richest in the city. And also all the Senators and Magistrates and Councillors and Gentlemen, for today at the hour of eight o'clock in the evening, all to be arrayed in clothes of most honourable colours; the which at the said hour all gathered in the chamber of the Most Excellent Signor Messr. L., and all the ladies in the chamber of the Madonna the Duchess Isabella.'

Art historians and biographers have ever since studied all the text and documents concerning this ball, in an effort to discover something more about Leonardo. Unhappily not a single one of the great painter's designs for the costumes or 'pageants' has survived, although this is hardly surprising, for neither carpenters nor costumiers could be expected at that time to treat the sketches and instructions as sacrosanct. There are however accounts of the production which speak eloquently of its richness. For example, Ludovico is said to have been wearing a 'tunic of mulberry coloured velvet with a mantle of black velvet lined with brocade of gold on a white ground'. It is also stated that his suit was in the Spanish style, this being one of the earliest references to the Spanish fashions which were to exert so strong an influence on European court dress of the sixteenth century.

Although we have some knowledge of the style of the dancing of the period no detailed record remains of the programme of this famous ball. Nevertheless we can construct some kind of picture of the occasion. Each group of people was seated around the great salon of the Sala Verde in specially appointed places, with Isabella between her husband and Ludovico, grouped with the ladies of the household. On either side were the ambassadors and their retinues.

The music consisted of wind instruments and drums, and the ball was formally opened with a Neapolitan dance. Isabella went to the middle of the floor with three of her ladies and there, with the ambassador of Naples, danced two sequences. Following this came the ballets. These consisted of groups of dancers from various countries, each of them performing one or more dances from their own nation after first having brought words of homage and greeting from their king. The first group was from Spain, and they were followed by Poles, then Hungarians, Turks (they were actually led, so we are told, by their ambassador and his company on horseback). But the Turks did not dance, for to do so in front of Christians would to them have been barbaric. Instead they retired to the side and sat on cushions.

Next followed masquers from Germany and France, all of whom took their place on the floor and performed in the manner of their country. And at the end of this part of the celebrations:

'The Most Illustrious Isabella commanded that everyone should dance, and so every dancer performed the same dance together, Spaniards, Poles, Hungarians, Germans and French: so were danced many dances. At the twenty-third hour came into the said festa eight more masquers, lightly clad, who were most vivacious and agile, and which made many scissor-jumps, with such play of the feet and leaping, which for a time were fine to see.'

When this part of the spectacle came to an end Isabella next commanded her ladies-in-waiting to dance, which they did, we are told, in the Neapolitan style. They were followed by the Spanish dancers, and once again all the nations had their turn. Then, a little before midnight, the spectacle planned and devised by Leonardo was introduced. Entitled *Il Paradiso*, this contained representations of all seven planets, the stars and the signs of the zodiac. Remembering Leonardo's prowess as an engineer as well as a painter we can well imagine that the machines and pageants for these effects were ingenious to a degree. Today we might think it strange that an artist of the stature of Leonardo should be called upon to execute such work as this, but painters of that time considered it a great honour and exerted as much effort, as much imagination, in the construction of wonderful pageants as they did in the creation of their masterpieces on wall, canvas and in marble. Leonardo himself, by all accounts, was something of a dandy and although we possess no knowledge of his work for *Il Paradiso* beyond the fact that the designed the effects and costumes, I like to believe that he also had a hand in the actual pattern of the dances, and that he perhaps even danced himself. Although none of his own designs for *Il Paradiso* have survived, we do possess other designs of his of a comparable nature and we do know to some extent how his work influenced costume design and even hair styles. For example, he appears to have been the first, and if not the first he certainly used the idea in a new way, to decorate the rather simple hair styles of that time with extra hair in the form of plaits.

In view of this I find myself ceaselessly frustrated through Leonardo never having attempted to represent the dance in his painting. To say that he was not interested in movement would be untrue, but his interest lay in the suggestion of power in the human body, not in the outward results of that power. In other words, at least from the evidence we possess, he maintained that the actual representation of movement was either not desirable or not possible on canvas, although in his drawings he sometimes expresses it. Had he thought otherwise, had he sought like Botticelli and others to show human beings in movement, think of the wonderful representation he might well have given us of dancers of that period. Perhaps he did in his designs for the costumes for *Il Paradiso*, but now we shall never know. He certainly did not in his costume designs for other occasions, for some of those are still in existence.

One year before this extravaganza I have just described there took place what is frequently referred to as the first ballet. This claim is not by any stretch of the imagination justifiable, for I have already described various entertainments which could be classed in the same category, even if not so lavish.

The spectacle presented by Bergonzio di Botta, a noted gourmet and keen dancer, in Tortona in 1489, had for its excuse a visit of Gian Galeazo, Duke of Milan, who was passing through with Isabella of Aragon, his new wife. Perhaps this affair has become known as the first ballet largely because its documentation has come down to us more firmly than that of others of the same period. In fact it was no more of a ballet than many other spectacles given during the previous hundred years, but was, in common with all such events, a kind of banquet ball during which special tableaux added variety to the dancing and other entertainment. I quote a contemporary description:

'When the Duke and Isabella walked into the banquet hall, from an opposite door entered Jason, with his Argonauts. By pantomime and to the sound of war-like music they expressed their virile pleasure in the Ducal presence, left a Golden Fleece (a roast, gilded lamb) before the pair, and retired. Mercury arrived, and in recitative, told of the craft by which he stole a calf from Admetus. Three quadrilles terminated his entry. Diana and her nymphs were succeeded by a litter upon which a stag, Acteon, sat. She told them that this youth, as a hart, was glad to be eaten by one so fair as Isabella. A symphony of strings announced Orpheus. The Thracian lyre for the first time since the loss of Eurydice was struck with joy, discovering such bliss as the Duke's, the Duchess's. A brusque note broke his song; it was Theseus, Atalanta and the Calydonian hunt. Their wild boar, duly slain, was offered by the Duke to carve. There was a course of fowl, disguised as Isis, throned on a car drawn by peacocks, followed by nymphs supporting platters of birds cooked in their feathers. Hebe poured her her devine nectar. Arcadian shepherds, Vertumnus and Pomon brought fruits. The Imperial epicure, Apicius, represented by his ghost, gave all the fantasy of gourmandise known to antique Rome. Then a spectacle of sea gods; the Lombard rivers offered up their fish-foods, dancing suitable figures. And so it went, entry after entry, until it terminated with a Bacchic rout.'

At intervals in the meal groups of dancers appeared, sometimes as an interlude itself and sometimes, later, to herald in the next course. These groups became known as *entrées*, a word common today in both ballet and the dining table. The French word is really *entremets*, which eventually came to mean the sweetmeats served at the end of the meal. The word is derived from the Latin *intromissum*, meaning the third course of a banquet, or simply 'something inserted into something else'. Later this kind of interlude, now transferred from the dining hall to the ballroom and thence to the stage of the theatre, was to become the intermezzi, which were originally the danced interludes in classic plays. Later still, after these interludes had frequently become more popular than the plays themselves, they were to develop into an entirely separate form of theatrical entertainment, the ballet.

An entertainment of this kind must have lasted at least four or five hours, and there are suggestions that many of them endured for much longer than that. Some students of the period have stated that we of today would have been unutterably bored with them long before the end. I simply do not believe it. Do we not today often sit through a formal dinner lasting about three hours. True we do suffer from ennui if the speeches are long and unfunny, but imagine how much more rich and varied were the entertainments of that time. The magnificent fabrics and extravagant fashions, the gossip of people who had not heard the news on the radio or read their newspapers an hour before; the delight in the beautiful dance movements, and the invention of the presentation of the many courses of the meal, to say nothing of the originality of the food itself, must have appealed to every sense. This was *la dolce vita* before it had turned into the kind of dull, continuous repetition without imaginative transmutations which was to produce the boredom and satiety of later periods. Nor of course were these entertainments presented with enough frequency to create boredom, for they were extremely costly even for the great princes and nobles of that time. Each event was planned months in advance and all the ingenuity of musicians, artists, chefs and others was devoted to make them outstanding events, a glory to the household from which they emanated.

Doubtless, then, the Duke of Milan and his lovely bride were still avid for such entertainment when they reached Milan after their regalement in Tortona. And this is where Leonardo's *Il Paradiso* was put on for their pleasure. Incidentally, the evidence is fairly clear that in *Il Paradiso* Leonardo was able for the first time to surpass the effects created by the Brunelleschi brothers, who early in the century had made their wonderful cloud and heavenly effects by means of ingenious wooden structures and subtle use of various kinds of wool. Now the great inventor, painter, musician, engineer, a man said to be so strong that he could twist a ring out of a strip of iron, and so sensitive in touch that the could wrest beauty out of his lute, created yet more naturalistic effects by means of structures capable of complicated movement. In the climax of *Il Paradiso* a curtain fell to reveal the full splendour of paradise, which took the shape of an enormous egg cut into two, the inside gilded to shine like heaven itself. Innumerable lights represented the stars, and, cunningly fitted into niches, were the seven planets; while around the outer rim of the 'egg' were the signs of the zodiac, with lights reflected through water contained within thin glass in order to achieve a luminous effect.

This kind of presentation naturally had a strong influence upon the theatre which was coming greatly to the fore in the fifteenth century. For many years much of the dance element on the ballroom floor and on the stage was to remain identical in figuration, if not always in pattern and skill. At this time the theatre gained by being able to produce the spectacular 'entrées' of all kinds of exotic dances presented at these balls. But apart from that the Basse Danse and the other dances of the time remained in vogue both as a social development and as a theatrical spectacle. It was to take time before the special needs of the theatre would separate the stage dance from the social dance so that the two became virtually unrecognizable one with the other.

In his *World History of the Dance* Curt Sachs has many interesting theories about the chain dance form. He claims that although it was ignored by contemporary technical literature it was nevertheless danced, even in courtly circles. His evidence, quite apart from our instinctive feelings that the linked processional and round form must go back to antiquity, is overwhelming, for painters of the period show this form of dance. Sachs himself instances Antonio Rosellino's altar relief of the birth of Christ in the Monto-oliveto church of Naples from about 1475. Botticelli's Nativity in the London National Gallery (dated 1500) is surely another very good example. Indeed Botitcelli provides the best source for a non-technical study of the stylized gesture and poses of the courts of the Medicis in the latter half of the fifteenth century. His groupings and the particular style of his subjects must frequently have been based on dance groups and figures. After looking at the beautiful chain round of the angels in the Nativity look at his Primavera, which was painted in all probability round about 1475. It seems likely that this, one of the most famous of his pictures, owes some of its symbolism to the pageants and spectacles lavishly staged by the Medicis. At any rate the Primavera can easily be interpreted as a rich charade in which two gods, in collaboration, bring about a meeting of two lovers in a wood. The god Boreas, the shadowy figure on the right, pushes the shy maid forward, past the figure of spring, towards the seemingly unaware young man on the left, at whom Cupid is aiming his arrow. The three graces dance, posed in a style which artists have adopted ever since the Renaissance, prompted of course by the fifteenth-century painters. That dance of the three graces cannot surely come straight from the imagination. The linked hands, the turn of the bodies, the raised arms, perhaps in preparation for an 'allemande', must surely be a keenly observed portrait of a dance figure. Even the highly stylized pose and gesture of Venus herself are probably taken from the highly artificial behaviour on the dance floor.

That Botticelli should however show the angels in his Nativity dancing a round is perhaps a little strange, for according to Castiglione's book of etiquette of Italian renaissance society this kind of dance was not to be performed in public, but only in private. In Petrarch's opinion, too, men and girls running about in a linked circle, turning and posturing, presented a ridiculous spectacle. What a happy circumstance that Botticelli paid no attention to these apparent demands of etiquette, for those angels are one of the most felicitous fragments in the whole of fifteenth-century painting, and certainly in our records of the dance. The theme of the picture is the single-minded one of the triumph of God and the destruction of evil, represented so ingeniously if at first glimpse so naively, by the slain creatures below. We rise through the paths of the ineffable joy around the infant Christ, protected by the trilogy on the manger roof. But the greatest felicity, the unbounded tranquillity, is saved for the angels dancing on the floor of the air. So joyous are they in the dance that they are constrained to open their lips in spontaneous song. That Botticelli used the dance form for such transcendent emotions is beyond doubt evidence of the power and influence of the dance at court. That the picture itself is dated 1500 is perhaps symptomatic of the glory of the dance of the fifteenth century.

Sachs believes that the most frequently mentioned dance of the century is the Moresque, at the same time admitting that it is the most difficult to classify and characterize. Yet Melusine Wood does not refer to it in any of her technical books, and Mabel Dolmetsch merely touches it in passing. Morisco is the Spanish name for a moor who remained in Spain after the Moorish conquest and who was converted to christianity. The reason for endowing the dance with this name, it appears, derives partly from the Spanish custom of performing certain dances as they were believed to have been danced in the Moorish courts; and partly from a mimetic couple dance in which occurs a mock sword combat between a christian and a mohammedan. This theme exists right up to the present day in certain Spanish festivals, and can even be seen in a classical ballet: the toyshop scene in the Royal Ballet's production of *Coppelia*.

The Moresca also appears in various double file processions in which there is no allusion to religious strife. In one particular Moresca two files dance towards one another with swaying movements and then return to their places. Their accompaniment is the castanets. Such double file dances are however common in many parts of the world, and were so from primitive times. We need not therefore necessarily endow them with an arabic common source. On the other hand there seems little doubt that the preference of fifteenth- and sixteenth-century Spain for this form was mostly due to this influence—an influence which became stronger after the physical danger of the invasion had passed, when cultural influences could be readily accepted and even embraced. It was a form, moreover, which exerted an influence on more than the social dance, for as it became increasingly stylized, it was assimilated into the rapidly growing theatrical art of ballet. It is therefore more than passing strange that this, one of the most 'foreign' of influences, one which started outside Europe, should give its name to a form which is regarded as the most indigenous of all forms: the British Morris dance.

In England however this dance was certainly not adopted by the court but remained with the peasantry, and it was the most characteristic form of rural dance in the whole of the century. Its characteristic form has always consisted of a group of men, frequently six, and a 'fool', a boy dressed as a woman and a man with a hobby-horse. At various times and in various places the costumes have become varied and fantastic, but the music normally consisted, until the beginning of this century, of flute, drum or bagpipe. Today in England the piano accordion has supplanted this combination.

The whole conception of the dance is one which stresses manly vigour, its basic step being a strong forward motion of one leg while the other maintains a skipping movement. The arms are swung with energetic rhythm and the basic figure is varied with occasional leaps. Today one very rarely sees the dance performed in a circle ground pattern, although it seems likely that this was the original form. Nowadays the dancers form into rows, often of three dancers in each.

At no time are women supposed to participate in the Morris, which from our point of view here takes it outside the purely social form of dance. In Spain a dance based on the classical form of Moresque is still danced in the cathedral. This is known as Les Seises and is performed annually by six choir boys.

The Piva, too, to which I have already referred, was at this time much performed by the peasantry. Its vigour appealed to the gentry of the time and they took up the dance with some enthusiasm, but appear to have dropped it almost completely by half-way through the fifteenth century.

These country dances undoubtedly influenced the whole outlook towards the social dance, giving it a new vigour and vitality. Even in this century, although not to the same extent as three hundred years later, the court dance at certain times, coinciding with its technical development, began to grow effete and lifeless. At such times the form can survive only if reinvigorated by a sufficiently strong outside influence. This kind of reinvigoration regularly appears in the history of the social dance.

The brilliant dancing masters, Guglielmo Ebreo and Cornazano, working on the firm foundation built by Domenico, worked out their refined and complex forms quite independently of the country dances of the peasants. These masters became highly respected members of upper society, and doubtless with their elevation in the social strata they added their own courtly embellishments to their dance instruction. Although he was teaching his pupils for the courtly balls and great occasions, not for the stage, these pupils were nevertheless very much on show, for as we have seen, several of the dances were of a mimetic nature and in all of them each couple would at some time or another be on the floor either alone or with no more than one or two other couples. These masters therefore aimed at extreme elegance and refinement, and a technique which required much patience and application for its mastery. The dancing places of that time, although the floor surface itself would consist only of polished stone or rough wood, must have offered a rich spectacle, with their tapestry hangings, their galleries and the multi-coloured and voluminous costumes, greatly varying in style and pattern, of the dancers. It is not difficult to relate the dancing master's philosophy to this setting. Wrote Guglielmo:

'Dancing is an action, showing outwardly the spiritual movements which must agree with those measures and perfect concords of harmony which, through our hearing and with earthly joy, descend into one intellect, there to produce sweet movements which, being thus imprisoned, as it were, in defiance of nature, endeavour to escape and reveal themselves through movement. Which movement of this sweetness and melody, shown outwardly (when we dance) with our person, proves itself to be united and in accord with the singing and with that harmony which proceeds from the sweet and harmonious song and from the measured sound we are listening to.

'The art of dancing is for generous hearts that love it, and for gentle spirits that have a heaven-sent inclination for it rather than an accidental disposition, a most amiable matter, entirely different from and mortally inimical to the vicious and artless common people who frequently, with corrupt spirits and depraved minds turn it from a liberal art and virtuous science, into a vile adulterous affair, and who more often in their dishonest concupiscience under the guise of modesty, make the dance a procuress, through whom they are able to arrive at stealthily at the satisfaction of their desires.'

Imagine what would have happened to the dance if this puritanical approach had been allowed full sway throughout the century. The very form itself would surely have disappeared, although it seems quite possible that Guglielmo did not hold quite such straitlaced views himself, but was conscious of the views of a large proportion of the aristocracy who maintained that dancing was undesirable and calculated to corrupt morals. Perhaps these dancing masters did not after all resist with undue force the vigorous innovations that really came almost direct from the soil.

THE DEVELOPMENT OF TECHNIQUE AND EARLY LITERATURE

Guglielmo prescribes six fundamental requirements for those who wish to dance with skill and accomplishment:

Misura (measures). This refers to the ability to keep time with the music, both rhythmically as well as in the tempo. One copy of the manuscript contains an illustration of a man and two women dancing, with a harp player providing the music. The harp and the lute, as well as the tambour, were mostly used for dance accompaniment at this time.

Memoria (memory). The ability to recollect all the steps and their order of sequence in all the various dances.

Partire del terreno (proportion of the floor). A careful observation of the size of the dance space. This was very important at this time. Remember that in some great halls there was still a central fire, with a hole in the roof to let out the smoke, whereas in other newer buildings the chimney was already exerting its influence on the dance. No longer did the assembly have to dance around that centre piece, but could when desired dance across the floor.

Aierel. This term is a little difficult to comprehend, but broadly speaking it must mean lightness and dexterity. It also refers to the swaying motion of the body necessary for the best interpretation of certain figures, together with a rise and fall through the use of the ball of the foot, not unlike that in use today.

Maniera. This term too is a little obscure, but it refers broadly speaking to the turn and adjustment of the body in relation to the direction of the feet. Guglielmo describes it thus:

'When one performs a single or a double step he should turn his body, so long as the movement lasts, towards the same side as the foot which performs the step, and the act should be adorned and shaded with the movement called *maniera*.'

Kinkeldy, modestly referring to it as a 'not very elegant but almost literal translation of Cornazano's explanation of *maniera*, gives the following:

'Remembering the steps and pacing them in musical time, you ought to give (a certain) aptitude to the things that you do, balancing and undulating with your body according to the foot that you move; as (for example) if you have the right foot to make a double step, you ought to balance on the left, which remains on the ground, turning your body slightly in that direction, and to undulate on the second short step, raising yourself gently (soavamente) on this step, lowering yourself with equal gentleness on the third step which completes the double step.'

In his brief description of *aere* Cornazano refers to the grace of movement that renders the dances pleasing to the eye of the onlooker.

Quite independently, and without knowledge of the work of these fifteenth-century dancing masters, a body of twentieth-century teachers worked out after the First World War a complex technique and science of movement in relation to ballroom dancing. They defined such terms, for example, as rise and fall and contrary body movement. Little did they realize that these same ideas had been put into technical definitions four hundred years before them.

Movemento corporeo is the last of Guglielmo's fundamentals. This refers, although not with any marked clarity so that we can fully comprehend its meaning today, to the carriage of the dancer, the act of moving with grace. Cornazano's *diversita di cose* exhorts the dancer to vary his movements, making some small and some large.

Doubtless it was the new vigour brought to social dance by the influence of country dancing which led Guglielmo to offer prudent advice to young ladies. He warns strongly against excesses of vigorous movement, concluding:

'Her glance should not be proud or wayward, gazing here and there as many do. Let her, for the most part, keep her eyes, with decency, on the ground; not however, as some do, with her head sunk on her bosom, but straight up, corresponding to the body, as nature teaches almost of herself. . . . And then at the end of the dance, when her partner leaves her, let her, facing him squarely, with a sweet regard, make a decent and respectful curtsey in answer to his.'

Guglielmo's contemporary, Antonio Cornazano, owed just as much to the teachings of the pioneer of them all, Domenico di Piacenza. Cornazano writes that he could repeat a dance without a mistake when it had been demonstrated but once. In view of Guglielmo's strictures about the necessity for a good memory this is a strong claim indeed; yet by no means an incredible claim when we realize that most outstanding dancers of today, whether social or theatrical, possess just this facility—an outstanding memory for the steps and patterns.

It is hardly surprising that terms used by both Guglielmo and Cornazano, as well as their actual descriptions of the dances, coincide in many details in view of the fact that both masters were either trained in one school or studied the same master work—probably both. Possibly Guglielmo held more lofty views of the purpose of the dance than Cornazano, although both considered their profession of the highest possible status. Cornazano was without doubt less frequently obscure than his contemporary, although at times both leave a great deal to the imagination. In common with teachers of more recent times, they evidently held the reasonable and justifiable view when they are writing that their readers were also going to undergo personal instruction, or at least to see practical demonstrations of what had been set on to paper. As a result of this outlook no single work of the fifteenth century provides descriptions which can be readily interpreted four hundred years later.

Guglielmo sets a number of tests for his pupils. Some are difficult to follow, but at least one of them is ingenious and would probably be of great practical assistance to many pupils today. He asks the dancer to try to dance a 'measure or two' against the musical time, for he maintains that this practice will sharpen his intellect and make him listen more attentively to the music. Another test of a similar nature is that in which he calls upon his students to begin against the time of the music and try to continue against the time. Guglielmo believes that the skilled dancer should be able to accomplish this difficult test.

In the final paragraph of his treatise on these fifteenth-century masters, Kinkeldy writes 'How Marguerite of Austria, Lorenzo the Magnificent, the lords and ladies of Sforza, Orbino and Este really danced, will not remain a mystery forever'. Although over thirty years have passed since he voiced that optimistic opinion, the mystery has still not been conclusively resolved; it is nevertheless true that a handful of teachers, with that rare combination, practical skill as dancers and an intellectual approach to research, have made a great deal of progress. Such authorities as Miss Joan Wildebloode, Miss Melusine Wood and Miss Belinda Quirey, although they do not yet agree as to every detail, have reconstructed dances of this century so that we can gain a pretty good idea from the demonstrations of their pupils as to what those dances really were like.

Towards the end of the century the French Basse Danse had become governed by rules, it seems, even more firmly laid down than in Italy. After learning the various movements, which were common to all the composed dances of this time, the dancers had merely to look at certain abbreviations in the printed descriptions in order to know what to do. These movements were as follows:

Reverence. The initial bow of the man and curtsy of the woman. In the printed description this was represented by a capital R.

Branle. Also a form of curtsy, similar to the Reverence, but performed during the dance, not at the beginning. Represented by a small b. Sometimes the Branle was known as the Conge, in which case it was represented by a small c.

Simple. A Simple was a walking step made by first moving one leg forward a pace, drawing the other leg up to it, pausing, and then continuing forward with the same leg. Represented by a small s, ss obviously referring to two successive Simples.

Double. A walking movement made on the balls of the feet and occupying four bars of music. First left foot forward keeping the weight well forward, then right foot forward, then left foot forward, concluding the movement by closing the right foot to the left foot and lowering the heels. Represented by a small d.

Reprise. This consisted of a Simple performed while moving in a backward direction and bowing slightly at the same time thus: Right foot a small step back; a little bow to the left side; normal posture again; left foot back to right foot. The Reprise was represented by a small r.

The foregoing descriptions are intended of course only to give a general idea of the movement and are by no means of a practical instructional nature. Anyone wishing to learn these dances should study one of the excellent books referred to in the Appendix.

One amusing custom during the fifteenth century—and it was a custom which extended in many parts of Europe into the sixteenth century—was the retention by the man of his hat on the ballroom floor. Instructions were laid down for its use, calling for him to doff it with his left hand before beginning his bow, and to hold it close to his side with the inside turned towards his body. He was then admonished to don it again as his foot closed at the end of his bow. Following that, in order to commence the dance the man tendered his right hand towards his partner, who placed her left hand in his. In this kind of hold the hands were kept low, and never raised above elbow level.

The cultivation of rise and fall (aierel) and the turning of the body in opposition to the moving foot, for example, were in the best dancers beautifully co-ordinated, just as they are in the best of the 'English Style' dancers today.

Indeed, in spite of the French concern with technique, Italy then held the position of England today. Although other countries sought the same skill and polish, the highest practical demonstration of the form was invested in Italian dancers. During the next century, however, England was to wrest this supremacy from Italy, and in spite of a decline from time to time, we have retained that supremacy ever since.

CHAPTER III

The Sixteenth Century

THE TEACHINGS OF ARBEAU AND OTHERS

The Dance is poetry with arms and legs. It is matter, graceful and terrible, brought to life and made beautiful by movement.

THE beginning of the sixteenth century heralded great advances in social life and mental outlook. In Gothic times the Church dominated most social activity; and during the previous century England in particular had been torn by civil strife. Now the Crown was not only to enhance its own secular glory, but also to increase its newly won ascendancy over the church. The Church of England was before long to become the focus of our national religion, with the monarch as supreme governor. The influence of Rome, although not dead, was on the wane, its power never to be rekindled.

Thus political, religious and social life centred more and more on the Crown. Even so the Tudors could never have governed effectively without the loyal and enthusiastic allegiance of the leading classes. The monarchy, taking on more and more responsibility, had need of a new aristocracy to assist in its great tasks. This means that the court of the monarch was both the prototype and the exemplar of the courts of the nobles. But there were in addition many other influences at work to widen the old world's vision and to sow the seeds of a hitherto unknown liberality of view and originality of thought. The discovery of America at the end of the fifteenth century added greatly to the world's experience, which soon began to manifest itself in a variety of ways. In the dance this new 'feeling' found an outlet in a greater freedom of movement and the introduction of exotic elements. The renaissance from Italy was also percolating through Northern Europe and thus leading to a loosening of restraint.

Another vitally important factor was the development of printing. Until this time a veil had hung over dance music. Now came a flood of such music from all over Europe. Not only at Court, but in the great houses which were to grow rapidly in number throughout the century, every nobleman kept his own orchestra.

The gap between the classes which had widened during the last century persisted, but nevertheless there were certain common folkloric elements which made a bond between the entertainment, and certainly the dances, of the two extreme classes. Broadly speaking the peasant class favoured the sturdy, even boisterous dances, flavoured strongly with pantomime, while the aristocracy were more addicted to style, posture and grace. As well as exemplifying their newly found security, brought about by a diminution of internicine strife, their dress at this time once again adopted a style which encouraged its wearers to indulge in a little understandable if not justifiable showing off.

The dancing master began to assume an ever growing importance in spite of the fact that he no longer controlled dance music. Indeed, music dictated its terms to the dance. Early in this century the time of music was shortened by half the value of the notes, and now for the first time came precise phrases to define musical form. Most dance music was arranged in four or five parts: viols, fiddles, alto, tenor, bass. More and more stress was placed on the treble.

The aristocracy continued to dance the Basse Danse, but the solemn nature of this form was now abandoned by the lower classes, who found the Galliard more to their liking. Later in the century the Pavane became probably the most popular of all dances, and this dance gradually took the place of the Basse Danse. The Pavane, also in triple rhythm, was sometimes written in 4/4 and sometimes 2/4 time. The fundamental style and movement of the dance was one of extreme dignity. At the outset the performers walked gravely round the room and saluted those who sat at the top. Its dignity is perhaps demonstrated by the fact that two musical compositions for the Pavane were dedicated to the Mother of God; and that no reference to this particular dance has yet been found in descriptions of contemporary folk and bourgeois life. One teacher exhorted students of it to enshroud their very souls with majestic dignity.

The actual figures of the dance were extremely simple, and only two in number, being known as advancing and retreating. Dancers formed into couples, with the gentleman behind his partner when retreating. Each step was made with a gliding motion and the entire dance was punctuated with frequent reverences for the gentleman and corresponding curtseys for the lady. At one point the gentleman danced solo, making a shallow curve towards the centre of the room, strutting like a peacock and saluting the lady opposite him before moving backwards to return to his own partner, to whom he bowed yet again.

The origin of the Pavane has now been established with some certainty in the court life of inquisitional Spain, which accounts for the sombre and religious mood of the dance. By the same token its dignity and spendour are suggested by the title, which derives from pavo, which means peacock. This relationship of the dance to the church brought to the music a certain chant-like quality. Dancing has in fact always played an important role in the ceremonies of the Spanish church.

The *Dictionnaire de Trevour* (1721) states that the Pavane is a grave dance borrowed from the Spaniards, and goes on to say 'performers make a kind of wheel or tail before each other, like that of a peacock, whence the name'. There seems little doubt that the Pavane retained its popularity from round about 1530 to 1676, there being various references to it in English literature at this time. In 1530, for example, Elyot wrote: 'We have now base daunsis, pavions, turdions, and roundes.' A few years later, in 1535, Lyndesay wrote:

> 'We sall leir now to dance
> Ane new Pavin of France.'

In the French and Spanish courts the Pavane developed into a processional pageant, and for many years it opened all ceremonial balls, being generally followed by the Galliard. But a dance of this character, simple in its fundamentals and with a clear-cut mood, must obviously develop in a variety of ways during its extremely long life, and there are various accounts of the dance being used in masquerades and other entertainments.

Although the Basse Danse remained in fashion well into the seventeenth century, by about 1650 its place had been taken almost completely by the Pavane, especially in Italy and France. Some authorities are still not convinced by the weighty evidence as to the Spanish origin of the dance and adduce facts which may set up doubt in the minds of those who are not convinced except by the irrefutable. Curt Sachs, in *World History of the Dance*, for example, refers to the strange confusion of the word Pavane with the 'similar sounding' name of the city of Padua. He also refers to a book of lute music published in Venice in 1508 which contains the music of the first Pavanes. The headings in this book are correct, but on the title page they are referred to as *Padoane diverse*.

Despite this evidence, however, there is really small doubt today that the Pavane did in fact have its origin in Spain, spreading rapidly from there all over Europe.

As its name suggests it was danced proudly, with a sort of strut. Male costume of the time enhanced its slight pantomimic effect, for with mantle and dagger, or the short sword favoured by many patricians, the male performer could suggest the spread of the peacock's tail. In view of the marked simplicity of the actual footwork of the dance, this pantomimic play afforded colour and variety. But the extent of the always mild play of this kind depended largely on the occasion, for after all the dance was intended primarily to express ceremonial dignity. The music of the dance was used in certain kinds of procession. The piper played a Pavane for example when a bride of some social standing proceeded to church, or when civic or ecclesiastic dignitaries went about their highly formal public functions.

As the century advanced, however, all dancing naturally became less severe, less formal in composition. The whole spirit of the age was towards a relaxation of formality. In addition, the mincing, highly artificial style begotten of the false sycophancy of the male towards the female, had already been challenged earlier in the century. The extent to which this new atmosphere of frankness reached later was indicated in the Shakespeare sonnets, in which the idea of male self-deprecation, and the adulation of one's mistress, has given way to a firmer kind of relationship and a new honesty. Donne in his turn went even further and showed some of the brutal cynicism, side by side with the idealism, of the new age.

In such an atmosphere the Galliard flourished. Right from the beginning it was a blithe and lively dance, living well up to its name. Its origin lies in *galach*, which means lively, a galliard being a gay dash- or ing person.

'Come, Madam, let's be frolick, galliard
and extraordinary brisk.'

The Galliard in all its phases always possessed a vigorous quality, its origin usually being attributed to Italy. Gathering strength and variety throughout the century, it achieved its greatest popularity from the last quarter of the sixteenth century to the middle of the seventeenth century. The first form of the dance was the Tourdion which, although it consisted of less violent movements, required a great deal of skill for its proper accomplishment. Possessing strong pantomimic qualities the Tourdion called upon both the lady and the gentleman to perform solo passages. Yet another form of the Galliard was the notorious La Volta.

THE TEACHINGS OF ARBEAU AND OTHERS

The only description to come down to us is that by Thoinot Arbeau, although possibly Cesare Negri's La Nizzarda is also a version of this same boisterous dance. Here is Arbeau's introduction to the Galliard:

'At the commencement of the galliard you must presuppose that the dancer, holding the damsel by the hand, makes the *reverence* at the moment when the musicians begin to play; the *reverence* done, he assumes a goodly modest attitude. To perform the *reverence* you will keep the left foot firmly on the ground and, bending the right knee, carry the point of the toe a little to the rear of the left foot, at the same time doffing your bonnet or hat and saluting your damsel and the company as you see in this picture. When the *reverence* has been performed, straighten the body and replace your bonnet; then, drawing back your right foot, bring and keep the two feet together (pied points). This is considered to be the correct position when the two feet are so disposed that one is on the right of the other, as you see in the picture below, the toes in a straight line, so that the body is equally balanced on the two feet.'

In La Volta the dancers rotated in close embrace, a type of hold which made the dance unique, for in all others couples danced either alongside or opposite each other, with some distance between them. But now they not only embraced, but sprang into the air as they turned, moving as one person. In order to accomplish this vigorous movement properly the gentleman placed his left arm around the right hip of his partner, his left thigh firmly against her right thigh, and his right hand beneath the busk of her dress.

Many people found La Volta bold and indecent, one contemporary writer going so far as to assert that a great many miscarriages resulted from its practice.

Arbeau, to whom we so frequently have recourse for sane and reasoned judgement, was not so concerned; but he wrote rather later in the century, when the dance had already been accepted by the nobility. In England, for example, Queen Elizabeth gave it respectability by dancing it at court with the Earl of Leicester—just as Queen Elizabeth II gave respectability to another form of dancing four hundred years later. Arbeau therefore merely wonders if it is proper for young girls to take such long steps, and voices some concern over the danger of dizziness because of the rapid and continuous turns. Later in the century it seems that each couple danced only one figure, making about three-quarters of a turn at a time. They then remained stationary, waiting, while other couples did the same figure, then prepared to start again. La Volta appears to have begun to diminish in popularity early in the seventeenth century, and to have disappeared altogether before 1650.

The greater freedom of thought and the increased prosperity of Europe, which had prepared the ground for such a dance as La Volta, naturally did not stop there, All dances were to some extent influenced by an outlook which was different from that in which they first flourished. The Basse Danse, born at the beginning of the fifteenth century, would have now been unrecognizable to its first performers. Other dances of the same period had of course disappeared long since, but even at the outset the Basse Danse was light in character, despite its slow and stately movements. Its small gliding steps and the frequent rise on to the toes lent themselves to an even lighter development, so that it could easily adapt itself to a less restrictive discipline. Both Arbeau and Antonius de Arena discuss the dance at some length, and from their descriptions it is abundantly clear that many changes had taken place. Fabritio Caroso too gives a number of figures, some of which call for hops and jumps which finally deprive the dance of the right to the title under which it embarked a century and a half before. Later still Negri describes three Basse Danses which again show an even wider divergence.

Earlier, in 1521, a treatise on the Basse Danse appeared as an appendix to a French grammar, opening as follows:

'Here followeth the manner of dancing of bace dances after the use of France and other places, translated out of French in English by Robert Coplande.'

This treatise which has been quoted in full by Mabel Dolmetsch in her excellent *Dances of England and France: 1450 to 1600* is well worthy of close study. Although some of the descriptions may be a little obscure, and have been the subject of some controversy, they nevertheless give a general idea as to how the dance was intended to be performed.

Shortly after the end of the century Negri, in 1604, describes three Basse Danses which also show an extreme divergence from the original pattern. The actual figures were laid down with extreme clarity and the contemporary authorities of each particular period do not appear to have been in very great difference of opinion as to the technique, although Arena states that all dances should start with the left foot and Arbeau is equally that the right foot should have this privilege. This seeming discrepancy may be the result of a change in fashion during the years which intervened between the two authorities, or it may be a difference of custom in various regions. On the other hand it is possible, if we are convinced by Mabel Dolmetsch's argument to the effect that Arbeau had never seen the Basse Danse performed, that the priest from central France was in error on this occasion.

The order of the figures was however a matter of extreme difference of opinion. According to Robert Coplande there were four paces: a single, a double, reprise and branle. The initial révérence was followed by two singles, one double, a reprise and a branle; but sometimes two singles were sandwiched between the double and the reprise. The double and the reprise were always odd in number. The dance, according to Coplande, always began with a single, after the initial révérence, and always ended with a branle. Sometimes the reprise was known as a demarché and the branle as a congé.

In the fifteenth century, the Basse Danse was divided into three parts (grand measure, medium and little measure) but by the time Arbeau was writing about it there were certain fundamental modifications and the inexorable rules were no longer enforced. There was also a sacrifice of grace and sinuosity, with an addition of hops and leaps. Arbeau refers to an occasional performance of the dance by three dancers, with the man in the centre, a form which naturally led to a certain complication in the exchange of courtesies. By the time of Arbeau, too, many dancers were taking even more liberties with the dance than the developments laid down by him and others permitted. Arbeau warned Capriol against certain practices, especially that of making the steps too large.

Arena and Arbeau agree that the Basse Danse was placed in the programme between the Pavane and the more lively dances. Arena's treatise is incidentally enlivened with passages of humour, whereas Arbeau is concerned with a straightforward but by no means dull teaching method. And it is Arbeau to whom we are chiefly indebted for our knowledge of the Branle, Arena providing only scanty information. Further, Arbeau is in all probability accurate, for he obtained his first-hand knowledge in Poitou, a leading home of the Branle.

In 1565, at a banquet given by Catherine de Medici at Bayonne, groups of dancers from the French provinces performed 'chaque à la façon de son pays'. In other words they performed their own folk dances. Dancers from Breton did *branls gais*, the name of Branle coming from an old balancing movement. The essential movements of the branle were a chain-like joining of the hands of all the dancers, who formed a circle or in couples in file. The title of the dance was derived from the verb *branler*, to swing from side to side, as a balancing movement which entailed this kind of action was an essential part of the dance. The English corrupted it to 'Brawl' and at one time, through this corruption, misinterpreted the nature of the dance.

Certain figures were common to all Branles, but within these figures a great deal of latitude was permitted and gradually a number of Branles became popular, some of them couple dances and others in chain form. A characteristic common to all Branles was a sideways movement in the nature of a chassé. Among them was the Branle de Poitou, in which the leading couple performed a kind of wooing dance, with a great deal of mime, at the end of which they returned to the end of the file, the miming procedure being then taken up by the next couple. It is said that every couple had their turn, but this must have caused each dance to last an interminable time, and probably many couples dropped out before their turn arrived; probably, too, there were pauses for refreshment.

The pantomimic themes were greatly mixed in these various versions throughout France, and it is in them that the form of the choral dance of the previous century is retained and developed. But although the French courts right from Henry III (1574-1589) to Louis XIV (1643-1715) favoured the Branle in its many forms, Italian society, at least of the first half of the sixteenth century, scorned it. Adopting the dance from the peasantry, French society danced it in groups, with three Branles at the beginning of a ball: a Branle double, sedate in nature, a Branle simple, of a more lively character, and a Branle gay, extremely rapid in its movements. The dance consisted of running, gliding and even skipping movements, the unrestrained and boisterous steps of the country folk now being tempered by the more artificial behaviour of society.

Each Branle was given a special title, some of them being composed for specific occasions. There were for instance the Branle de Malte, Branle de lavandières, Branle de pois, and Branle de hermites. The themes and the steps were mixed in such a manner as at times to seem inextricable one from the other. But because of the varying tempi Arbeau laid down that the Branle double form was suitable for old people, the Branle gay for young married couples and the Branle de Bourgogne suitable only for the youngest members of the assembly. Arbeau also stated that the order of dancing a suite of Branles, in which they were usually performed, was Branle double, Branle simple, Branle gay and Branle de Bourgogne. Musically the same melody was employed for the first two forms, with a melodic variation to provide for the change in pace. Incidentally this adaptation of the melody to the dance, typically medieval in character, led eventually to the development of the suite and finally therefore to the sonata and symphonic forms. During the sixteenth century, however, the transmutation from to one the other was confined solely to this melodic variation, which could be used in a great number of intricate ways.

One of the most popular dances of the second half of the sixteenth century—and indeed, although in three different forms, for about two hundred years from 1550—was the Courante. With the possible exception of the later Minuet, no other dance has remained in the programme for such an extended period. Its origin probably lies in Italy, although it is possible that it sprang up simultaneously in France as well as Italy. There is however evidence which establishes with certainty that in one of its forms it was imported to France from Italy by Catherine de Medici. Descriptions are extant of many Courantes, but none of them gives the atmosphere and feeling of the dance more aptly than Sir John Davies' long peom, *Orchestra*, published in 1596:

> 'What shall I name those current travases,
> That on a triple dactyl foot do run
> Close to the ground with sliding passages,
> Wherein the dancer greatest praise hath won,
> Which with best order can all order shun:
> For everywhere he wantonly must range
>   And turn and wind with unexpected change.'

One year later Thomas Morley describes the same dance as 'travising and running', while another writer was of the opinion that its characteristic movement 'recalls that of a fish when it plunges lightly through the water and returns to the surface'.

The music for the earliest form was written in 3/4 time and consisted very largely of rapid, tripping passages of eight notes. Yet a few years later Arbeau gives the music in 2/2 time. It is not clear when this further change came about, but during the seventeenth century, as the Courante grew in favour with the aristocracy, the music became slower, a little more solemn, and was written prolifically in triple time.

If Sir John Davies' poem gives us a good idea of the characteristic feeling of the dance, we must once again refer to Arbeau for a colourful non-technical description of the pattern and theme:

'In my young days there was a kind of game and ballet arranged to the Courante. For three young men would choose three girls, and having placed themselves in a row, the first dancer would lead his damsel to the end of the room, when he would return alone to his companions. The second would to the same, then the third, so that the three girls were left by themselves at one end of the room and three young men at the other. And when the third returned, the first, gambolling and making all manner of amorous glances, pulling his hose tight and setting his shirt straight, went to claim his damsel, who refused his arm and turned her back on him; then, seeing the young man had returned to his place, she pretended to be in despair. The two others did the same. At last all three went together to claim their respective damsels, and kneeling on the ground, begged this boon with clasped hands, when the damsels fell into their arms and all danced the Courante pell-mell.'

But before the end of the sixteenth century this pantomimic element had disappeared from the Courante, largely it seems because of its lack of sincerity and obvious artificiality. Instead, the pattern of the dance was firmly developed with an alternation of two simples and one double, first to the left and then to the right. This gave the dance a zigzag ground pattern, variety being achieved partly by a considerable latitude in the speed of the music. In this form the dance lived lustily right through the next century.

Arbeau's musical example is of the utmost simplicity, but it is strangely given with a duple beat. None of the great composers appear to have written music for the dance in anything but simple time, more often in 3/2 than 3/4. Dolmetsch comes to the conclusion that Arbeau regarded the accented beat as twice the length of the other; as steps were taken only on accented beats, this would thus amount to quick triple time. A yet further classification, known as the instrumental form, developed from the others. One measure of 6/4 time was made out of two measures of 3/4 and, with the number six as the least common multiple, changes of rhythm were obtained by writing some measures in 6/4 (two times three with the beat on 1 and 4) and some in 3/2 (three times two with the beat on 1, 3 and 5). There was no hard and fast rule as to when these changes in rhythm should occur, but it seems that the last measure was invariably in 6/4 and the penultimate in 3/2. This rhythmic device does not however appear to have been inspired by the dance itself, but rather to have stemmed directly from the composers. François Couperin undoubtedly wrote most of this kind of Courante music, although both Bach and Rameau were also responsible for some splendid examples. Thousands of tunes were to be written for the dance in the next century, the dance itself having lost the right by that time to term itself, in Shakespeare's words, 'swift', becoming instead a slower, more solemn affair, the favourite of the aristocracy, successor to the Pavane and precursor of the Minuet. But in the sixteenth century Arbeau says that the Courante preceded the Allemande, the reversal of this order coming with Bach in the next century.

After the Courante the Canaries were the chief form of sixteenth-century courtship dance. The earliest example of this dance comes from Spain, where it was regarded as the father of Jota. The Canaries consisted of bold and even bizarre movements, one of them being a skip and stamp of the heel and toe. In form it seems to have been related to the Schuhplatter and other wooing dances of eastern Europe. Arbeau gives the music in 2/8, although there are many examples in a dotted 3/8 time. In one early sixteenth-century form the couple danced through the hall, when the gentleman left his partner and danced backwards, then forward and back again. The lady then did the same, so that each has a long solo passage.

The Gigue, said by Shakespeare to be 'hot and hasty', is the quickest of all dance forms of the sixteenth century. Like the Courante, it was also written frequently in 3/8, although there are many examples in 6/8, 9/8 and 12/8. The music is written in rapidly moving groups of three notes thus setting up the rhythm of a galop. Composers soon found that they could produce an exciting effect by the use of this with the title of Gigue to which no performer could possibly have danced.

Various claims are made for the origin of the dance. The name itself possibly derives from *giga*, a small stringed instrument known in Italy. But the word can also mean a leg or limb. Other authorities claim British origin for the dance, asserting that the Italian references are to the instrument only. To throw a little more obscurity into all this uncertainty, the common term for violin in Germany is *geige* (fiddle) and the fiddle is the instrument most commonly associated with the Gigue.

Although most of the court composers of the sixteenth and seventeenth centuries wrote Gigues, the dance itself never appears to have won the patronage of the court. Nevertheless English literature of this time abounds in references to the dance, treating it to a wide variety of spellings in the process. Sir Henry Sidney, writing from Galway to Queen Elizabeth about the Anglo-Irish ladies, refers to them as 'very beautiful, magnificently dressed, and first-class dancers' and expressed great enthusiasm over their skill in dancing Irish Jigs. That was in 1599. Over a hundred years later Playford refers to the pleasure found by the gentlemen of the Inns of Court in dancing Jigs. But by that time the dance had undergone many changes.

In the early English theatre the play frequently ended with a Gigue, but this meant both the words as well as the music and the dance. Poetically a Gigue consisted of any light rhythm with an irreverent context. There may be some connexion between this and the development of the Gigue until it became the final movement of the musical suite.

Although the influence of France and Italy, followed closely by Spain, has been most powerful in the development of European social dance, that of Germany has been of great importance, even if not in so extensive a field. Such a dance was the Landler, which derives its name from Landl, a mountainous region of Austria. In common with certain other German dances, a very close hold was employed during most of the dance, a feature that was frowned upon by the Latins, who in many stages of their history have viewed demonstrations of this kind with disfavour. The continuous turns of the Landler, carried out in a small space, were also peculiar to the Germanic races, and there seems little doubt that this kind of dance, perhaps the Landler in particular, led to the Waltz which played such an important part in the English social dance scene of the nineteenth century and, with important modifications, continues to influence very strongly the dance of the present time.

Germany, in fact, was so far outside the main stream of social dance development that travellers between the two parts of Europe often wrote in amazement of the strange forms of dancing to which their travels had introduced them.

In the Landler, and in other dances of a similar nature, the close hold I have referred to consisted of the man holding his partner with both his hands around her, in a kind of embrace, and often with faces touching. As in the present day, this kind of hold was modified according to taste—and dependent upon the degree of familiarity permitted. An engraving by Aldegrever, for example, shows the man with his arm around the neck of his partner, his cheek against hers.

Although the Landler originated with the peasants it is, strangely, a gliding dance, although it is probable that in its earliest form the gliding element was not so marked. In certain communities the man occasionally let go of his partner and clapped his hands in time with the music. The girls then formed into a circle on the outside of their partners and danced round while their men continued to clap. At a given moment the circle would break up and the girls find their partners and resume their gyrations. At other times the girl would turn under her partner's raised arm, usually retaining hold of the hand. This is common today in a number of the dances which have come down to us from Victorian and Edwardian times, and which are comically misnamed 'old-time' dances. This movement is aptly described, prosodically rather than technically, by Nicholaus Lenau in *Der Steyrertanz*:

> High o'er the maiden's head
> Then raises he his arm;
> His finger as a pivot,
> She circles round about
> Like strength to beauty joined.
> How straight ahead he dances
> In noble attitude,
> And causes then the maid
> Light whirling from the right
> To glide beneath the left.
> His nimble partner now,
> Must circle at his back,
> Dance round and round about him
> As if he wished to be
> As if he wished to say,
> Encircled by his love,
> 'Describe for me the circle
> of all my hopes and joys.'
> And now the blissful couple
> Take hold each other's hands
> And with a supple movement
> Slip through each other's arms.
> His eyes are fixed on her
> And Hers see only him.
> Perhaps they mean to say,
> Why can't we two, united
> In one another's arms
> Spend all our life together
> In such a dance as this?

At village weddings this turning dance took on an ever increasing licence, especially when the wine had flowed. As always happens with any uninhibited form of dance, there was a great deal of condemnation of it, one town council going so far as to threaten summary punishment upon those who went too far. Even when this kind of turning dance was adopted by society, however, it successfully resisted any kind of adulteration, the church and municipal council protesting in vain against its suggestiveness. In fact, its slight love-pantomime element, coupled with its vigour and rhythmic exhilaration, brought new life into the formalized dancing of the time.

But Germany was not responsible for all this freedom. The English court had already welcomed, as we have seen, La Volta, and kissing and embracing in English dances were by no means uncommon; nor, for that matter, in France either. There are records of protest and reprimands from both Italy and France in connexion with an alleged abuse of this practice. In 1583 Phillip Stubbes in *The Anatomie of the Abuses in Ailgna* writes:

'For what clipping, what culling, what kissing and bussing, what smooching and slabbering one of another, what filthie groping and uncleane handling is not practised in those dancings.'

But kissing of a chaste and restrained nature was at this time considered good manners. Shakespeare's Henry VIII, for example, inviting Anne Bolyn to dance when as a masquer he meet her at Wolsey's party, says:
> 'I were unmannerly to take you out
> And not to kiss you.'

'To take you out' means to dance together.

Towards the end of the sixteenth century the dance of the courts, enriched and enlivened by the adoption of peasant movements and rhythms, became yet freer in its forms; what had once been occasions for the practice of high formality and dignified if sometimes rapid and intricate dances now enjoyed wider variety and ever increasing freedom. It was inevitable that this freedom should sometimes lead to abuse, but generally speaking there can be no doubt that the dances of the end of the century were livelier by far than those by which it had been heralded. But the wheel contined to turn; coming events and a new outlook would soon bring with them a comparable transformation in dance fashions.

The last twenty-five years of the century were marked by a singular artistic activity, for by this time in Europe the great renaissance of learning, inspired by the achievements of Greece and Rome, had not only reached the whole geographical area, but had also achieved its highest peak of perfection. Indeed, in one or two areas, perhaps, a decline had already begun. For our purposes here, however, we can be sure that spectacle, entertainment and feasting on a lavish scale, and music, had never before been conceived in such extravagent and imaginative terms.

The composers of this time were by no means conscious that they were creating a new art form, for they were seeking enthusiastically to recreate the drama of classical Greece; just as a hundred years earlier Mantegna had believed himself to be recreating the art forms of Greece when he painted his great series, *The Triumph of Caeser*. The composers, in the result, proved to be equally unwitting pioneers as the Paduan painter. Almost accidentally, it seems, they made discoveries which led directly to the development of symphonic music. At this time the instruments of the orchestra were developing in various ways and certain instruments other than strings now began to occupy the attention of composers. This development brought about a substitution of the major and minor keys for the modes which had until now been employed.

Throughout the century in Italy masques and processions, together with great feasts for which elaborate preparation was made, and for which famous painters were frequently engaged to design and fabricate decoration and costumes, were growing in magnificence. Towards the the end of the century the theme was taken up enthusiastically by the French court, who then sought to improve, at least in spectacle, the entertainments presented by the House of Medici, in which house Lorenzo 'The Magnificent' had been responsible for the most lavish of these entertainments. It is therefore understandable that every dance historian spends considerable time in enlarging on what is generally believed to be the most spectacular of all these affairs.

The occasion was the celebration of the marriage of Marguerite, sister of the Queen of France, to the Duc de Joyeuse in 1581. This gave the queen mother, Catherine de Medici, just the opportunity she wanted to surpass a spectacle recently sponsored by her son, who had engaged Ronsard the poet, musicians and painters to devise masquerades, ballets on horseback and other extravaganzas.

Catherine's *valet de chambre* was a man named Baldassarino da Belgiojoso, an Italian violinist who had been in her employ for about twenty-five years. He had originally come to the French Court as the leader of a band of violins which were soon to become known as *Les vingt-quatre violons du Roi*. At this time it was by no means unusual for a musician to hold a post comparable with that of Belgiojoso in Catherrine's household; just as in more recent times outstanding sportsmen have been given nominal employment by tycoons and insurance companies. Be that as it may there is no doubt whatever that this particular *valet de chambre* exerted considerable influence on his powerful mistress in artistic matters. In the production of this entertainment to celebrate the nuptials of the Duc de Joyeuse and Marguerite, he appears to have been given an entirely free hand and an open purse.

Incidentally, soon after he arrived in France Belgiojoso called himself Baltazar de Beaujoyeux, and this is the name by which I shall now refer to him, as it is under this identification that a record of the entertainment has come down to us. The title of the entertainment is Balet Comique de la Reine, and although it is by no means the first time this kind of spectacle was presented, it is probably the first time that an attempt was made to base such an entertainment on a firm story and to relate that story through the combined media of dancing, music and verse. Instead of a mere masquerade we now had something which, however vaguely, had pretensions to drama. Although there is of course no record of the actual dance forms, the libretto of the work was published, having become today a rare and key work in the literature of the dance, and particularly of ballet history. As the libretto also contains eight plates which show the ballet in progress, together with musical notation of the melodies, we can gain an approximate idea of the spectacle—especially as we also know that it took place in the hall of the Petit-Bourbon in Paris, which was about a hundred feet long and fifty feet wide.

At one end of the hall, beneath a rich canopy, sit the royal family, the rest of the packed audience being arranged along the sides, some on raised tiers, the others at floor level. At the far end is a representation of the palace of Circe, the sorceress who turns her lovers into beasts. The floor is reserved for the performers. On the right of the royal seats is the arbour of Pan, a grotto flanked by illuminated trees; and on the left a golden vault, which forms a rostrum for the musicians.

After the instrumental overture to the entertainment a gentleman comes fleeing out of Circe's palace. Reaching the centre of the hall he stops and mops his brow, still in terror. After a short pause, during which all present are able to admire his costume, made of cloth of silver decorated with semi-precious stones, short cape and sword, he catches his breath and addresses himself to the king. After briefly philosophizing on pride and happiness he begs the king of Peace and Abundance to save him from the power of Circe, who had first turned him into a lion and then, temporarily relenting, turned him back into human form. Next the dreaded Circe appears and regrets having softened and sings 'The Complaint of Circe having lost a Gentleman'. After this she retires, with the look of a very angry woman, to her grotto to give way to the

1. Most of our scanty knowledge of the dances of classical Greece derives from low reliefs and paintings on vases, of which the above is a good example in the late sixth-century style. The flute player himself appears to be dancing, and the female dancer is wielding clappers in each hand.

2. Roman Pantomimes caught by the sculptor in dancing pose. These creatures, however, exemplify the corruption of Roman entertainment and are by no means to be compared with Bathylus and Pylades, those two great figures of Roman history.

3. A detail of Botticelli's famous painting of the Nativity in the National Gallery, London. Although the angels are ostensibly shown in flight, it seems clear that the great Florentine painter has conceived the whole idea from a round dance of the period. The painting is dated 1500.

4. This picture is a reproduction from one of the exquisite drawings from the Roman de la Rose in the British Museum. It is by an unknown Flemish artist of the fifteenth century. Illustrated here is a Basse Danse in which the artist seeks to show Love Leading the Dancing in the Garden of Pleasure.

5. An engraving from a painting by Israel van Meckenham, *circa* 1475. In the background Salome's grisly deed is depicted while in the foreground a stately ball is in progress. The musicians' rostrum appears to offer them scant room, and evidently the artist has taken considerable licence in representing a contemporary ball scene.

6. At Penshurst Palace in Kent there is an oil painting which depicts Queen Elizabeth dancing La Volta with the Earl of Leicester. Above is a reproduction from a wood-cut of the two central figures in that painting. A comparison with the painting shows the figures in the wood-cut to be reversed, a natural sequence when the engraver copied from the painting and then took off his prints.

7. A painting by Giulio Romano, who lived during the first half of the sixteenth century, and who was one of the creators of the mannerist style. Giulio worked chiefly in Rome and it is interesting to compare his conception of a round dance with that of Botticelli (Plate 3).

8. A contemporary artist's impression of the Duc de Joyeuse' Ball in 1581.

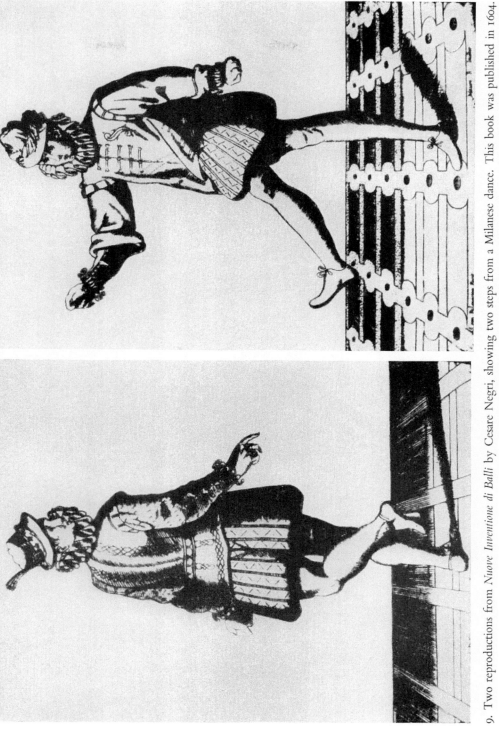

9. Two reproductions from *Nuove Inventione di Balli* by Cesare Negri, showing two steps from a Milanese dance. This book was published in 1604.

10. Two reproductions from illustrations in Antonio Cornazano's Treatise published in 1600. They show the way in which the hands are held in some Italian dances.

11. Painter David Teniers lived from 1582 to 1649. Here is a reproduction from a painting of his in the Alte Pinakothek, Munich. Its title is *The Village Wedding*.

12. King Charles II dancing with his sister, Mary Princess of Orange, during a ball at The Hague, held probably on the eve of his return to England at the Restoration (1660). They are dancing a Courante.

13. Pictures by the Flemish painter Antoine Wattau (1684-1721) are frequently used to illustrate the style of dancing of that period. The title of the original of the above is *The Pleasures of the Ball*.

14. This picture is reproduced from an engraving in Kellom Tomlinson's book *The Art of Dancing* published in 1735. It represents a figure in the Minuet, and on the floor is an example of the dance notation used in the Feuillet system.

15. William Hogarth painted a number of dance pictures, in all of them showing acute observation. The above, painted some time after 1745, was inspired by the Wanstead Assembly.

16. Here is another work by Hogarth, taken from an engraving which appeared in his *The Analysis of Beauty*, published in 1753. It depicts a country dance.

THE TEACHINGS OF ARBEAU AND OTHERS

Premier Intermede, a procession of sirens and tritons who, holding their tails under their arms, join together in song as they march round the floor. Next a float is wheeled on in the form of a fountain in four tiers, bearing on it Thetis and Glaucus with attendant nymphs. Among these are the chief dancers, the princess de Lorraine and various duchesses. After a brief exchange in verse between Glaucus and Thetis the groups descend from the fountain and dance what is referred to as the *première entrée de ballet*. Starting in lines they form themselves into twelve different geometric figures, although no record appears in the libretto as to the shape of these figures. However, we do know that at the end, in two crossing lines, they are struck into immobility by Circe with her wand, only to be freed shortly after by Mercury in a passage called *Entrée de Mercure*, who descends on a cloud. Perhaps he danced, but probably not, for the record shows that he made a speech abundant in flattery to the King of Peace, and sprinkled a holy herb over the enchanted nymphs in order to release them to continue their dance. Next come eight satyrs to form the *deuxième intermede*. They run round the hall singing the while, with a choir in a vault responding to their couplets. While they are thus engaged another float in the form of a forest containing four pastoral virgins appears and the Satyrs and the Dryads combine in further song. Following this comes more verse, the nymph Opis soliloquising and discoursing concluding by calling upon Pan to rescue them from Circe. The Four Virtues now make an entry, heralding the third *intermede*. Next comes yet another float in the shape of the Car of Pallas drawn by a serpent. Pallas seeks the help of Jupiter himself, who then descends *deus ex Machina*, the machine being in the form of an eagle. All the gods, goddesses, nymphs and satyrs who have taken part now bring the entertainment to a fitting climax by joining in a grand assault upon Circe's palace. After Jupiter has smitten her with a thunderbolt she is led captive to the King. Then, as a magnificent finale all the nymphs and others dance in wonderful figures and patterns over the entire floor.

But the entertainment had only just begun. Now all the leading characters come, two by two, down the centre of the floor in order to pay obeissance to the king. Then all together the assembly of 'entertainers' joins in a ballet consisting of forty figures: 'accurate and considered in their diameter, some square, some round, in various forms: in triangles within a smaller square.'

At the end of this spectacular entertainment came general dancing, in which the performers mingled with the audience. The final part, in which the whole crowd danced the social dances of the time, must have been spectacular indeed. I have not attempted to describe the costumes of the performers, but they were rich beyond belief. Neither would the court dress have been mean, despite the impoverished state of the country at this time. The cost of the presentation of the Balet Comique itself must have been excessive in the extreme and doubtless in some way aggravated the disgruntlement of the people.

Although it was the first time that a spectacle of this kind had so completely unified the various elements of singing, poetry, music, masquerade and dance, thus leading the way to the opera-ballet of the next century, the Balet Comique must have been nevertheless a monstrous form of entertainment, consisting as it did of a long drawn-out procession of scenes, dances, music and song, lasting six hours, from ten in the evening until four the next morning. The dances in the 'balet', as distinct from those performed at the end, were not strictly speaking social forms, although the figures would obviously have derived from the dances then in vogue. Mostly these dances were in rounds and excessively long. The first actual ballet consisted musically of a kind of Basse Danse, obviously specially patterned at the behest of the arranger of the dances. Next came a Tourdion to be followed by a Clochette, similar in rhythm to a Gavotte, and later a Branle. Even if they were not regarded as suitable for the ballroom floor, however, there can be little doubt that what was performed on that occasion was avidly copied by courts throughout Europe. Steps done during the 'balet', would be carefully observed by the audience, and movements originated in it taken far and wide, to exert an influence comparable to that exerted by the music. of which of course a more accurate record has come down to us.

The dances themselves were of an extremely elaborate character, requiring the performers not only to execute the steps common to the social dances of the time, but also to create as ensembles a diverse series of geometric patterns. Today exactly the same kind of situation exists in connexion with formation dancing—made popular through the medium of television—in which the dancers perform the figures common to the various dances of our time, but either in unison or in varying patterns. The arrangement of the various patterns for the Balet Comique must without doubt however have been simple if not rudimentary, for the robes in which the ladies were clad, carrying symbols of the creatures they represented, did not permit much freedom of movement. In all probability the most exciting part of the spectacle, as far as the dance element was concerned, must have been the constantly changing patterns of richly clad figures.

THE TEACHINGS OF ARBEAU AND OTHERS

Arbeau's *Orchesography*, to which I have referred with some frequency, appeared in 1588, seven years after the production of the *Balet Comique de la Reine*. In fact Arbeau was a pseudonym for a canon of Langres named Jehan Tabouret. The only other work traced to the canon is devoted to mathematics and astronomy, which was a fitting background for one investigating the dance, for geometrical pattern played an important part in the dance at this time—and later. Nearly two hundred years later Jean Georges Noverre, the great choreographer who left behind one of the most famous of all works on ballet of the eighteenth century, *Les Lettres sur la Danse et Sur le Ballet*, exhorted would-be ballet-makers to study those two same subjects. Be that as it may, Arbeau's book was a good deal more detailed than any of those written in the previous century, and it is possible today to reconstruct with some confidence in the accuracy of such reconstruction, most of the steps and figures he describes, as well as the rhythm and music.

The work is written mostly in the form of a dialogue between the master and his imaginary pupil, Capriol. Capriol is a young man who already possesses some skill in fencing and tennis, but knows nothing of the dance. He has come to Arbeau, he says, because he wishes to please a young lady in a way that befits an eligible young bachelor. Arbeau undertakes to instruct him provided he abides himself in patience, and first outlines the various classes, commencing with the antique (of which Arbeau probably himself possessed but small knowledge) before coming to grips with the dances of the time.

Antonius de Arena was an Italian who in 1536 published a fascinating little book, partly in macaronic verse with insertions of French and Italian. Although it is by no means as thorough or comprehensive as the *Orchesography*, The Arena work, which bears the long title, *Ad Compagnonies qui sunt de persona friantes bassas dansa et branles practicantes*, adds here and there to Arbeau's picture. Fabritio Caroso was another Italian; he was responsible for a work entitled *El Ballerino*. This work too is not very rewarding, for it contains vague descriptions only of mimetic dances which were not among the most popular of their time.

Yet a third Italian to colour the sixteenth-century scene was Cesare Negri of Milan who published a work on the dance in 1602 entitled *Le Gratie d'Amore* and in 1604 producing a revised edition under the more appropriate title of *Nuovi inventioni di Ballo*. Because he includes his own portrait as a frontispeice Curt Sachs comes to the conclusion, with some justification, that Negri suffers from 'self-complacency'. Be that as it may his technical descriptions are plainly derived from

Caroso, although he has minutely described several of the dances of his own composition.

It is Arbeau, in fact, who must have the last word in this century, at any rate as far as style and technique are concerned. He very clearly defines various positions of the feet and how best to achieve these positions—positions necessary in all dances. In making these definitions he proves to us today that here were the turned out positions which were eventually to form the basis of the classical ballet. It is often erroneously supposed that these positions originated in the ballet and that they were then borrowed for the ballroom in the nineteenth-century social dances. This is certainly not the case. These positions laid down here for the first time on paper by Arbeau were thus practised in the ballroom four hundred years ago, before ballet as such was known. The form of balletic entertainment which developed in the next century derived its movements directly from the social dance forms, and it was not until that century was well advanced that the social dances were developed for stage purposes beyond the reach of the skilled performer on the dance floor.

In addition to laying down the principles of the social dance in his *Orchesography* Arbeau also provided his young student with a great deal of suitable music. In conclusion Capriol thanks his master for having taken so much trouble with his instruction, to which Arbeau replies:

'I should like to have been able to make the result equal to the wealth of my sincere affection for you. In the future I hope to give you the airs and movements of several ballets and masquerades which have taken place in this town. We will deal with these in a second treatise as soon as we have leisure to do so. However, practise these dances carefully and you will become a fit companion of the planets, which dance of their own nature, and of those Nymphs who Marcus Varro said he had seen in Lydia come out of a pool and dance to the sound of flutes, and then return to their pool. And when you have danced with your mistress you will return to the great pool of your studies and gain profit from it, as I pray God give you grace to do.'

Thus, although the impetus for European social dance emanated from Italy, the two most important works left during this century for the clarification of our pictures of the dance of the time, are the *Balet Comique de la Reine* and the *Orchesography*, both of French origin, although it is clear that their subject matter owes a great deal to Italian influence.

CHAPTER IV

The Seventeenth Century

THE MINUET AND A VARIETY OF FORMS

So much of dancing, at least, as belongs to the behaviour and a handsome carriage of the body, is extremely useful, if not absolutely necessary.
The Spectator, May 17th, 1711

FOLLOWING the Elizabethan age of constant excitement with its great artistic achievement, its mental and physical development, the next hundred years, as far as it is possible to generalize over the temper and outlook of such a long period, was one of meditation and introspection. It was in fact almost as though so much had been accomplished in the preceding century that now an equally long period was required for its assimilation.

In social dance forms this change in temperament is clearly demonstrated in a number of ways. As late as 1588 for example Arbeau was still teaching a vigorous thrust of the leg in various figures, together with jumps and other uninhibited movements. But now vigour succumbed to restraint; angularity gave way to smoothness, jumps to gracious bends, firm steps to glides, the feet retaining contact with the floor. Everything was marked by an avoidance of haste. By halfway through the century the *douce manière* had become the dominant force if anything so unforceful could be described as a force, and the whole outlook of the dance had eschewed the vitality of the Elizabethans for the polish, refinement and suavity of the new age.

Throughout the sixteenth century dances in 4/4 time were in the ascendancy, only the Galliard, La Volta and a few Branles being left in triple time. Now the Courante, which was the most important dance of this century, although born in the previous century in triple time, changed to 6/4 time. Curt Sachs gives as the reason for this the inclination of the baroque to seek its expression in breadth rather than height, finding parallels in painting and dress. In all probability this factor did exert its influence, but it is not true to say that duple time is not appropriate for breadth of movement, as several dances of the present age which can in fact be claimed to bear some resemblance to the Courante and the typical gliding motion of seventeenth-century movement, are in duple time. Our Foxtrot, for example, is perhaps the closest possible translation of seventeenth-century movement into the terms of the twentieth century.

One must look further than this for the reason. In this century dance music no longer remains the servant of the dance. Until now dance forms had dictated the measures of the music; dance and music had more or less developed side by side. But now the widespread development of printing gave music an advantage which it would never again relinquish. After first determining the form of musical time and being the mainspring of the early musical suite, the dance would henceforward follow the composer rather than the composer the dance. At last the development of technical skill and knowledge became acquisitions which each individual composer could add after a detailed study of the work of those who went before. The dance too developed a kind of notation, quite apart from the printed word, but this kind of notation simply did not compare with that for music. As a result it must be admitted even by the most rabid dance enthusiasts that music now began to outstrip the dance in its establishment of tradition, theory and practice. Today the dance is really no longer in the race, from an intellectual point of view, as anyone who has studied a little counterpoint and harmony, as well as having witnessed hundreds of dance classes and ballet rehearsals, can testify.

The Allemande and the Courante were of course already well established in the last century, but from 1620 French lute books contain a Sarabande, a dance to which I will refer later. From this time it also seems to have become common practice to preface a suite of dances with a prelude. The musical suite now therefore became Prelude, Allemande, Courante (this dance was often performed twice) Gigue and Sarabande. What was later to grow into the classic order of these dance rhythms was also developed at this time: Allemande, Courante, Sarabande, Gigue.

Thus the musical suite laid down a number of strongly contrasted dances. Halfway through the century the idea of the variation of movement being accompanied by one main theme was practically discarded for both rhythmic and melodic contrast in each item of the suite. This innovation was finally to develop into the classical suite so brilliantly exploited by Bach and Handel. Lest I have perhaps given the impression that music now began to divorce itself from the dance, however, I must add that throughout the seventeenth century the most popular form of instrumental compositon was dance music. Each country has a bewildering variety of styles in this kind of composition, for the hundreds of itinerant musicians were constantly introducing the forms of one country into another. Again it can be seen quite clearly that this was a time for musical as well as dance consolidation; the forms which had come into being during the previous century were now being brought together and varied, but without a great deal of new thought, at least until towards the close of the century.

Parallel with this consolidation of the discoveries of the past, and their exploitation in new ways and in new combinations, this century was perhaps notable for its differentiation between the active and passive elements of our life. In Europe philosophers came to be regarded purely as thinkers; no longer were they expected to be men of action as well. The poet retired from active life and the soldier who was also a poet would be eyed askance. Perhaps Milton would after all have been more rigorously persecuted for his republican principles in an age when Moore and Galileo were looked upon as men of action as well as philosophers.

In seventeenth-century dance the dichotomy soon became evident, for as dance itself grew more complex, as distinct from being more active, amateurs gave way to professionals. Members of the court, who had been looked upon as the criterion of dance standards, now gave way to professional performers, so that by 1661, when Louis quatorze set up his Royal Academy, the social dance had developed such a complicated technique that it required long and arduous study, and was enlisted into court spectacles as professional entertainment.

From this time the French influence on the dance became the most important. French standards of execution began to set examples to the world, and in Paris a set of rules grew up, together with technical principles which roped the social dance into a benevolent bondage from which it would rarely, and then only briefly, ever again escape. Louis' academy consisted at the outset of thirteen dancing masters who sought to free themselves from the guild of musicians. Already dancers were fighting against the increasing domination of music—it is a fight which has continued ever since, although more in theatrical dancing than that on the ballroom floor. But hard though a few have waged the fight, from those seventeenth-century masters to Lifar in the twentieth century, who has made ballet not to music but 'just noises', the fight remains a futile one. Even in the ballroom groups of dance teachers have from time to time tried to 'invent' dance movements, and even rhythms, persuading musicians to set their accompaniment to those movements. Usually the result has proved an abysmal failure despite the fact that Stravinsky once said that he gains a great deal of inspiration from the rhythms of the human body in movement. Perhaps, after all, the dance is still in its intellectual infancy, and will in time develop a theory comparable with that of music, and thus create its own rhythms, freeing itself from the bonds of the composer. In England John Weaver, at the end of the century, was probably the first to base the dance and dance instruction on a scientific knowledge of the motions of the body. But here too this increased technical and theoretical knowledge also led to a decline in spontaneous expression; and indeed to an ever increasing dependence upon music.

One of the most popular dances of the seventeenth-century programme was the Gavotte. Originally this was a peasant dance which appears to have emanated from the inhabitants of Gap, which is situated in the Higher Alps, in the province of Dauphine in south-eastern France. As the natives were known as Gavots it is not difficult to see how the dance acquired its name. The Gavotte was first introduced to the French court in the sixteenth century, when a part of the entertainment was the performance of dances from the various provinces, the performers being clad in the costume of the province. Originally the Gavotte consisted of a succession of Branles mixed with movements from the Galliard. Arbeau describes the dance thus:

'. . . a collection of several Branles Doubles which musicians have chosen and arranged in a sequence. . . . To this sequence they have given this name of Gavottes. They are danced in duple time (2/2) with little jumps in the manner of the Branle da Haut Barrois, and consist of a double to the right and a double to the left like the Branle Commun. But the dancers divide the doubles, both to the right and to the left by passages taken at will from the Galliardes. When the dancers have danced a little, one of them, with his damsel, goes a little way apart and makes several passages in the middle of the dance in the sight of all the others; then he comes to kiss all the other damsels, and all the young men kiss his damsel, and they return to their proper order. Some accord the privilege of kissing to the leader of the dance alone, and to the damsel who is his companion. And at the end, the damsel having a chaplet or posy, presents it to one of the dancers who has to pay the musicians.'

At court the Gavotte inevitably underwent various changes in step, pattern and style, gradually losing a great deal of its roughness, as well as its natural vitality, at first becoming formal and stately, and finally stiff and artificial to such an extent that it would probably not have been recognized as having its origin in the dance which the Gavots had first taken to court.

In *Polite and Social Dances* Mari Ruef Hofer states:

'The Gavotte appeared as a welcome reaction after a long period of strenuous etiquette devoted to dances of undoubted tedious elegance. One can fancy a younger generation of royalty seizing with avidity upon this new terpsichorean delight. It soon became the fashion to follow the stately measure of the old dance of ceremony, with the lighter and more vivacious graces of its rival. . . . Who could devine that this pleasant breaking away from the stern formalities of court and caste might presage so dire and devastating a calamity as the not far distant French Revolution?'

Father Mersenne, in 1636, describes the dance as consisting of one or two rounds, after which the first leader bows to his lady, performs eight steps in front of her, bows again and then returns to his place with her. All the couples repeat this sequence in succession, then all bow together and take the ladies back to their seats. By this time every shade of roughness had been cut out of the dance. Its uncouth element gave way to formality; and even then devitalization did not cease, for in turn formality was supplanted by extreme artificiality; until finally the exchange of kisses demanded in the early peasant versions of the dance now became an exchange of posies. In short the Gavotte at court became symptomatic of the prevailing atmosphere of sentimentality and romanticism. But this deterioration was not to develop fully within the century of our present survey. Although the seeds of adulteration were sown at this time, they did not flower until the nineteenth century.

The music for the Gavotte was in two-part form, although as the dance developed a three-part form was added, this becoming known as the Musette. The time of the music was in 2/2 or 4/4. As it commences on the third quarter there was a mild element of syncopation. Mattheson in *The Perfect Conductor*, says:

'Its emotion is truly a real exultant joy. Its time-measure is indeed of an even sort but such a one as consists of two half-beats; even though it, at the same time allows itself to be divided into quarters; yes, even into eighths. I would wish that this distinction were taken heed of a little better, and that one would not be able to call most of them a *bad measure*; it does happen. The hopping character is a legitimate property of these Gavottes; by no means the running I seem to see the mountain folk jumping about on the hills with their Gavottes.'

How far is this conception of the Gavotte from the dance into which it actually developed a hundred years later. By that time it had become so refined, its technique so complex, that famous ballet masters such as the Gardels, the Vestris, father and son, were to dance it on stage as part of their virtuosity and gradually it was absorbed into the vocabulary of theatrical dance. An idea of the changes experienced by the dance in its long history can be gained by a study of Arbeau's description in his *Orchesography*—this is the oldest extant description—and the later Gavottes of the stage, and even those performed in the French courts of the early eighteenth century.

Another dance which enjoyed a long life and several changes in character was the Minuet. It began as a lively rustic dance in triple time, and seems to have first seen the light of day in its original form in Poitou. *Menu* means a little step, and towards the end of its career the Minuet suffered corruption into a mincing, highly artificial form of movement so far removed from its original robust form.

The style and the figures and the posture most highly developed in the practice of the Minuet have probably had as great an effect on the movement of ballet as the rhythm of the music for the dance has exerted on music. Indeed there seems little doubt that in the seventeenth and eighteenth centuries the Minuet provided the greatest impetus to musical development. At Versailles the most popular order of the musical suite became Branle, Courante, Gavotte, and Minuet, although by the time the dances had been elevated with the music to this station they had all conveniently forgotten their rustic origins.

In the performance of each of these dances at court the dancers formed into a column of couples, with the king and his partner, or the next lofty in rank if the king were absent, first at the head of the line. the dance continuing until they came back to the head again. At this stage the king would withdraw, though the others might by now have got so much into the spirit of the dance as to desire to continue.

In Paris the Royal Academicians of the dance appear to have become a little fearful of the Minuet, for they recognized it as a serious threat to the supremacy of the Courante, a dance which, as we know, they had nurtured with great care. In order to placate them the Minuet was referred to as the daughter of the Courante, although this in no way affected the gradual displacement of the Courante in favour of the Minuet, both in the orchestra and on the dance floor. Indeed, when the sonata form evolved from the musical suite the Minuet was the only dance form which survived in it. The basic suite had been Allemande, Courante, Sarabande and Gigue. Later five or six part suites included the Minuet form. These additions were known as intermezzi and soon began to have very little rhythmic reference to the dance form from which they stemmed. This same comment can also be passed on the dance form itself, for the Minuet of the late eighteenth century, expressing the artificial behaviour of that time, and reflecting very clearly the decline of the French court, is hardly identifiable with the dance from which it originally sprung. At this time, too, the Minuet was taken up by ballet masters with even more enthusiasm than that with which they had embraced the Gavotte. Gardel, Pécour and Pierre Rameau, great ballet dancers and teachers, exploited the dance to extend the rapidly growing vocabulary of balletic movement.

The French court did not however finally adopt the Minuet until about 1670, following which it became a part of the social life of the country for over 120 years. At first Lully, the great composer and dancing master, developed both the music and the dance, and he it was who wrote the first Minuet melodies. These were in eight-bar phrases. This form was adopted by most of those who followed him, although Allesandro Scarlatti did a great deal with a six-bar form. Purcell, Handel and Bach all composed beautiful Minuets, but by the time they had finished with it the musical form had left the dance far behind, and bore little relation to it.

As we shall see, the death of the Minuet came about in France towards the end of the eighteenth century solely, as is naturally so often the case, through a transformation in social conditions and a new moral temperature. Even then its death struggles were powerful enough, for it was revived in 1891 for about ten years, although in a new form. Ironically, I think, had it retained at the end of the eighteenth century more of the style with which it began its life outside the place of its origin, it would have gone on for another hundred years.

Louis Horst, in his fascinating book *Pre-Classic Dance Forms*, refers to the Minuet as a highly artificial dance of the rococo period. Aptly he quotes Mari Ruef Hofer:

'An attempt to write all that the Minuet implies would necessitate compiling the social history of France during several centuries; the manners, customs, art, music, and ceremonies of the period of the Grand Manner, as well as manifold steps and forms invented on its behalf.

Arriving as a climax in the art of the dance, in a period of luxurious national life, its very name suggests the refined magnificence of the courts of the kings in whose century it flourished. Millions were spent in its production; musicians, poets, decorators, artists and costumers exercised their combined powers to set forth its perfections. Its despotic ceremonial governed kings and queens, and its etiquette decided the fate of statesmen more often than their ability in statecraft. The dancing teachers of that day were autocrats to whom all bowed and deferred.'

Dance historians, and for that matter technicians of the dance, have so frequently stressed the artificiality of the Minuet, however, that today we are prone to see this dance in a false light. As a result enlightened teachers of the present time are seeking to bring this popular and false image of the dance into its right perspective. Writing in *The Ballroom Dancing Times* of May 1961, Belinda Quirey said:

'These private images (and, alas, public performances) range from a vision of a dainty china figure, a Dresden shepherdess in panniers and pointe shoes, to that of a lovelorn damsel with a limp white wig and limp large feet; from the Pizzicato mincing of the "ever so coquettish" to the undulating curtseys of the swoop and swoon school.

'. . . All I will say is that they bear about the same relation to the Minuet as the crinoline dolls that hid the telephones of my childhood to the Venus de Milo.'

In the same article Miss Quirey compares the reign of the Minuet with that of the Waltz. Although the Waltz has enjoyed a longer ballroom life, from early in the nineteenth century to the present time, it has not during that time reigned supreme, but has had to take second place, for all but a short period of its life, to other dances. The Minuet, on the other hand, lasted altogether only about 120 years, from the 1670s to the French Revolution, but during that period it appears to have undergone no change in tempo.

The basic figure of the Minuet consists of a bending of the knees, with the body held well over them, the feet turned out from each other, with all the weight held over one foot while the other remains slightly raised from the floor, followed by a slight lilting motion of the body from side to side, changing the weight from one foot to the other, keeping the body well braced and the heels raised slightly from the floor. From this position the weight is taken over one foot, the heels touching, and the other foot raised some inches from the floor.

The Minuet continued to dominate the ballroom until halfway through the eighteenth century, appearing for the last time in dance literature in a dance manual published in 1767. A dance book in 1798 refers to the severity with which the Minuet had by then been judged for some years. The dance of the same title taught in the nineteenth century, was far more artificial and mincing than that practised in the seventeenth and eighteenth centuries. Refugees in England from the French Revolution were engaged to teach young ladies in various kinds of educational establishments, and there is little doubt that they added their own niceties, subtleties and variations. They had after all to earn their living, and throughout the history of the professional teaching of dancing it is clear that teachers have always taken strong measures to justify their professional existence—measures which have in artistically impoverished times taken the form of intensifying and complicating technique in order that the craft should become a 'skilled mystery'.

A dance of considerable importance, in spite of the fact that it is not mentioned by Arbeau, is the Sarabande. Although the music for this dance was in 3/4 time it possessed similar characteristics to the Pavane: pride and gravity. Originally it appears to have been a religious and processional dance. It was adopted by European courts for their own social purpose later than the Pavane, although there seems to be a distinct possibility that it reaches much further back than the Pavane, even to the twelfth century. There is still a great deal of uncertainty as to its origin, and a number of authorities are of the opinion that in spite of its later religious associations it had a dissolute youth. Although there is not any indisputable proof, the Sarabande appears to have an Arabic-Moorish origin. One authority, the padre Maridana, who lived from 1536 to 1623, wrote:

'Among other inventions there has appeared during late years a dance and song so lascivious in its words, so ugly in its movements, that it is enough to inflame even very modest people.'

The Sarabande became in the fifteenth century a dance for courtisans and was later suppressed. There is no clear evidence or description of how it was transformed, or by what kind of evolution, before it came to play a part in religious drama. The dance appears to have been introduced into the French court round about 1588 and became extremely fashionable during the reign of the sad king Louis XIII. Cardinal Richelieu is said to have danced it in order to gain the favour of Queen Anne of Austria, wearing bells on his feet and playing the castanets. This story, whimsical and appealing though it may seem, is, however, to say the least, apocryphal, for to manipulate both bells and castanets with but a modicum of co-ordinated sound and rhythm would have required greater skill than Richelieu could conceivably have acquired. He is not after all reported elsewhere as a dancer or a musician of any accomplishment.

In the first quarter of the seventeenth century the music of the Sarabande was firmly established as the third movement of the suite; and then became the slow movement when the suite evolved into the sonata. One of the oldest Sarabandes is that by Couperin (1630-60), and Gluck composed a number of them. After that, however, the Sarabande seems to have been completely neglected by composers until Eric Satie produced one in 1887. In England we do not find any description of the dance until the Playford edition of 1703. From that description it is evident that there was a great deal of advancing and retiring.

According to Curt Sachs the Sarabande was considered so indecent and repulsive at the end of the sixteenth century that the singing and reciting of the words and music became punishable by two hundred lashes and six years in the galleys for male offenders, and exile for women. Despite a lack of explicit detail of the movements of the dance at this time, there does appear to be general agreement among contemporary writers that the dance consisted of sexual pantomime of unparelled suggestiveness. Before 1620, however, so great was both the change in outlook and the transformation of the dance, it became part of a comedy in the Spanish court; and no later than 1621 it was rejected by ladies of fashion as being outmoded. There are records of its being danced in Paris in 1625, but it seems likely that little of the Spanish form of the dance now remained except for the castanets and leg bells. Of the steps we now possess no real and reliable knowledge. By the end of the seventeenth century the dance had almost disappeared from society, although it was kept alive in the theatre in a variety of forms, none of them probably coming very close to the form in which it had acquired its ill-fame.

A lively dance of a shallow nature which nevertheless demanded a great deal of physical skill was the Rigaudon. A great deal of uncertainty exists as to its origin and even its name is shouded in some doubt. In the next century, descriptions of various Rigaudons show the dance at that time to be courtly and perhaps even artistic, but these forms were but distantly influenced by the original, and were performed quite differently in various areas.

The music was either 2/2 or 4/4 time, with a light character. In this form both the music and the dance were highly popular for some years in Provence. Indeed, some authorities claim that it had its origin in Provence as a dance of the peasants. Be that as it may, it seems at first to have been accompanied by the tambourine. Another theory is that the dance gained its name from a ballet master, Rigaud, who is said to have imported it to Paris during the reign of Louis XIII. Probably there is some truth in all these claims, with the result that, in common with many other dances, the Rigaudon owes its seventeenth-century form not to one source but to several.

The light and volatile rhythm of the Rigaudon lent itself to virtuosity and no matter how the dance began its life it became eventually a most suitable vehicle for the dancers of the French court, now highly conscious of their unsurpassed skill and anxious at all times for an opportunity to display it. If it had ever been a circle dance it certainly remained so no longer, but the dancers ran, hopped and turned, interspersing their more energetic phrases with a balancing movement that required a highly artificial line and poise. The dance became for a time extremely popular in England and there may be some grounds for the belief that the Sailors' Hornpipe was strongly influenced by its movements. But this would have been the original Hornpipe danced in various British ports, not the ultimate form which was developed from that original and presented on the stage in the nineteenth century by T. P. Cooke.

In some parts of Europe the Rigaudon appears to have been divided into two parts; the first consisted of a couple dance, and the second of couples in double file round the room. This last part may have represented a return to its original form, in which it was said to have been a circle dance.

Later the ballet master Dufort developed a theatrical figure from a characteristic Rigaudon movement, using a changing step and leaping movement together, and naming them the *pas de rigaudon*. This may account for the fact that many years after the dance itself had passed into oblivion the music was considered supremely suitable for the accompaniment of various kinds of exhibition dancing.

After the Rigaudon the Passepied was the lightest of the court dances. The figures of the dance itself were not more subtle than those of the Rigaudon, but the music was of a rather deeper significance, according to Louis Horst approaching the solid gaiety of the Galliard. As I have already stated, every French province possessed its own Branle, and the Passepied was the Branle of Brittany, where it was also known as the Trihory. In this early form it has a place in Arbeau's *Orchesography*, and from the description was a pantomimic dance with a strong dramatic flavour. One early seventeenth-century authority describes it as follows:

'The Passepied is so named because in such a dance one must beat and place one foot over the other.'

Another teacher laid down that the dance 'ought to fly close to the ground'.

A common expression was to 'run a Passepied'. It seems most likely to me that the dance derived its name from the crossing and recrossing of the feet in a series of gliding steps.

Normally the Passepied consisted of ten figures, the dancers starting by facing each other and joining hands. The first actual movement was a pas de basque in which the dancers first put one shoulder forward, then the other following this movement by a change of places in a turning step. Another and very attractive figure was a series of turns made while the dancers 'pawed the ground with one foot, their arms around each other's necks'.

This is another dance which came into outstanding favour during the reign of Louis XIV when the ladies and gentlemen of the court frequently dressed themselves as shepherds and shepherdesses. A great deal of theorizing has been indulged in about this propensity of the court, the most likely it seems to me being the desire to show some innocence and simplicity during a reign of the highest sophistication. That great diarist Madame de Sévigné was a skilled and enthusiastic adherent of the Passepied and wrote in a letter to her daughter in 1671:

'I am sure that you would be enraptured to see Lomaria dance the Passepied, and the violins of the Court would make your heart ache. I wish you could see the manner in which M. de Lomaria lifts and replaces his hat. What grace! What precision! The Passepied could make me weep because it brought back to me such sweet memories which it was impossible for me to resist . . .'

In England the Passepied became known alternatively as the Paspe, and is described under this title in the twelfth edition (1703) of Playford's *The Dancing Master*, although other dancing masters continued to use the full French title. Playford describes the ground pattern of the dance thus:

'First couple cross over to the second improper, then the figure through the second couple to the second proper, then cross over to the third improper, then the first couple cast up to the second improper, and cross over below the second couple to the first improper, then the first and second women change places, and the first and second man the like, then the first and second couple all hands half round, and the first couple cast off to the second improper, then the first woman cross over below the third woman and come between the third couple (the first man at the same time cross over and go above second man and so between the second couple) then the first woman in the middle of the third couple hands all three abreast (the first man the same with the second couple at the same time), then meet and set, then the first man hand his own and turn to the second proper.'

Proper refers to the men and the women being on their own sides, that is the side at which they started the dance; Improper, by the same token, means when they are on the other side.

Most composers at the beginning of the seventeenth century employed duple time for their Passepied compositions. During the century, however, the music changed in form and eventually, in common with the Minuet, became a dance in triple rhythm.

'Its essence is near to that of lightmindedness . . . but it is the kind of lightmindedness that has nothing sinful or displeasing, like that of many a female, who though she may be of a somewhat shallow character, thereby loses none of her charm.'

Various dances, including the Minuet and the Courante, were played two or three in succession, *en suite*, and this mode was also frequently adopted with the Passepied. This led in time to a marked change in the steps of the dance itself, and even in its character, so that by the time the Passepied reached the next century, we find it in a modified form with a great deal more technique but less vitality.

The further one lives into the seventeenth century the more separate one from another do the dances appear to grow, with the result that, as I have stated, the musical suite gradually developed into a group of dances related only by their rhythmic and figuration contrasts. Midway through the century the principle of the retention of one theme in the musical suite, varied in rhythm, gave way to less closely related rhythmic and melodic contrasts. Developments in the dance patterns themselves, although not of course slavishly following these musical developments, did inevitably undergo changes. These were motivated not through the growth of dance itself, but also because of this gradual change in the nature of the accompaniment. It is possible therefore to refer to a dance which at the beginning of the century would be hardly recognizable as having the same ancestry, much less being the same dance, at the end of that century.

An excellent example of this kind of change is to be observed in the Bourrée, which is first found at court as a folk dance halfway through the sixteenth century. A hundred years later it was to be seen in artificial dress, appearing in a ballet, with steps and figurations as artificial as the other social dances of the time. In the early part of the seventeenth century, if not later, it became one of a family of three dances: Gavotte, Bourrée and Rigaudon. In common with the other two, which I have already discussed, the Bourrée was in a lively 2/2 or 2/4 time, but each of the three dances in the group was provided with a highly individual opening. Of the three the Bourrée was the most lively and vital, which is not surprising in view of its emphatically peasant origins, some authorities claiming that it started life as a rustic clog dance in Auvergne. As so often happens, an examination of the word itself proves nothing, for there is a variety of theories. Perhaps the most likely explanation is that of the painstaking Mattheson in his *Der Vollkommene Capelmeister*, published in 1739:

'The word *Bourrée* in itself really means something stuffed, filled out, sedate, strong, weighty, and yet soft or delicate—which is more adapted to shoving, sliding, and gliding than to hopping and humping. This is in agreement with the qualities of the Bourrée, namely: content, pleasant, untroubled, tranquil, listless, gentle, and yet agreeable. Since there is now a well-known dance which in honour of a bride is called la mariée, it might well be that the people of Biscay, where the Bourrée is quite at home, and where there are seldom any plump pretty figures, imported this dance to please somewhat that sort of woman and named it that. Truly, it lends itself to no type of figure better than to an undignified one. However, these are only conjectures which for the most part tend to perplexity.'

Mattheson's definition coincides with that of the dictionary for the verb *bourrer*. But there is also an identically spelt noun, meaning faggot of twigs or brushwood. Ironically, although most dance historians deny any association, some dictionaries refer to the 'dance from Auvergne' under this heading. However, at least one authority supports this theory, Lapaire (La Bourrée 1921) tracing the dance back, although not with certainty, to ancient Gaul, when during a festival, Jour des Fagots, men danced with flaming torches around huge fires.

In 1676 Madame de Sévigné described the Bourrée as the most beautiful dance in the world. At the same time she added that it was not danced at Versailles. Despite its undoubted excellencies, for some inexplicable reason it never proved very popular either with dancers or composers. Soon it disappeared from the ballroom, although musically it is to be found in the suite. Composers frequently followed one Bourrée with another. Louis Horst claims that the greatest Bourree of them all occurs in Bach's second violin sonata, and few will disagree with him. Strangely, very few modern composers are keen to employ the Bourrée.

No kind of detailed technical description of the steps has ever been discovered, and perhaps the 'literary' description of a musician, Marius Verspuy of Auvergat, who wrote a number of Bourrées, was the most colourful. Once again I am indebted to Louis Horst for the following quotation from Versepuy:

'The Bourrée constitutes a veritable little scenario of which love is the theme. It would be difficult to give an idea of the Bourrée except to say that the dancers seek and flee from each other. However, the roles are different. The man, bold and proud, dances with a determined air, stamping and clapping and shouting. The woman, at once audacious and timid, attracts her admirer and avoids him, using calculated ruses and tender artifices. One appears earnest, and the other coquettish. The couples mix, cross, swinging the head and body, raising the arm, snapping their fingers and noisily hammering out with their feet the beat given out by the bagpipes or the hurdy-gurdy. Rhythm is essential in the Bourrée—to the point where it alone suffices. In the absence of the bagpipe, one may see one of the dancers perched on a table singing the air while he vigorously pounds out the rhythm with his foot. Finally his humming dimishes, he no longer sings. His heel suffices to keep the couples going until dawn.'

No more is known of the actual steps of the Chaconne than of those of the Bourrée. First referred to towards the end of the sixteenth century, this dance was already popular throughout Spain at the beginning of the next century. In its early stages it appears to have been another of those uninhibited dances, and was stigmatized as passionate and unbridled. The Chaconne which later graced the ballet could certainly not be condemned in those terms. And the dance of the same name that was taken up by the French and turned for some years into the concluding dance of the ball, can have possessed but little resemblance to that early form. In common with one form of the Bourrée the executants danced in two lines, the gentlemen on one side, the ladies on the other. For the first eight bars the lines advanced and retreated, then one couple danced a different figure. Following this the dancers would repeat the opening eight bars, then the next group or couple would have their turn. And so the dance would continue until all had enjoyed their turn.

Related to the Chaconne and usually treated with it by musicologists, is the Passacaglia. This too developed into a slow dance with three beats to a measure. Its origin cannot with certainty be attributed to Spain, as there seems to be an equal possibility that it stemmed from Italy. We know no more of its actual steps and figurations than we do of those of the Chaconne. From a musical standpoint the two became very early in life almost indistinguishable one from the other, and there is no doubt whatever that the musical forms of both stemmed directly from the dance forms.

Keyboard composers of the seventeenth century, and for that matter of the early eighteenth century, made wide use of both forms, setting their melodies on a firm ground base, this foundation occasionally finding itself transferred into the upper part. Each section consisted of not more than eight measures, and frequently of only four. Lully, Rameau and other well-known composers of this time frequently terminated their operas with Chaconnes and Passacaglias, although once again the stress was almost completely on the music and not at all upon the dance.

Choral dances are frequently looked upon as a particularly English institution. It is of course true that this kind of dancing gained tremendous favour in Britain, and in the 1728 edition of Playford about 900 such dances are listed. Yet the origin of the choral form goes back to antiquity, and the dance itself appears to have been founded on a theme of love and the combat of men for love. In this theme lies undoubtedly the advancing and retreating element which is a feature of choral dancing, together with the frequent uniting and separating of the dances. In such a form there is nothing singularly British; it crossed the channel in the same way as many other customs, but this one for some now inexplicable reason found more than usually fertile soil, and after winning great favour with the people in their towns and villages, was eventually elevated to the court at the end of the sixteenth century. In the last years of Elizabeth there is little doubt that it was danced at the court by masters and servants in the same assembly.

During almost the entire seventeenth century the Choral Dance, with numerous but mostly small variations, played its part in the social life of the country. Then, at the beginning of the next century, at last discarded by the English, it recrossed the channel to win new favour in France. But by this time it was not unnaturally dressed in somewhat different guise. In the first place its name became *contredanse française*, and after that Cotillon. There is an amusing if apocryphal account of how the dance changed its name to the French for petticoat. The rapid turning movement of one of the figures revealed this undergarment of the ladies, which was not indecorous, for the petticoats of the time were beautiful works of art in themselves and were in fact designed to be so revealed. That surely gives one very good reason for the popularity of the dance. Part of the chorus of a popular song of the time was as follows:

> 'Ma commère, quand je danse,
> Mon cotillon va-t-il bien?'

A contemporary French dancing master described a hundred Cotillon figures. And now, once again, the two-way traffic was repeated, for in this new form the Cotillon was in the next century to invade England, and in turn eventually to lead to another kind of social dance which we shall discuss later, the Quadrille.

During the century the music of the Gigue, a dance, as we have seen, well established in the last century, became a firmly established member of the classical suite, because of its lively nature usually coming last. Earlier in the century some complaint appears at various times to have been made about its extremely robust nature. Playford made such a complaint, and in 1650 Thomas Mace wrote: 'Jigs are light and squeamish things only fit for fantastical light-headed people.' But these are isolated complaints and there is no doubt whatever that the Gigue provided for many years a concluding highlight in the dances of nobles and commoners all over the Isles. Although he was writing about the music, Matteson's summing up of the four chief emotions aroused by the Gigue can perhaps be more aptly ascribed to the dance than to its accompaniment: 'fury, or passion, pride, simple eagerness and a careless temperament.'

In the opinion of a seventeenth-century writer:

'I know of no dance in which so much loveliness, dignity, and charm are united in the polonaise. It is the only dance which becomes exalted persons and monarchs and which is suited to courtly dress. This dance is marked by poetic feeling and the national character, the outstanding trait of which is a ceremonial dignity. It does not express passion; it is a solemn procession.'

Paul Nettl in *The Story of Dance Music* claims that the Polonaise was one of the most popular dances from the sixteenth century to the twentieth century. It must be remembered, however, that Doctor Nettl is more concerned with the music of the dance than the dance itself and, as he says, the music was very popular among renaissance composers. Bach wrote nearly fifty of them and the nineteenth-century ballet composers included them in their scores, with the result that the formalized Polonaise for the stage can still be seen in twentieth-century revivals of certain ballets. In Edwardian ballrooms, too the stately Polonaise was frequently to be seen. But that form of Polonaise stemmed from that which had developed in Poland from the earlier versions. As the national dance of Poland it was first known in the masculine gender as Polonais. Evelyn Porter in *Music through the Dance* writes:

'In 1573 Henry of Anjou was crowned King of Poland, and in the following year he received the nobles of the country in great state in the castle of Cracow. The nobles took their wives by the hand and made them parade before the king, stepping in rhythm but without a stereotyped form. It was not conceivable that on such an occasion the musicians would have been allowed to produce an unknown rhythmic effect. Rather they would use music which was considered to be the best of the national repertoire. From that time the stately procession of the Polonaise was the customary overture to all court balls, and all ceremonial occasions. In the eighteenth century it had become the acknowledged national dance, and was a part of every festivity of the country.'

This certainly does appear to be a plausible suggestion of the origin of the form of the dance, for the stately rhythm undeniably dictates the slow, measured walk and that typically eastern European movement of the bent knee as the other leg stretches out with the toes raised and well pointed. But doubtless even before 1573 a similar custom existed of showing off one's womenfolk, and their finery, to the king. It also enabled the men to show off their own well-shaped legs and proud deportment at the same time. A Polish nobleman of that period would have worn for such occasions the elegant top boots and tight breeches which simply invited this kind of movement; and both his tightly belted tunic with its many tassels across his chest, and the heavily boned bodice of his consort, with its corsetlacing tied on the outside, would have been of the finest quality brocades, velvets and silks. Although the long and richly embroidered skirts of the ladies would have put rapid movement at a premium, the men enjoyed many a wilder skirmish at this time, but always they would return to their true dignity, of which there could be no finer physical expression than the careful, deliberately posed steps of the Polonaise. We shall however return to this dance when we reach the nineteenth century.

Frequently the host of a great ball led the dance by taking his partner and escorting her, not only round the salon in which the dance was to take place but also through other rooms in his house and, doubtless only if the weather was favourable, through the garden as well. On the return of the leading couple into the ballroom the host would surrender his partner to another, at which all the men moved one place down. Sometimes the procession would continue for hours, so that the ladies had frequent changes of partner. Those gentlemen who were really keen on the dance, as distinct from its social possibilities, gradually developed a number of ingenious steps, gestures and postures. But all this kind of ornament never once succeeded in concealing the display of chivalry and noble bearing associated, however fallaciously, with the Middle Ages.

Vivid accounts have been left of various great social occasions of the seventeenth century during which dancing formed an important part of the celebrations, but it seems to me that no single one of them typifies either the form of such occasions, or the spirit of the age. I am tempted to try to put on to paper some impressions of one of the great events presented at Versailles during the reign of Louis XIV, but the 'sun king', much though he did for dancing, was essentially an outdoor man, and those fabulous presentations, consisting of lavish spectacles, gargantuan feasts, games, joustings and dancing, scarcely typify anything except the prodigality of the monarch and his seeming unconcern for the abject poverty of so many of his subjects.

The difficulty is made greater when we remember that during a large part of the century Europe was creating what came to be known as the Golden Age. Until the last part of the century the thought of writers and painters was directed more to the open air than for many years.

As far as painting is concerned, indeed, we now saw what was virtually the birth of the landscape. Until this time painters had been concerned only with giving their sitters an outdoor environment; now the landscape itself frequently became the subject, with figures included to animate it. Claude and Poussin, for example, were producing their great works in bewildering profusion. Claude thought so little of the misty, mythological figures which are sometimes difficult to find in his canvases, that he frequently allowed others to paint them in for him. Poussin, on the other hand, took enormous interest in his figures, and often depicted them as though they were dancing. Yet not one of his figures ever looks as though it is actually moving at all, but that it has been frozen in the position in which it has been painted.

THE SEVENTEENTH CENTURY

In the previous century Sir John Davies had written his long poem *Orchestra* consisting of 136 seven-line stanzas on dancing, and in fact glorifying the dance to such an extent as to claim that it had been invented by true love. In this century we had the purism of Cromwell who, although not nearly as condemnatory of dancing as various writers have suggested, certainly did not encourage the joustings, feasts and extravagant celebrations at which dancing played a vital part. In England, as in France, entertainment frequently took place outdoors and the English Court masque came into its own. Ben Jonson composed the words for a number of such masques, and Milton towards the end of his youth, in which he wrote the most beautiful and idyllic verses before puritanism and republicanism caused him virtually to abandon poetry for twenty years, until in fact the Restoration in 1660, wrote the most beautiful of them all when he created *Comus* in 1634. The motivating force behind this particular masque was Henry Lawes, Milton's friend and a fine composer of music. He was commissioned to compose a masque for a special occasion at Ludlow Castle, in Shropshire, on the Welsh border, by the Earl of Bridgewater, who had recently become President of the Council of Wales. Now to Milton and Lawes add Inigo Jones, who created the special stage architecture, the pageants for the piece, and it is clear that the greatest creative artists in their own field were interested in this kind of entertainment.

Comus was given in the grounds of Ludlow. Today we can still read the magnificent verses; we can, although fewer of us do, refer to the musical settings of the songs in *Comus*, for they are in the British Museum. But what of the dances? Of those we have not a single concrete piece of information. All we can be reasonably sure of is that they were the social forms popular at this time. The actual patterns would be modified to suit the action of the masque. Processional dances would play a prominent part, and dancing would alternate with spoken or mimed scenes.

This form of masque flourished in the first half of the century, and was by no means extinguished either by the arrival of the Commonwealth or the Protectorate. Today, however, it would be regarded as a hopeless confusion of different elements. Although the masque laid claim to bring together the arts of music, architecture and poetry, it was seldom created for the sake of art, but purely as a spectacle for a specific occasion. Many a masque was in fact performed but once, and the dozens written by Jonson were intended for no more.

England at this time was enthusiastic about the masque, although some of this enthusiasm can perhaps be attributed to a revulsion against the savage attacks made on stage plays by various over-energetic puritans. Such puritans probably condemned *Comus*, although Milton was himself one of the greatest adherents of Puritanism.

Originally the masque had consisted of a masqued dance, but by this time the only concession made to this origin lay in such a dance towards the close of the entertainment, this being usually performed by noble amateurs. As to the masque itself, this consisted of a medley of pageant, music, both vocal and instrumental, and scenery. The theme would be invariably taken from mythology, allegory or farce, and be enacted by means of dance, song and dialogue.

In most writers today the dance element receives short shift. Take for example Oliver Elton's thorough and fascinating introduction to the Clarendon Press edition of the poem of *Comus*:

'... is not its success precisely in proportion to Milton's success in making a clean sweep of the cumbrous and transient elements of the masque, and in keeping its poetical element supreme over such of its other elements as he retained.'

The dance may have been transient, but in perhaps more typical masques than *Comus* dancing was at least one of the most important elements, of not frequently the most important of all. Enid Welsford, whose *The Court Masque* is the most authoritative book on the subject, says:

'Both in the French ballet and the English masque, however varied the forms of entertainment might be, there was one constant factor: the *raison d'être* of the whole performance was the arrival of noble personages disguised and masqued to dance a specially prepared dance. They might dance other dances as well, either all together or in groups, but there was one special dance in which they all took part which was the centre of the whole thing, and that dance was known in France as *le grand ballet*, in England as the main or grand masque dance. The chief features of the costume of the noble masquers were also very similar in the two countries. An important difference must, however, be mentioned. In France *le grand ballet* was a grand finale. In England it almost always occupied a more or less central position, and was followed by *revels* (i.e. ordinary ballroom dancing between masquers and audience) and by the final dance of the masquers, known as the 'going off' or 'the last dance'.

The 'specially prepared dance' to which Miss Welsford refers does not mean that new steps would necessarily be invented, but that the accepted steps of the time would be put together in a particular way, and that the ground pattern would be specially devised; just as in the sequence dances of our own time, there are very few actual new figures, each dance consisting of different combinations of the same figures, together with one or two original movements.

The masque was brought to England under the influence of the Stuart queens. All of them seem to have regarded the continental entertainments of a similar kind as an essential part of court life, with all the richness, inventiveness and grandeur of these entertainments reflecting the wealth and power of the country.

Inigo Jones had by this time travelled extensively on the continent, especially in Italy, and he brought back a number of ideas developed from those he had seen in Italy, particularly in engineering feats by which pageants could be manipulated to produce their gods and goddesses *ex machina*, and the latest innovations in scenic perspective. In this way the glory of this aspect of the Italian renaissance was transformed and translated for English enrichment. This particular development led rapidly to the theatrical evolution of the proscenium arch, and the bifurcation of dancing into its theatrical application on the one hand, with its growing technique and spectacularity, and on the other hand the slower development of the social dance.

Queen Anne and the ladies of her court frequently appeared in the masques devised by Inigo Jones and Ben Jonson; and this led in turn to the anti-masque. In 1609, Jonson wrote 'A Celebration of Honourable and True Fame, bred out of Virtue' for Queen Anne and his introduction to this masque is accordingly addressed to her. No clearer explanation either of the origin of the anti-masque or its form has ever been given elsewhere.

'And because Her Majesty (best knowing that a principal part of life in these spectacles lay in their variety) had commanded me to think on some dance, or show, that might precede her and have the place of a foil, or false masque: It was careful to decline, not only from others, but mine own steps in that kind, since the last year, I had an *anti-masque* of boys; and therefore now devised that twelve women, in the habit of hags or witches, sustaining the persons of Ignorance, Suspicion, Credulity, etc. the opposites to good Fame, should fill that part, not as a masque, but a spectacle of strangeness, producing multiplicity of gesture, and not unaptly sorting with the current and whole fall of the device.'

Although of course there were far more entertainments of this kind under the Stuarts, which naturally led to similar if more modest entertainments in the great houses up and down the country, the advent of Cromwell by no means stifled these secular pleasures. Indeed, it is claimed that Cromwell himself danced until the early hours of the morning during the wedding festivities of one of his daughters. In 1653 an official masque was performed in honour of the Portuguese ambassador. This contained a great deal of dancing as had *Comus* nineteen years earlier.

Thus the masque, complete with its anti-masque, played an important part in the presentation of dancing, and its popularization throughout the land. It did not however play much part in the development of the various forms of social dancing. Whatever developments took place in the masque were to influence theatrical entertainment and from now on the two forms of dance were destined to grow further and further apart.

The social dance in the new world not suprisingly followed the patterns of that in Europe. When in 1620 the Puritans landed in the Mayflower their aim was the establishment of a calvanistic society. But not all the settlers in North America, particularly those in the six North East Atlantic states which comprise New England, were Puritans, for there were many Quakers and others who were strongly opposed to their beliefs and practices. Even so, it was not only the influence of these dissidents which enabled the dance to flourish there, although this influence did undoubtedly free it from certain inhibitions, for the Puritans were by no means opposed to dancing. They went so far as to encourage dancing, in fact, where according to their interpretation it would have been encouraged in the bible, condemning it strongly when it appeared to them to conflict with bible teaching. In consequence, for a number of years some of them were strongly opposed to mixed dancing, whereas others, more liberally minded, fought against only what they considered to be amorous and lascivious forms of the dance.

The Puritans, and others in North America, were guided to a large extent in their dance education by Playford's book, with its descriptions of simple folk dances. Those who were keen to see the dance firmly established as part of the American way of life urged its advantages in the instruction of good manners, for manners were considered by the Puritans to form an important part of the moral life. But during the first fifty years of the settlement it seems that dance teachers who set up in business were frequently of not much credit to their profession.

THE SEVENTEENTH CENTURY

However, one in 1685, when complaints had been made against him, claimed that in his art he could teach more of divinity than any of the local preachers. But his bold assertion did not help him, for he was fined £100, although we are told that rather than pay he fled from the colony.

Outcries against mixed dancing continued across the Atlantic right through the century, but history should have taught its opponents better. Mixed dancing as a natural form of expression and relaxation was then, as it remains today, too firmly established as a natural human activity to suffer suppression for long. By the end of the century mixed dancing was accepted by communities through the length and breadth of the land; ministers began to approve of dance schools, especially those which undertook to teach children the rules and practice of good behaviour.

In the south the ruling class appears from the outset to have viewed the dance with tolerance and even with favour. Here before long it was regarded, as in Europe, as a necessary part of one's education. The planters and others lived in very sparsely occupied territory, and a visit between neighbours, who invariably lived several miles apart, was often the occasion of a party in which dancing played an important part. Dancing masters were soon in considerable demand to teach the forms favoured in the courts of Europe. How wonderful a spectacle it must have been when those spacious wooden homes of the Virginians, with their chandeliers and English furniture, were inhabited by numerous familes, all clad in their very best finery, to perform those dances.

One of the most important works on the social dance of the seventeenth century is that by F. de Lauze entitled *Apologie de la Danse* and published in 1623. It is a work which offers much food for thought to students of society as well as students of the dance. From the point of view of dance, it concerns the early part of the century, containing a great deal of material which throws light on the transitions in technique and style which were developing from the dances of the previous century. We are greatly indebted to Joan Wildeblood for the appearance in 1952 of a new edition of this work, which in this edition is given in the original French together with Miss Wildeblood's English translation, a brilliant introduction and some illuminating notes in which she compares certain statements and theories of authorities such as Arbeau, Mersenne, Caroso and others.

Little is known of the life of de Lauze; in fact we are not even sure if he actually practised as a professional dance master. Apropos of this he himself says:

'It is true that the dance is not my only calling, nor certainly is it my resolution to die in exercising it. But at a time and in a country where I find myself compelled to put into practice that which springs from my inclination, and which I had previously learnt for my particular amusement and as a manner of exercising, it is my boast to be able to acquit myself in it knowingly, and at the same time to satisfy those who follow me.'

It is unfortunate that his actual descriptions are extremely difficult, in many cases impossible, to follow. He does not believe in illustrations, for he says:

'Those who believe that to teach dancing properly from a book necessitates numerous illustrations, in order to describe more plainly the movements which should be observed in dancing, are in agreement with that Orator of old, who, having to harangue in open Senate on an atrocious deed, committed this clumsy fault of setting up a painting before the eyes of the Judges, trusting more in the dumb strokes of a dead painting, than to the energy of living eloquence.'

This seventeenth-century author *cum* dancing master lays down precise details and instructions for bows and curtseys, and for salutations for all occasions. This is the first time details of this kind were published —at least as far as one can ascertain today—and although some of the instructions are vague it is possible to gain an excellent idea of the form of these civilities, which were at this time, in an age of growing artificiality, of paramount importance.

Another piece of evidence, this time concerning the turning out of the legs, is of considerable significance. De Lauze insists that ladies as well as gentlemen should maintain this 'turn-out', disagreeing with those masters who apparently argued that as the long dresses of the time concealed the lady's feet it was not necessary for them to be turned out. In the first few paragraphs of his section on 'The Method for Ladies' he says:

'... as no one will deny me that the action of the body in dancing naturally follows that of the feet, I am assured that if they pay attention to the movements which are made, as much with the shoulders as with the rest of the body, when opening or closing (the feet), of if they make a comparison between the grace of one who, in dancing, keeps the toes turned in with she who will have them outwards, that they will approve of my advice.'

In fact throughout his treatise de Lauze is seemingly more concerned with the style, deportment and movement of his pupils than he is with the actual steps of the various dances which come under his only vaguely descriptive pen. Dancing masters of that time were not unique in expecting their readers to know the steps and movements. For the acquisition of control and style de Lauze advocates at one point the use of a table for support during the practice of certain exercises. This has prompted Miss Wildeblood to state in her introduction that although one cannot claim because of this that de Lauze originated the idea 'we find here the theory which in time became formulated into the practice of *exercises à la barre*, which is the backbone of technical training in Ballet'.

One of the keys to de Lauze's teaching lies in his expectation of perfect balance in his students. The following would I think tax many of our most highly skilled participants in dance competitions today:

'... stopping on the right toe, make him carry the other in the air, the leg well stretched, in order to make a *temps en rond* (circular step), which will be carried to the side, whereof the movement should proceed from the hip in order to be well executed. One must bend a little on the other leg and rise again on to the toe. After which *temps* one must make a chassé off the ground to the same side, then spring on the left foot, carry the other, the leg well stretched, not in front as some do, who by this means incommode the lady, but to the side in the air, to carry it with the same *temps* on the ground, the leg crossed in a manner that the calves touch.'

De Lauze is also insistent upon the need for grace of the arms. It is certainly a reflection on the style of the normal dances of the twentieth century, in which because of our firmly closed hold, arm movements are virtually eliminated. After reading de Lauze's colourful exhortations about the arm movements of the time, one cannot but feel a strong sense of loss. Perhaps, too, this loss accounts in some small part for the revival of the so called old-time dance forms—that is the forms of the Victorian and Edwardian periods, in which the arms played an important part.

De Lauze is no less exacting in his demands upon the balancing powers of the ladies. The following is included in his instruction to them on the curtsey:

'... having the arms negligently extended to the sides, she should, with the utmost smoothness that is possible, bend both knees equally, not in front as many do, who by holding their toes together acquit themselves very badly, but out to each side. If she wishes to descend very low and remain there a while, the body firm and erect, then she will raise her heels, supporting herself on her toes while she bends her knees.'

During all this de Lauze demands a constant regard for modesty. As she begins this feat of balancing which constitutes the curtsey, the lady must look at the company, but is instructed to lower her eyes as she bends her knees, not lifting them again until her knees are straight. On no account must she regard any person for this savours of effrontery. By this time the technique of social dancing had developed as far as possible within the styles of dancing then current. For example, already skilled performers could execute *entrechats six* (at this time this meant the crossing of the feet while jumping in the air, each crossing representing an *entrechant*, or caper as it was known during the seventeenth and eighteenth century in England); and I have already quoted de Lauze as witness of the demands made upon dancers for an excellent ability to balance.

In spite of this degree of virtuosity, however, the seventeenth century demanded far more stress upon style and smoothness of movement than upon the kind of acrobatics into which dancing degenerates from time to time. What was danced in the sixteenth century, and for that matter in the first years of the seventeenth century, with tremendous energy and vigour, was gradually toned down, with grace and deportment taking the important place at the expense of high spirits and uncontrolled enegy. In the continuation of the cycle this process was inevitably to lead to a corrupt and artificial manner until the revolt against the excesses of mannerisms and foppishness was to lead in turn to a violent swing of the pendulum towards less artificiality and more natural movement.

Students who wish to compare the technique of the sixteenth century, as laid down by Arbeau, with that of the early seventeenth century, as laid down by de Lauze, will find in this book much profitable study, although in several matters de Lauze is infuriatingly vague and ambiguous.

Today, with our keenly organized examining bodies and our determination to eliminate unqualified teachers from our midst, it is amusing perhaps to remind ourselves once again that nothing is new and that history is only a constant process of repetition. Listen to de Lauze:

'... None should have the liberty of teaching, whether in public or in private, without a certificate from people who would be chosen for this purpose, before whom it would be obligatory to render some proof of the justness of their actions, together with their capability.'

From this fascinating book, and from the insistent stress upon the paramount importance of style by the leading masters of our time, it seems clear that the atmosphere surrounding the cult of social dancing was much the same as that of the thousands of skilled teachers and their pupils today. The only difference—and it is a fundamental difference—was that at this time the leaders of society were also the leaders in dance fashions, whereas today the leaders of society are, generally speaking, least skilled on the floor. This sweeping generalization is true of Britain, America, and several countries in the Commonwealth, but not, strangely enough, in Germany, or to a lesser extent Denmark, where the dance seems to be most popular among the higher reaches of society.

CHAPTER V

The Eighteenth Century

THE GROWING TECHNIQUE

Dancing is an elegant, and regular movement, harmonically composed of beautiful attitudes, and contrasted graceful postures of the body, and parts thereof.
JOHN WEAVER in *Anatomical and Mechanical Lectures on Dancing*

EARLY in this century a father wrote in *The Spectator* an account of the activities of a dancing academy at which his daughter was a pupil. This contemporary view gives a vivid impression of the attitude of parents towards dancing, the attitude of dancers themselves and some idea of the kind of dancing in vogue.

'I am a man in years, and by an honest industry in the world have acquired enough to give my children a liberal education, though I was an utter stranger to it myself. My eldest daughter, a girl of sixteen, has for sometime past been under the tuition of Monsieur Rigadoon, a dancing master in the city; and I was prevailed upon by her and her mother to go last night to one of the balls. I must own to you, sir, that having never been at any such place before, I was very much pleased and surprised with that part of his entertainment which he called *French dancing*. There were several young men and women whose limbs seemed to have no other motion but purely what the music gave them. After this part was over they began a diversion which they call *country dancing*, and wherein there were also some things not disagreeable, and divers emblematical figures, composed, as I guess, by wise men for the instruction of youth.

The moral of this dance does, I think, very aptly recommend modesty and discretion in the female sex.

But as the best institutions are liable to corruption, so, sir, I must acquaint you that very great abuses are crept into this entertainment. I was amazed to see my girl handed by and handing young fellows with so much familiarity, and I could have thought it had been my child. They very often made use of a most impudent and lascivious step called *setting to partners*, which I know not how to describe to you but by telling you that it is the very reverse of *back to back*. At last an impudent young dog bid the fiddlers to play a dance called Moll Patley, and, after having made two or three capers, ran to his partner, locked his arms in hers, and whisked her round cleverly above ground in such a manner that I, who sat upon one of the lowest benches, saw further above her shoe than I can think fit to acquaint you with. I could not longer endure these enormities, wherefore, just as my girl was going to be made a whirligig, I ran in, seized my child, and carried her home.'

Consider the differences between this period with those of a hundred and fifty years earlier and a hundred and fifty years later. Certainly today a father would get short shift from his daughter, and probably from his wife, if he were to attempt that sort of high handed, dictatorial behaviour. Yet the beginning of the eighteenth century is packed with contradictions, for at this time ladies of society were wont to assert their gentility by coarse language. By and large the fair sex, as it was then often termed, was regarded as frivolous and inferior, although the courting of the female by the male reached extreme heights, or depths, whichever way one looks at it, of extravagance. Mostly too it was an age in which form was of infinite importance. Etiquette was taken to ridiculous lengths and in literature the ideas themselves frequently seemed to be of less importance than the language in which they were expressed. There was also a great deal of circumlocution, as anyone who has read Pope's unerringly measured couplets will vouch; and even a poet such as Thomson who eventually took literature out of the coffee houses where it had for years been enshrined and into the open countryside, wrote in the kind of extravagant terms wherein he could concoct such circumlocutions as 'the feather'd tribe domestic' for chickens.

More important for our purposes is the new attitude the people of this time were bringing towards the human body. In the first half of the century there is little doubt that a false prudery prevailed, leading to a great deal of artificiality in movement as well as in the customs of society. Hogarth might be able to expose the vice and corruption lying beneath all the finery of that society, but its grandeur and dignity also had to be exhibited. The starving rogues outside Calais Gate, the mad and filthy wretches in the debtors' prison, did not for long trouble the conscience of society. Other painters, and even Hogarth himself, could show the dignity, the richness and the useless show of society. The charming, formal landscapes of Canaletto were there to display both the splendour of the residences and the means of transport, covering it all with an air of assured wealth so that the slaves rowing the fine barges across the Thames glorified their owner rather than expose the immorality of the age. Even the working people of the time were recorded as genteel and posturing in imitation of their betters. Look at Hayman's beautiful painting of the Dance of the Milkmaids on May Day, now in the Victoria and Albert Museum. Did milkmaids ever really look like this, and dance like this, even on high days and holidays. There is no reason to suppose that the peasantry was anything but robust in its ways of life; indeed, had it been anything else surely it would have given up the ghost, for living conditions and the standard of the food for the populace would else have killed them off like flies.

The artificial attractions, the formality and the posture of the conversation piece which thrived at this time, is a measure of the quality and development of the social dance, with all the contradictions implicit in the time. Moliere's dancing master in *Le Bourgeous Gentilhomme* could say:

'There is nothing so necessary to man as the dance. Without dancing a man can do nothing. All the disasters of men, all the fatal misfortunes of which history is full, the blunders of the politicians, the mistakes of the great commanders, all this comes only from not knowing how to dance.'

But that dancing master, in common with his creator, did not have to believe what he said, for he was seeking to sell lessons to his *nouveau riche* patron. The introductions to the many long and complex books of instruction throughout the century can for the same reason not be accepted as a true indication of the value placed on dancing by society of the time. Indeed, one teacher about two thirds the way through the century became conscious of the ridiculous claim made by some of his contemporaries, and as a result opened his own book with an acknowledgement of the ridiculousness of the teacher who claims for dancing more importance than it warrants.

This shift in outlook towards the human body, or at least towards movement in the dance, is typified in the dress which became more and more popular as the century progressed. Louis XIV, that keen dancer, had eventually abandoned the art, probably because of his growing obesity. This meant that the court, not only of France, but of the whole of Europe, gradually followed suit. On stage the dance now became the exclusive property of the growing band of professionals. La Fontaine towards the end of the seventeenth century was the first professional ballerina, and she was quickly followed by two others in great contrast one with another. Marie Camargo was really the first to make the gap between the court and the stage dance unbridgeable, for she developed a number of figures which were not suitable for the ballroom floor. Until then the ballet, which played an important part in court entertainments, consisted of little more than the ballroom figures performed with perhaps greater skill than on the dance floor. Now Camargo and others who followed her made the stage dance a more skilled and undoubtedly a more energetic mystery. Although, as has frequently been stated, Carmargo was not the first in the century to shorten her skirts in order to display the speedy brilliance of her footwork and those *entrechats* with which she is sometimes credited as the originator, she did without question set a seal on this particular fashion, as is to be seen today in that delightful picture by Lancret in the Wallace Collection. A glance at some of the pictures by other contemporary artists, both of France and England, illustrates that throughout the century ladies' dresses were heavy and voluminous. The men, on the other hand, adopted for an equally long period the tight knee breeches and coats ending just above, level with, or just below the knee, according to the whim of the moment, with richly decorated cuffs, brocaded waiscoats and any amount of foppery. While they thus possessed freedom to move energetically their mental attitude was strongly opposed to this kind of horseplay, with the result that their manners and movements became ever more artificial, with delicate gestures and hand motions which became the subject of a complicated technique.

This outlook was to grow more and more pronounced until the whole way of life, with its extreme artificiality and defiance of nature was to be blown sky high by the French Revolution.

Frequently it has been argued that this style of dress was primarily responsible for the style of the dance, but such an argument overlooks the fact that fashion itself was not arbitrarily dictated by some eighteenth-century Dior, but was an expression of the ethos of its own time. In that age of reason, frankness had to be reined within the formal behaviour of the age. Everything must bow to form, and if form is allowed to govern ruthlessly for too long form gives way at last to formality for its own sake. Thus, the enormous hoops to swell out the skirts of the women, skyscraper headdresses, high heeled shoes, and the rest, were the inevitable growth of fashion governed by form rather than feeling.

Round about that time it is true, fashion had taken a new turn, among the most important developments being a shortening of the skirt for some occasions, and thus, one might imagine, to a greater freedom of movement. But it is necessary only to glance at a few examples of the extraordinary head styles of the same period to realize that violent movement would have caused a major disaster. Today we may smile tolerantly at the frivolity of feminine hats and curious coiffures, but compared with some of the styles in the late rococo and the period of the French Revolution our styles of today are prudent to the point of self-denial. Hair was piled up to absurd heights and topped with indescribable decorations. The stride was allowed greater length but the body must glide if disaster was to be avoided.

With limitations of this kind imposed upon human movement, social dancing evolved more and more elaborate methods of performing the actual steps and managing the arms. Lengthy books were published by several of the innumerable dancing masters who now come into fashion. Naturally most of these masters possessed a profound knowledge of the ballet, for in spite of the ballet's new professional status, the social dance still retained the fundamentals of the technique from which the ballet had developed. This development of technique was doubtless encouraged by a new impetus in attempts to record dance movement on paper. Many had tried for perhaps two hundred years before the eighteenth century to set out dance movements in some way different from a purely 'literary' description, but it is believed that the first to achieve marked success in this direction was Charles Beauchamps, a dancer who became the first director of the school of dancing attached to the Academie Royale de Music which was founded in 1666. Beauchamps created the dances in a number of ballets which enlivened the action of Moliere's plays and which were set to Lully's music. In 1681 he partnered, as the girl, Louis XIV in *Le Triomphe de l'Amour*. Quite apart from his pioneering efforts with dance notation, he is also generally believed to have created the basic five positions first employed in social dancing and later to become the very basis and foundation of classical ballet.

In fact, no matter to what extent he may have developed the use of these fundamental positions, he certainly did not create them. I have already discussed Arbeau's influence, but in much earlier works than that and in a great deal of sculpture the dancers can be seen with their feet turned out. What Beauchamps did do was to establish these positons, to integrate them scientifically into dance technique and finally to codify them for posterity.

But unfortunately Beauchamps did not himself publish the results of his developments and today nothing is left of any notes he may have written. It was left to a successor, Raoul Auger Feuillet, to take the credit for the first detailed method of notation. In 1701 Feuillet published his *Choregraphie*. In it he pays no tribute to Beauchamps, and certainly does not admit any debt to him, but others were quick to attribute much of the work to Beauchamps. An English dancing master in a preface to a translation of Feuillet in 1706 wrote:

' 'Tis to Monsieur Beauchamps, nevertheless, that the invention of the Art is wholly owing. This I can assure you, on my Word, since he himself taught me the Grounds of it above Eighteen years ago, but 'tho through an unaccountable Negligence he delay'd the publishing of it from Time to Time, it must needs be no small concern to him to see that another has all the Honour and Advantage of what cost him so much Study and Labour.'

Be all that as it may, it is to Feuillet that our gratitude is due today, for without his efforts we should be the poorer in our knowledge of what the dances of the time were like. Indeed, it is from this time that we can reconstruct with fair certainty, although of course by no means guaranteed accuracy, several historical dance forms. Further, we must I think accept that Feuillet did not merely crib Beauchamps but that he added to and developed that master's inventions. At any rate Feuillet has written a complete exposition of the writing down of dances, including body movements and arm positions. For his purpose he developed a system of conventional signs and characters. The system proved highly successful and the book (the first edition in small quarto, consisted of 106 pages) soon ran into a second enlarged edition. In 1704 Feuillet published a sequel containing actual descriptions of a number of dances. Some of them are for women, and these are placed first as they are considered easier, and some for men. There are Sarabandes, Entrées, Chaconnes, Passacailles, Gigues, Minuets, Bourrées and several others. These dances are taken from stage performances and the names of the eminent dancers who performed them are given. Many social dancers would doubtless have been inspired to emulate these great professionals, although in some cases modifying the forms in keeping with the decorous demands of the ballroom.

One of the greatest dancing masters in England during the first part of the century was John Weaver. He was however far more than a teacher of dance, for he was the first, preceding Noverre, to whom the credit is still frequently given, to create the *ballet d'action* in which dance and dramatic action were closely integrated. In addition Weaver did a great deal to develop the technique of theatrical dancing, building of course upon the movements of social dancing. Much of his writing is still pertinent today.

The extent to which stage, or theatrical dancing as Weaver called it, owed its development to social dancing is to be found in the fact that one of Weaver's most important works, *Anatomical and Mechanical Lectures*, was based firmly on the teachings of Thomas Caverly, considered by several contemporaries to be the greatest dancing master of the time. Unfortunately Caverly did not commit his teachings to paper, or if he did they have either been destroyed or are lying undiscovered in some dark place. Here is an extract from Weaver's *Essay towards an History of Dancing* which shows clearly the closer relationship between movement on the stage and on the dance floor of this time.

'Serious *dancing*, differs from the *Common-Dancing* usually taught in Schools, as *History* Painting differs from Living. For as the *Common-Dancing* has a peculiar Softness, which would hardly be perceivable on the Stage; so *Stage-Dancing* would have a rough and ridiculous Air in a Room, when on the Stage it would appear soft, tender and delightful. And altho' the Steps of both are generally the same, yet they differ in the Performance: Notwithstanding there are some Steps peculiarly adapted to this sort of Dancing, viz Capers, and Cross-Capers of all kinds: Pirouettes, Batteries, and indeed almost all Steps from the Ground.'

Weaver then goes on to discuss the quality of the various movements in this kind of dancing, remarking somewhat self-contradictorarily that 'it is of all other (dancing) the easiest attained . . . but yet this Difficulty attends it, that a Man must excel in it to be able to please.'

Another great dancing master of the first half of the eighteenth century was Pierre Rameau (not to be confused with his contemporary Jean-Philip Rameau, the composer). Little is known of him except that he was according to his own statement in his most important book, dancing master to the Queen of Spain, Elizabeth Farnese, second wife of Philip V, who was known as one of the most ambitious royal ladies of the century. In *Le Maître à Danser* Rameau provided us with one of the key books on ballroom dancing of the period—indeed, one of the most important books in the history of dance literature. Here for the first time was set out the technique upon which both theatrical dancing and social dancing were to be based for nearly two hundred years. Although he could not justly lay claim to any skill in the art of 'limning', the diagrams he included were perfectly clear and were used by others who followed him.

When *Le Maître à Danser* was translated into English in 1728 a skilled artist was employed to copy these illustrations, which he did with considerable success. It is however unfortunate that this English edition does not contain the reproduction of a painting of a court ball which enhances the Paris 1725 edition.

The title page of *The Dancing Master*, the English title of course, following the fashion of the time, outlines the contents after providing a sub-title, 'The Art of Dancing Explained':

'Wherein the manner of Performing all Steps in Ball Dancing is made easy by a new and familiar Method. In Two Parts. The First, Treating of the proper Positions and different Attitudes for Men and Women, from which all the steps are to be taken and performed; adorned with instructive Figures: With a Description of the Menuet Figure, shewing the beautiful Turns and graceful Motions of the Body in that Dance. The Second, of the Use and graceful Motion of the Arms with the legs in taking the proper Movements and forming the Contrasts, with Figures for the better Explanation. The Whole containing Sixty Figures drawn from the Life, and cursiously Engraved on Copper Plates.'

This translation was excellently carried out by J. Essex a London dancing master.

In England it was not until towards the end of the reign of Queen Anne (1702–1714) that stage dancing began to grow in popularity. John Rich, a famous impresario of the time, was chiefly responsible for this development, for he it was who imported a number of famous French dancers. At the same time pantomime was begininng to take the public fancy and this naturally lent itself to the exploitation of vigorous and exciting dance. Mark E. Perugini in his *Pageant of the Dance and Ballet* held also that various articles in *The Spectator* in support of this development, together with the writings of John Weaver, were of great assistance to the cause. Even so Steele could still write in *The Spectator*: 'It would be a great improvement, as well as embellishment to the theatre, if dancing were more regarded and taught to all the actors.' A similar plea is not exactly rare today. Robert Helpmann once said during his period at the Old Vic during the Shakespeare Folio seasons: 'All dancers should be taught to act, and all actors taught to dance.' Weaver too complained in *The Spectator* (how welcome such devotion to dancing would be in any of the 'quality' periodicals of the twentieth century) of the depths to which dancing had fallen. He also was referring chiefly to stage dancing, and deplored the 'capering and tumbling' that in those days in common with our own, were often exploited to the detriment of good style and beautifully executed figures.

Although, like other dancing masters who had committed at least some of their teachings to paper, Rameau was chiefly concerned with social dancing, his work is closely interconnected with theatrical dancing. From his book we can learn for the first time something of the essential style of movement of the period, not merely the steps and figures. Indeed, he makes frequent references to the actual leading stage dancers whose particular style should be emulated in the acquisition of skill in the social dance. Rameau in fact appears to have developed his system of dance instruction more from observation than from his own original theories. He says:

'My views on dancing have been acquired not so much from personal experience, as from the practices of the great masters with whom I have had the fortune to associate.'

From this statement Lincoln Kirstein, in *Dance*, draws the conclusion that Rameau was more of an observer than a technician. Such a conclusion is I think hardly justified by the facts, except in so far as every dance master throughout history has had first to observe and assimilate the teaching of others before he himself could make any worthwhile original contribution to the development of his subject.

Like the French the English at this time sought more after technical brilliance, both in theatrical and social dancing, with very little attempt to express any kind of emotion in the movements of the dance. Rather they aimed at clarity, regularity and balance. Weaver, after referring to the various physical qualities necessary for the good dancer, asks the performers to consider chiefly 'a nice Address in the Management of those Motions, that none of the Gestures and Dispositons of the Body may be disagreeable to the Spectators'. Nowhere in fact does he refer to any emotional cause and effect.

By this time the chain form of dance had virtually disappeared from the ballroom itself, and was reintroduced in the form of country dancing. Circle dancing and double file dancing had likewise been refined, so that they had by now almost denied their lowly origins. Leaping movements, as I have already indicated, were taboo. Everything is dictated by the five positions, with an excess of formality, absence of violent movement and the feet regulated so that never more than the length of one foot separated them. Not only was the Minuet itself the ubiquitous and popular dance, but its characteristic step was introduced as the *pas de menuet* into many other dances.

Returning to the eighteenth-century ballroom, *douce manière* was the order of the day. What in effect happened during the first half of this century was that generally speaking the dances of the last half of the previous century were continued, but were now provided with a growing complexity of technique and high formality, and robbed of any more profound expression of human feeling.

But this kind of dancing was not allowed all its own way. Country dancing which, as we have seen, had won a great deal of favour in the second half of the previous century, now came more than ever into its own. In 1728 the eighteenth edition of Playford's *The Dancing Master* made its appearance in two volumes. The first contained '358 of the Choicest Old and New Tunes now used at Court and other Publick Places', the second 360 more of the same order. But now the country dance, or Contredanse as it was frequently known, had undergone an even higher degree of refinement than when the first edition of Playford's book had appeared halfway through the previous century. Aristocracy had taken this form of dancing to its heart to such effect that the simple circle and chain dance from which this form had emanated had now developed into a endless number and variety of figures of considerable complexity. And with this variety and the extreme technical skill of the Minuet the social dance remained content for the best part of the first half of the eighteenth century. Dufort's *Trattato de Ballo Nobile* (treatise of the noble dance) contained only descriptions of the Minuet and the Contredanse. Although it is clear from his descriptions that the Contredanse consisted of movements quite simple in themselves, and therefore did not gain his unqualified approval, it is equally clear that a great deal was made of the co-operative work among the couples and the involvement of the individual in the set. It was said that every human being with normal limbs and common sense was capable of performing it, but to these qualities should have been added a good memory for the mastery of the various figures.

The Cotillon developed a great number of figures and eventually turned into a forfeit game in which kisses had to be given by ladies unable to execute certain figures. As this kind of dance grew more complicated it gradually developed into the set dance of the nineteenth century.

THE GROWING TECHNIQUE

The Country Dance of England, the Contredanse of France and the Contradanza of Italy were all one and the same thing, except of course for certain small national and regional divergencies. The form originated in England, the Country Dance being found much earlier than its French and Italian counterparts. The form was imported into France towards the end of the seventeenth century, when two French dancing masters, Isaac and Lorine, returning to France after a prolonged visit to London, introduced the form into the court of Louis XIV. A manuscript copy of the English airs and a description of some of the figures made for the king by one of these masters is still in existence.

I have spoken of the 'form' of country dancing, but this is perhaps hardly correct, for these was no such thing as a definite country dance. Instead there were many series of dances consisting of figures made in geometrical pattern. These forms originated on the village green but soon percolated through to the aristocracy and seem to have been popular in these forms at the court of Queen Elizabeth. But it was not until the eighteenth century that they really came into their own throughout Europe. During the greater part of the century many collections of country dance tunes, often with abbreviated descriptions, were issued by most music publishers. Usually these books contained about twenty-four dances and were produced in a small enough format to fit into the dancing master's pocket. At every important ball these country dances became an important feature, and there is an account of how Louis XV at one of his great banquets and masquerades, wandering among the dancers, stayed for some while to watch an English country dance performed by the daughters of some rich merchants. There is however no record that the king himself ever practised such dances.

During the first half of the eighteenth century, although ladies could use coarse language and behave in other ways which we in our enlightened time should consider ill-mannered, to say the least, leaping was considered ill bred. Partly of course etiquette followed the dictates of fashion, for as we have seen the clothes of the lady of fashion of this time would scarcely have permitted her to cavort with much freedom. Those with an excess of energy therefore released it on the dance floor by means of running sequences made with rapid steps. Any kind of broken rhythm or strongly accented syncopation was out of the question because of the nature of the instruments, which were harpsichords or clavichords and viols.

Although the nature of the dances remained to this extent circumscribed both by etiquette and fashion, the balls and social occasions at which dancing took place gradually became less formal. France led the way in this development. The end of the reign of Louis XIV was far less brilliant and grandiose than its beginning, for his country was by that time heavily in debt. Instead of the magnificent and incredibly costly occasions of the court, therefore, there now developed numbers of much smaller affairs arranged by the princes and nobles in their own estates in the provinces. Although these were naturally more intimate and less magnificent than those earlier celebrations of the king at Versailles, however, these provincial balls, based on the Versailles, pattern, were sometimes even more carefully worked out even if on a far smaller pattern and fraction of the expenditure.

Apart from those of royal and noble blood there had by this time, early in the eighteenth century, arisen a new class of bourgois merchants and bankers whose newly won wealth enabled and encouraged them to present functions of their own. Pulling themselves up the social scale they commissioned music, decoration and costumes from fashionable composers and artists, hoping no doubt to be able to grace their lists of guests with imposing names. In this way the court-centred taste of the sun King, the dictatorial magnificence of one man, gave way to the wider patronage of many who were not quite so sure of themselves as to dictate quite so definitely to those whom they had commissioned to carry out their desires. Gradually the musical influence of Lully became diffused with that of Jean Philipe Rameau, the decorative power of Le Bruhn and Le Nain with that of Lancret and Watteau. But the moderate extent of this advance can be gauged when we remember that so far there was little hint of the extravagances of Fragonard and his contemporaries which were going to turn the wheel full circle.

Between the decline of Lully and the rise of Rameau, both of whom in their different ways stressed the values of dramatic and poetic elements, music took first place, and this gave the dance a much needed boost. Italian composers and instrumentalists developed a greater skill in the playing of instruments and in the appreciation of music itself. At the same time, because of the diminution of the dramatic and lyrical elements in the opera ballet of the time, dancing began to play a more and more important part. This in turn led to a greater interest in the social dance, which after all was still exactly the same in basic form as the dances one saw on the stage.

This species of opera ballet consisted of the kind of opera in which orchestral music and dancing played an equally important part as the vocal element. Dramatic action was reduced and the plot formed little more than the basis upon which to build the musical themes and more and more elaborate dance patterns.

The standard of the eighteenth-century social dance reached its greatest level of achievement during the first twenty-five to thirty years, following which it suffered, generally speaking, a gradual decline. Through the rest of the century the Country Dance of England and the Cotillon of France continued to gain popularity, but standards fell for the simple reason that technical accomplishment had by now passed from the amateurs who sought their pleasure on the ballroom floor to the professionals who sought high skill on the stage. There can be little doubt, although no diaries or other records have been traced to confirm the theory, that the noble amateurs, finding themselves less skilful than the professionals gave up the competition; and after a while this meant that instead of skill in the social dance being regarded as an asset, it became instead to be a little *infra dig* to possess any skill on the floor at all. This factor in itself accounts in part for the growing popularity of the Cotillon and Country Dance, for these required little actual physical skill in performance.

Only the Minuet of the 'virtuoso' dances remained, and performance in that deteriorated sadly. With the French Revolution amateur virtuosity was extinguished altogether, as were the manners of the court among the bourgeoisie. One obvious example of this is the difference between the regal taking of the raised hand of the lady by the gentleman with the more informal slipping of the lady's arm through her partner's bent arm.

Nevertheless, whatever the prevailing standard, dancing itself, both on the stage and in the salon, was held in considerable favour, and Queen Anne herself employed dancing masters to instruct her. One of of them, a 'Monsieur l'Abbe' is said to have been a highly skilled performer on the stage. But it was common at this time, and much later for that matter, for the great stage dancers to instruct in social dancing. Queen Mary, for example, could remember quite well having been taught by one of the most famous of all the nineteenth-century ballerinas, Marie Taglioni.

Early in the century John Weaver presented at Drury Lane an entertainment entitled *The Tavern Bilkers* which consisted of 'dancing, action and motion' only. This proved so successful that he followed it with other entertainments of a similar nature, *The Loves of Mars and Venus* in 1716 perhaps being the most successful of them all. Doubtless this development of Weaver's invention also assisted the innovations of Rich who staged a series of pantomimes at Lincoln's Inn Field, reaching a climax with the *Beggar's Opera* in 1728 in which dancing and mime were married to suitable music and which played a fundamental part in the development of the plot. As diversions in these productions frequent dances were included in their own right, and Marie Camargo made her London debut in a piece entitled *Les Caractères de la danse*. In it she performed a Courante, a Minuet, Sarabande, Gigue, Chaconne, Rigaudon, Passepied, Louvre, Mussete. These dances were of course firmly based on the dances of that title that were performed on the ballroom floor, but now, as performed by Camargo, they departed a long way from that basis. With her remarkable virtuosity Camargo performed all sorts of figures, as well as the *entrechat*: sharp cutting steps, jumps and beats which enabled her to 'decorate' the ballroom steps until probably in a short time they became virtually unrecognizable as the foundation of the same dance. Noverre, the famous dancing master and choreographer, later said that Camargo would dance only to lively music in order to display her speed and agility. In fact Camargo undoubtedly succeeded in accelerating the speed at which the dance of the stage was now divorcing itself from the dance of the ballroom.

In Russia too the same kind of pattern can be traced. The first public theatre was not opened there until 1703, in Moscow. In the early years of the century Peter the Great had already introduced masquerades and dances such as the Courante, Minuet and Pavane to his court. The first ballet was presented there round about 1727, when members of the court presented an entertainment that would qualify for this title at the Winter Palace. Shortly after that public performances were put on with professional performers in the People's Theatre. Dancing masters from France and Italy were imported and during the reign of Anne (1710–40) a school of dancing was opened for poor children. Surely this early development must have influenced the growth of the great Russian ballet.

Across the Atlantic, taking their fashions from England, the colonists were just as keen on the dance as those they had left behind them in the mother country. Strangely enough, dancing schools were forbidden for some years into the eighteenth century, but whatever misguided attempts were made to suppress dancing itself were doomed to failure. I have already referred to unsuccessful attempts in the previous century to abolish the dance around the maypole. From the same source of information we learn that dancing was encouraged in Conneticut ordinations but forbidden at Massachusetts weddings. It seems, however, that the objections from the law and church were not against dancing generally but against 'lascivious dancing to wanton ditties with amorous gestures and wanton dalliances'. For in Boston in 1713 a ball appears to have endured from the very early evening until the early hours of the following morning. None other than President Washington himself danced for nearly three hours, without, apparently, once taking the weight off his feet. Towards the end of the century a vicar in *Letters to a Young Lady* strongly counsels dancing as an appropriate feminine exercise.

All through the century the battle continued, ministers declaiming against it, moralists proclaiming in extravagant terms its grave evils, laws being passed to prohibit it, while more and more the people learned how to do it. As the century wore on large sections of the people were growing considerably in wealth, for the slave trade, the rise of commerce and the rapidly increasing value of land concentrated large fortunes in the hands of a comparative few. Their immediate reaction was naturally to build themselves bigger houses and to wear better clothes as a sort of badge of superiority. But with wealth came more time for leisure pursuits. The theatre and music began to develop halfway through the century, although the enlightened rich had always to meet the disapprobation of those, larger in numbers than themselves whose intellectual deficiencies caused them to see nought but evil in such pursuits, and whose life outside the making of money was centred in the church.

In 1706, for example, in Philadelphia, the Quakers at a monthly meeting discussed the amusements of the town and voiced the following denunciation:

'Friends are generally grieved that a dancing and fencing school, are tolerated in this place, which they fear will tend to the corruption of their children.'

In pursuance of this pious resolution they took more active measures by petitioning the Governor to put a stop to such evil practices. Continually they coupled dancing not merely with what one would have thought at worst was the harmless practice of fencing, but with plays, games, lotteries and music.

Nevertheless, despite these dire warnings and denunciations the dance of the salon and the dance school had become firmly established as an integral part of America's polite society. In 1796 a contributor to the *Philadelphia Minerva* deplored the fact that young girls were sent to dancing lessons before they could properly read or write. 'Dancing was calculated to eradicate solid thought,' he said. 'In fact, versatility of mind, hatred for study, or sober reflection, are the inseparable companions of dancing schools, and the masteries resulting from them are virtually incalculable.' Dancing was then sufficiently popular and firmly established to have supporters who quickly attacked this bigoted opinion. Replied one of them, a female hiding behind the name of Amelia:

'Whatever captious cynics, in the delirium of their spleen, may allege to the contrary, dancing is incontestably an elegant and amiable accomplishment: it confers grace and dignity of carriage upon the female sex . . . it invigorates the constitution, enlivens the role of the cheek, and in its result operates as silent eloquence upon the hearts of men. Nature gives us limbs, and art teaches us to use them.'

Other correspondents of both sexes supported her, and it was agreed that it was the abuse of dancing, not dancing itself, which deserved censure. It was equally agreed that dancing was a healthy and pleasant pastime for both sexes.

But the struggle continued in various parts of the vast country right through the century. In a book quaintly titled *The Gentleman and Lady's Book of Politness and Propriety of Deportment, Dedicated to the Youth of Both Sexes* published in 1833, the author, a Madam Celnart, cited the case of Elizabeth Smith from Kentucky, who was banished from the church because she permitted dancing in her house, although the minister did not apparently 'find it inconsistent with the gospel of Christ for her to carry on a distillery of spirits'.

But despite all the warnings and injunctions from points throughout the land, dancing continued to flourish. Dance schools opened in many areas in large numbers and even in ordinary schools dancing was sometimes included as a part of the curriculum. The dance seems to have become as popular in many schools for 'young gentlemen' as fencing, at that time an accomplishment deemed highly desirable in a gentleman of breeding, in spite of protests from certain quarters. In common with doctors, lawyers and preachers, dancing masters—there were also a few dancing mistresses, several of whom were women retired from a theatrical career—journeyed from town to town, giving courses wherever they were in demand. In many cases too a teacher would undertake to instruct an organized group, leaving those responsible to obtain the room and the music, and the fees, so that all he had to do would be to arrive and give instruction for a predetermined length of and simply to obtain his dues without any responsibility than to take his class. This particular method continues to operate with large success in the U.S.A. right up to the present time, although elsewhere, admirable method though it seems to be for the teacher, I have heard of it only sporadically.

As the century advanced Country Dances (Playford's manual was in great demand throughout) were intermingled with the Minuet and other dances accepted in the salons of London and Paris. The dance school also came to be regarded by parents, and by a number of educationalists, as a place where good manners and etiquette could be imparted. This element of dance instruction was probably responsible in part for the keen desire of many large groups of citizens to install a dance school in their area. Newspapers frequently carried advertisements to the effect that a dance school would be welcomed and that a teacher would receive ample encouragement. Often these advertisement themselves led to heated controversy. In the *Providence Gazette* in 1763, following an advertisement of this kind, one correspondent believed that they might just as well seek to set up a 'public stew or brothel'. A number of letters followed, some for and some against.

Towards the end of the century, as the frontiers of the settlers were pushed further and further to the west, dancing masters were to be found in numbers throughout the new cities as well as the old. Some of these were of French birth, having fled from the Revolution. Naturally they taught the dances which had been favoured by fashionable French society. One would imagine that the gentility and artificiality of such dances would have found little favour in the feet of this rugged new people, but in fact the settlers were avid after the fashions and protocol of the old world. I quote from *America Learns to Dance*, by Joseph E. Marks III from which a great deal of my information about the history of dance across the Atlantic has been culled.

'As they (the French dancing masters) travelled from city to hamlet, they taught the fashionable dances of their native land. The dancing masters not only taught the minuet, cotillion, rigadoon, country dances, hornpipe steps, reels and jigs, but also they taught the genteel manners and graces of head and hand and thereby contributed more to the education of the young boys and girls than just a knowledge of the fashionable dances of the day. After a boy or a girl had gained some knowledge of the basic curriculum, they then turned to the dancing master so that he might 'finish' their education by teaching them manners, a graceful carriage, and deportment in genteel company.'

As to instructional books on the dance there is ample evidence to show that the works of John Weaver and Pierre Rameau (in translation) had made the journey from Europe to America with the dancing masters and that many families owned a copy of one or both of them. Naturally, as the dance became more and more a desirable accomplishment, a demand grew for more balls, frequently known, as in England, as assemblies. And with the increase in the number of balls so grew the demand for instruction. In spite of America's constant endeavour, at least in its moral outlook, for human equality and the avoidance of class distinction, it is clear from the diversity of public and private dances that class distinction was as rife here as in Europe. Up to 1776 it was considered a very high honour indeed to receive an invitation to the Royal Governor's Ball, and as a rule only persons of high rank were so honoured. In *American Journey* Moreau de Saint-Mery wrote:

'There is great snobbery in Philadelphia, where the classes are sharply divided . . . This is particularly noticeable at balls. There are some balls where no one is admitted unless his professional standing is up to a certain rank.'

As in England a number of dances were organized by the dancing masters—and dancing mistresses too. One of these ladies in Williamsburg in 1738 announced an assembly in which there would be 'several grotesque dances never yet performed in Virginia'. She also advertised a raffle, for which one of the prizes would be a 'likely young negro fellow'. A rival dancing mistress thereupon included in the advertisement for her assembly that 'There will also be set up to be Raffled for, a likely young Virginia Negro Woman, fit for House Business, and her Child'.

It is quite apparent from the newspapers and journals of the time that the social dance was far more favoured in the south than in the north. In fact it seems that whereas a number of authorities continued to frown on dancing in the north, passing laws of prohibition, or at least of restriction, upon it wherever possible, in the south it was generally speaking fostered and developed. In educational establishments particularly does this generalization appear to have been true.

The high ranking society balls, abundant in protocol and privilege, did not perhaps allow a great deal of scope for real pleasure on the floor. The dancers and onlookers of both sexes would be far more concerned with keeping up with the Joneses than with releasing their inhibitions by means of the dance. As so often happens it was left to the lower, less restricted, classes to enjoy themselves. Very few of them were able to afford the cost of dance lessons, with the result that they picked up their skill by learning from one another and by observation. At these popular dances it was by no means uncommon for a group to consist of grandparents, parents and children.

One of the spontaneous causes for a dance lay in the communal spirit which existed between groups of farmsteads. One family would help another whenever the need arose—perhaps even several families would converge upon one farm in case of illness or other emergency. At the end of a long spell of work in such circumstances it was common practice to hold what was known as a bee or frolic. This consisted chiefly of a hearty meal followed by a dance in which a great deal of harmless merriment was not allowed to detract from the sheer physical pleasure of hard and skilful dancing. One writer enthuses about the frolic thus:

'I really know among us of no custom which is so useful and tends so much to establish the union and the little society which subsists among us. Poor as we are, if we have not the gorgeous balls, the harmonious concerts, the shrill horn of Europe, yet we delate our hearts as well with the simple negro fiddle . . .'

In the south the negroes too had their own dances, for it must not be supposed that it was only their slavery and frustration which invested them with a sense of rhythm believed by many to be the most sensitive in the world. They brought with them this love of the dance and they aped the movements of the white man as well as enjoying their own simple forms long before the eruption in Saint Louis which was to influence so strongly the social dance forms of the whole world.

But for the Americans themselves the century saw a marked development in the dance. Whereas at the opening of the century there had been very few schools of dancing, by the end no city was without a number. Although there were those puritanical spirits who through fervour or ignorance of the dance itself still railed against its practice, they had diminished in numbers from a multitude to a handful—a handful what is more who were never again to cajole a patient hearing from the people.

London society during a large part of the eighteenth century was as keen on spectacle in the form of masquerades and great balls as Louis XIV had been a little ealier. At the end of the war with France in 1748 there was an immediate exchange of visitors between the two countries, although there appear to have been more from London to Paris than the other way round. As Horace Walpole said:

'All our milliners, tailors, tavern-keepers, and young gentlemen are tiding to France for our improvement and luxury.'

Owing to the clearly laid down forms of the social dance at this time in both countries, each of them differing in technique but very little, it is not possible to trace the exact form of the influence on the style of dancing. There is no doubt, however, that this exchange of visitors gradually led on both sides to an increased artificiality in both style and movement. Each sought to impress the other, each exaggerated the already artificial style of the period. It took no more than a few dandies on either side to sow corruption, for after all only the comparative few were deeply interested; the majority were quite content to follow clumsily and superficially, if at all, the example set by these 'experts'.

Possibly this artificiality of the dance accounts for the fact that neither of those keen observers of society, William Makepeace Thackeray nor Jane Austen, have anything whatever to say about the dance although important scenes in their works are concentrated around the ballroom floor. In *Emma* for instance Thackeray writes at great length about the Duchess of Richmond's Ball in Brussels on the eve of Waterloo; and in *Northanger Abbey* a number of Catherine's adventures, trifling though they may appear to us today, occurred either at the Assembly or as a result of her meetings in that hotbed of gossip and intrigue. Yet neither of these two authors tells us about what was happening on the actual dance floor. They can discuss the appearances and manners and characters of their characters, but immediately these characters set foot on the floor observation seemingly undergoes suspension, except for arch and meaningful glances. Of the steps the characters performed not a word is said.

Similarly, in that section of *Bleak House* which describes the characters of two gentlemen who are among the most famous dancing masters of fiction, the Turveydrops, father and son, Dickens makes no specific reference to a single movement. The old Turveydrop, with his constant use of the mystic word 'Deportment' was doubtless a fake, but the son, christened Prince in honour of the Prince Regent, worked twelve hours a day.

' "Go on, Prince! Go on!" said Mr. Turveydrop, standing with his back to the fire, and waving his gloves condescendingly. "Go on, my son!"
'At this command, or by this gracious permission, the lesson went on. Prince Turveydrop, sometimes, played the kit (a small bowed stringed instrument, a "pocket fiddle" used by eighteenth- and nineteenth-

century dance masters); sometimes played the piano, standing; sometimes hummed the tune with what little breath he could spare, while he set a pupil right; always conscientiously moved with the least proficient through every step and every part of the figure; and never rested for an instant. His distinguished father did nothing whatever, but stand before the fire, a model of Deportment.'

Dickens, percipient, analytical, and being deeply absorbed in the activities of every kind of human being, can find no more to say about the actual dance than that.

Perhaps the most interesting account of what is often referred to as the Waterloo Ball is that written at first hand by Lady de Ros, third daughter of the fourth Duke of Richmond, who was the host. It will be seen that this lady also fails to mention anything whatever about the dancing, although her reasons were the extremely valid ones that she was more concerned with the horror of the event than with any interest in it as a social occasion. She is therefore to be excused for providing us with no conception of the programme but a full list of the invitations.

The dances remaining in general favour through a large part of the century, then, were the Minuet, Allemande, Passepied, Bourrée, Rigaudoon and Gavotte. Of these the one which experienced the greatest change from its form in the seventeenth century was the Minuet, although such change did not come about until well into the second half of the eighteenth century. At this time, probably through a delayed influence from the 'exchange visits' between travellers in France and England, a new way of dancing the Minuet was introduced. Until then only one dance bore the title of the Minuet; its figuration was meticulously laid down and the style of dancing it equally definite. Now came the so-called 'figured' Minuets which were specially composed dances featuring a number of different steps and making legitimate claim to the title Minuet only because the Minuet step itself was retained, although frequently performed rather differently from its original form. There was also a form of Minuet known as Minuet Country dances, danced 'longways' progressively down the room. These various kinds of Minuet naturally led to a less rigid and disciplined form. And finally there was the solo Minuet, in which, as the prefix suggests, the dancer had to perform alone. Frequently this was used in the test held by many finishing schools for young ladies where a high standard was sought after. Whereas young gentlemen were careless, even deliberately clumsy, on the floor, far heavier demands were made on young ladies. Indeed, it was sometimes so difficult for these skilled young women to obtain partners at all, much less partners of their own standard, that special Minuets were composed by some masters for groups of three or four ladies. In 1711 a well-known master named Pemberton published a book entitled *An Essay for the Further Improvement of Dancing*. In this work, as in others during the century, a great deal of discretion was allowed in the actual interpretation of the dance; either the full and authentic Minuet step could be used or a simplified version of it.

Perhaps the reason for the high standard demanded of the young lady in school lay in the fact that at her first ball as a debutante she was expected to dance the Minuet with her partner alone on the floor as a sort of exhibition—before the terrifyingly critical gaze, remember, of the mothers of other debutantes and their friends.

The Minuet continued to play an important part throughout a large part of the century, varying descriptions of it appearing in dance books until 1767. Following that it went very much out of favour, and would certainly have been harshly judged in the period which followed the French Revolution. In England, however, it was still taught in the early nineteenth century, the reason for this being that the French dancing masters and the nobles who fled to England, were able to teach it to a society which was developing a new gentility. A number of the French masters sought to earn a living at our girls' 'seminaries' and only a fleeting knowledge of the world of Becky Sharp is necessary to realize how the artificialities of the Minuet would have flourished in that milieu.

But naturally the French masters, confident that few could question them on the matter of authenticity, invented new ways and new styles, and even new figures, so that the Minuet of the nineteenth century in England bore only small resemblance to that of mid-eighteenth-century France.

In France, although the Minuet could no longer find the artificial and courtly atmosphere necessary for its sustenance, dancing masters in the 1880s were nevertheless able to revive not only the Minuet but also the Gavotte and the Pavane as set dances at charity balls, presenting them as show pieces in fancy dress. To English visitors no doubt these affairs gave an entirely false idea of the actual life and thought which followed the Revolution.

CHAPTER VI

The Nineteenth Century

REVOLUTIONS AND SCANDALS—AND THE BIRTH OF A NEW STYLE

Dancing is an art because it is subject to rules.
VOLTAIRE

THE great industrial revolution began with a series of inventions in the eighteenth century. The flying shuttle and the spinning jenny did more than accelerate the speed at which textiles could be manufactured; they began to change the whole structure of society. But important as they were these two inventions were small indeed when in 1769 Watt was at last able to invent an efficient machine for the purpose of turning steam into a mighty and obedient servant. Naturally it took some time for this strange new servant to be conditioned and acclimatized to man's use; in 1815 our cotton imports were worth £82,000,000 and in 1860 they had reached £1,000,000,000. The wool trade, our staple export during the century, experienced a similar transformation in the same period.

At the same time the population increased more rapidly than ever before. At the time of Waterloo the inhabitants of England numbered 13,000,000; by 1871 that figure had doubled. More babies were surviving and the people were living longer. By and large we were better fed and better clothed. But as is the case with all rapid development, there were at the same time many inequities. Great wealth thrived on great poverty. It is not so much that actual poverty was greater than before, but that the comparison made it appear greater. The new rich classes thrown up by the industrial revolution were kept warm and well fed by the poverty of those below stairs. New houses of the wealthy boasted magnificent halls and wide staircases, while immediately behind them enormous trays were carried in darkness up the narrowest possible spirals of metal steps.

THE NINETEENTH CENTURY

When the 30,000 British returned to their own country after Waterloo they found many changes; a more efficient farming industry but far fewer smallholders and an ever increasing migration to the industrial towns. Transport, although still time consuming and even in places hazardous, was improving rapidly, with the result that the communication of customs and new ideas became a much faster process than in the previous century.

Such vast and momentous changes in material life inevitably wrought equally tremendous transformations on social activity. London remained the centre of fashion, but other towns were quick to follow. The aristocracy developed dandyism and a taste in clothes. The new and prosperous class of industrialists and manufacturers began to learn social niceties and extravagances from the aristocracy, but at the same leavened custom and fashion to their own more vigorous way of life. This new vigour also meant that almost throughout the century there would be a constant seeking for the new and novel, ideas would be tried out and discarded, fashions would go from one extreme to another. For this reason only the most powerful forms of expression, and those most characteristic of their times, would stand the remotest chance of longevity.

The greatest change in masculine dress was the transformation of knee breeches into trousers. Up to the end of the eighteenth century it seems that not a hint of this garment had graced an aristocratic leg, although the people of France had to some extent favoured a kind of trouser during the period of the Revolution. Then in 1815 in Britian it made an appearance that was almost immediately to become notable for its variety. There were trousers that swelled out from the hip to taper down to a tight fit round the ankles; there were trousers which finished above the ankle and trousers which grew wider as they approached the feet, sometime flapping about the ankles. Many experiments were conducted by fashionable tailors of the time before the trouser manifested itself in the not unreasonable narrow limb-following line in which it finally saw out the nineteenth century.

The billowing dresses of the ladies which were in vogue before the Revolution gave way during the course of about twenty years to long and clinging but not unduly tight skirts and a high waistline. Well before the end of the previous century ridiculous excesses in hair styles had succumbed to a more natural style, with the hair frequently brought up on the top of the head in a series of curls.

About twenty-five years into the nineteenth century, however, dresses became shorter, the skirts being flounced out from the waist,

REVOLUTIONS AND SCANDALS—BIRTH OF A NEW STYLE

usually with the aid of whalebones. In the first few years of Queen Victoria's reign starched petticoats were employed to aid the volume of these dresses, and these increased in size as one woman vied with another. By the middle of the century the crinoline had come into its own and a little later adopted its most exaggerated form. In revulsion against that came a return to the eighteenth-century styles, or rather extremely free adaptations of that style. By 1880 the bustle was very much *à la mode*, and as the century drew to its close, fringes, trains, furbelows and all kinds of decorations came more and more into favour.

Men's coats were at the beginning of the century cut away sharply in front, in a style reminiscent of the rapidly disappearing tails and the almost defunct morning dress of today. Lapels were wide and collars deep, while waistcoats, often in rich and colourful material, were short and square-cut. As the century matured the tail coat gradually gave way more and more to the informal lounge suit which was the forerunner of today's almost invariable fashion, although for evening functions with any social pretension at all evening dress remained *de rigeur* right to the end of the century, and well beyond.

During the first decade many dance resorts continued to favour the Country Dance, the Minuet, Contredanse, Scotch Reels and the Ecossaise. In common with various other Scottish accomplishments the two last named forms appear to have found more favour in France than in Scotland, and there even seems to be some doubt as to whether the Ecossaise was in fact known in the North. It may well be that this dance is of French origin and that it was set to Scottish music. At least we know that it was at first danced to the sound of bagpipes, although, as maintained by at least one highly experienced musician of the period, it bore no real resemblance to the Strathspey or the Reel, the only authentic Scottish dance music. Those eminent authorities, the late Cecil Sharp and A. P. Oppé in *The Dance*, claim that Ecossaises were danced in England from about 1780. It seems that they were 'very similar to English Country Dances but executed more energetically, to a faster tempo, and often to Scottish tunes'. To add a little more confusion, Beethoven, Chopin and others wrote Ecossaises which have nothing Scottish about them whatever. Be all that as it may the dance itself took the form partly of a Reel and partly of a Country Dance. During one passage the gentleman found himself with two partners.

The Minuet had been virtually killed in France by the French Revolution, but as we have seen, numerous members of the French aristocracy who fled to England sought to gain a living by teaching etiquette and dancing, especially in girls' schools. In the early part of the century this dance, which had during the last century become mincing and artificial, kept pace with the corruption and decadence of the French gentry themselves. There is little doubt that those refugees, far from moderating its mannerisms, now exaggerated them still further—dazzling their pupils with science, as it were, in order to justify their own existence and perhaps extend their course of instruction. In this connexion it is interesting to record that during the Congress of Vienna it was decided to revive the Minuet, yet according to reliable records it was only with the greatest difficulty possible to find a couple who could even remember the authentic movements.

During the last twenty years of the century the Minuet was to undergo another revival, when a number of French dancing masters resuscitated it, together with the Gavotte and the Pavane. But here again artificiality was the keynote, for the revival was not to enrich true ballroom dancing, but merely to present these dances of the past as demonstrations at fancy dress and charity balls. Naturally all kinds of 'improvements' on the early eighteenth-century form were considered necessary for the entertainment of the audience, with the result that the revived dances bore little resemblance in movement, and less in feeling, to the originals. In one figure in the Minuet revival, for instance, the gentleman actually knelt on one knee, an idea far from the classical ideal in which the Minuet enjoyed its richest period.

The music for these revivals was, however, usually that which had accompanied the originals. It was, after all, far easier to revive the music, which enjoyed an infinitely superior notation than the dances. Thus, when Louis d'Egville, a well-known dancing master towards the end of the nineteenth century, produced a Minuet, it was accompanied by the 'Menuet de Bourgeois Gentilhomme' music written by Lully for one of the dances in Moliere's play *Le Bourgeous Gentilhomme* which was first produced in 1670.

Towards the end of the eighteenth century a number of places known as assembly rooms had come into being. The earliest of them were undoubtedly erected in watering places such as Bath, Epsom, Tunbridge Wells. When the aristocracy left London and other big cities for the purpose of taking medicinal waters, they sought to surround themselves with their customary creature comforts and entertainment. They could not take Almack's with them, but there were those who were quick to see the possibility of diverting into their own pockets some of the wealth which was carried to these resorts. The life in such places was one of complete leisure, and often, judging by

REVOLUTIONS AND SCANDALS—BIRTH OF A NEW STYLE

the literature of the period, of considerable boredom, with the result that the devotees of the waters were also keen if not skilled exponents on the dance floor.

At the beginning of the century, then, these assembly rooms catered for a very exclusive clientele, and the form and etiquette followed largely upon that of Almack's. Invariably each ball opened with a Minuet and continued with Country Dances, Contredanses and Cotillons. See Appendix IV.

At court too the Minuet remained the ceremonial dance and both opened and closed the great occasions. In 1813 a big ball was held by the Prince Regent at Carlton House to celebrate the Battle of Vittoria in the Peninsular War. P. J. S. Richardson in *The Social Dances of the Nineteenth Century*, the only work written this century to cover exclusively that lively period, makes the point that no ball was given to celebrate El Alamein. This does perhaps seem rather strange, especially as the Royal Albert Hall is packed every year for a different kind of commemoration of that victory. But in the last war, unlike that of the Peninsular, we were all involved, not only the armed forces. The cause for rejoicing was therefore far more deep rooted, and took wider and more prolonged forms.

Into the ordered and artificial atmosphere of the early nineteenth-century dance scene the first breath of fresh air, one could almost say scandal, came with the advent of the Waltz. An English dance calendar of 1801 states: 'The English dances have no character. All they consist of is kicking and leaping to the measure, and this is falsely called dancing.' Was it then strange that in all the transformations taking place in social and industrial life, the dance should not also seek reinvigoration, and that it would shortly express in its own way the new vigorousness, the restlessness and sense of adventure of the times? No more apt expression of at least one vital side of the character of the people could have been found than in the Waltz. This dance was not a product of the century, and appears to have been born as a social dance in the suburbs of Vienna and in the Alpine districts of Austria. The first Waltzes possessing a definite musical form have been traced to a little after the middle of the seventeenth century, but well before that a form of waltzing had been practised in Austria and Germany by the peasants. This however was only the preliminary. The climate was not yet suitable, and not until the Industrial Revolution was well under way did the time became ripe for the true flowering of the dance. History followed its normal course, even so, and at the outset the dancing masters were vehemently opposed to this revolutionary new form.

In 1767, for instance, a French master, condemning it soundly, stated that the Waltz had no relation whatever with 'la Bonne Danse'. Another master, of a more cynical turn of mind, said: 'I can imagine that the mothers are fond of the Waltz, but not that they permit their daughters to dance it.'

At one time there seems to have been something of a battle between the French and Germans as to its origins. At that time the French claimed that the Waltz sprung originally from La Volta whereas the Germans maintained that the Drehtanz (turning dance), in which couples dance face to face, holding hands, was the true progenitor. It is strange, in view of this controversy, that most French dictionaries today, including Larousse, refer only to its Germanic origins. In old German the word Waltzen means to wander or to stroll, or even to turn or to glide. As early as 1760 the word is used in connexion with an order prohibiting this form of turning dance. In an encyclopaedia published about 1805, the following definition and comment appears:

'The verb *Waltzen*, whence this word (waltz) is derived, implies to roll, wallow, welter, tumble down, or roll in the dirt or mire.

What analogy there may be between these acceptances and the dance, we pretend not to say; but having seen it performed by a select party of foreigners, we could not help reflecting how uneasy an English mother would be to see her daughter so familiarly treated and still more to witness the obliging manner in which the freedom is returned by the females.'

In the German Landler, the accent occurs on the second beat of the second bar of the phrase. The first popular tune which could be claimed to be in true Waltz rhythm was a revival in 1780 of the ancient 'Ach! du lieber Augustin!' In a slightly different rhythmic form but with a virtually unchanged melodic line this became in the twentieth century 'The Frothblowers Anthem' in which form it was popular in England, France and Germany.

Outcries against the Waltz came from almost every quarter and in every land in Europe. It is said that in Mecklenburg in 1749 the queen turned away in disgust when the dance was first seen in court, but that the king was charmed. At the Russian court it was not even introduced until after the death of Catherine. Not until 1798 was it danced by the mistress of Paul the first.

In England the outcry was just as loud and perhaps even more prolonged. Byron's bitter comment when he saw his wife dancing the Waltz with another man that they looked like 'two cockchafers spitted on the same Bodekin' has frequently been quoted, but the following poem by him is not so well known:

> No decent David, when, before the art,
> His grand pas-seul excited some remark:
> Not love-lorn Quizote, when his gaucho though
> the knight's fandango friskier than it ought,
> No soft Herodias, when, with winning tread,
> Her nimble feet danced off another's head:
> Not Cleopatra on her galley's deck,
> Display'd so much of *leg*, or more of *neck*
> Than thou, ambrosial Waltz, when first the moon
> Beheld thee twirling to a Saxon tune.

At last, however, in 1816, the Waltz in England gained formal approval when it received the official sanction of the Prince Regent. But even this acknowledgement from the highest quarter did not satisfy *The Times*, which had conducted sporadic but fierce attacks upon the seemliness of the dance. Following the announcement of this sanction that staunch defencer of public morals in its issue of July 16th published the following condemnation:

'We remarked with pain that the indecent foreign dance called the *Waltz* was introduced (we believe for the first time) at the English Court on Friday last. This is a circumstance which ought not to be passed over in silence. National morals depend on national habits: and it is quite sufficient to cast one's eyes on the voluptuous intertwining of the limbs, and close compressure on the bodies, in their dance, to see that it is indeed far removed from the modest reserve which has hitherto been considered distinctive of English females. So long as this obscene display was confined to prostitutes and adulteresses, we did not think it deserving of notice: but now it is attempted to be forced on the respectable classes of society by the evil example of their superiors, we feel it a duty to warn every parent against exposing his daughter to so fatal a contagion. *Amicus Plato sed Atagis amica veritas.* We pay due deference to our superiors in rank, but we owe a higher duty to morality. We know not how it has happened (probably the recommendation of some worthless and ignorant dancing master) that so indecent a dance has now for the first time been exhibited at the English Court; but the novelty is one deserving of severe reprobation, and we trust it will never again be tolerated in any moral English society.'

THE NINETEENTH CENTURY

Almost immediately after the Revolution the Waltz appears to have gained favour in France, where social dancing among the bourgeoisie, if not the proletariat, was gaining a powerful hold. By 1789 it is said that there were nearly seven hundred dance halls in Paris alone. In view of the scarcity at present one wonders what happened to them. Although it is not for a moment to be supposed that many of them were of the size of the great public dance halls today in Britain, several of them according to a contemporary artist's impression, were capable of containing very large numbers of dancers.

By this time dance floors had acquired a high polish and many of the better ones were laid in the parquet pattern. This naturally meant that the movement of the dancers themselves became both smoother and faster, the feet gliding along the floor instead of being raised as in a normal walking movement. Leaps by the dancers and wide intervals in the music were gradually, but not too gradually, transformed into smooth and flowing sound and movement patterns.

Various writers have made the point that with the Waltz there was also introduced into the social dance the closed hold which has exerted such a powerful influence upon most social forms of dance ever since. It would perhaps have been more correct to refer to this feature as a 'reintroduction' for as far back as the sixteenth century we have seen that in at least one dance, La Volta, a similar kind of hold was in favour. At the outset this so-called close hold in the Waltz was of a sufficiently circumspect nature to allow ample 'daylight' between the couples, and it was not for about a hundred years that dancers became so daring as to allow their bodies actually to come into close contact with each other as they rotated giddily round the floor.

It is sometimes claimed that the Waltz was not seen in English ballrooms until 1812, but this is not strictly true. In one form, with entwining arm movements, and including an Allemande figure in which the lady turned under her partner's raised arm, the dance found some favour here at the beginning of the century. Developments have continued well into the present century. Today in fact we have three distinct forms of Waltz, each being identifiable with the others only because of a common rotary element and the triple measure.

To what extent the speed of the Waltz was governed by the music and to what extent the movements of the dancers governed the speed of the music cannot be determined, especially as tempi varied greatly and as there were several varieties of movement. Musicologists claim that Weber, with his famous pianoforte piece *The Invitation to the Dance* composed in 1819, laid down the ideal speed, which was crotchet = 76.

This would have been considered slow later in the century, for with the development of the Viennese Waltz this tempo was more than doubled, and even with the dance which became generally accepted in the ballrooms right up to the beginning of the first world war the tempo was still round about crotchet 130, although by that time musicians continued to measure tempi in that method, dancing masters were adopting one more suitable for their own requirements by naming the number of bars of music played in one minute. Today in the nineteen sixties, the tempo of the so-called modern Waltz is 32 bars a minute, the Viennese Waltz is 56 bars a minute, and the so-called Old Time Waltz is 48 bars a minute.

In the 'set' or square dances which became popular in Victorian and Edwardian periods, the Waltz played a vital part on most of the figures. In the Lancers it was widely used and the instructions for many dances of these times conclude with the words 'four bars of Waltzing'.

In *The Invitation to the Dance* Weber showed for the first time how to extend this kind of music away from banality into an attractive composition in its own right. A hundred years later, in fact, a great Russian choreographer, Michel Fokine, found it of sufficient merit for the musical accompaniment of a ballet, *Le Spectre de la Rose*, which was first danced by Karsavina and Nijinsky, and which is still often performed today. Following Weber's excellent example other composers began to produce a stream of Waltzes, some of them for instruments alone and others for the human voice accompanied by the pianoforte. But 'Invitation' remained the favourite both in the ballroom and in the salon for many years. After Weber perhaps Chopin is the best known composer of brilliant Waltz music, although today when we hear his melodies in the ballroom as distinct from the concert hall, they are distorted for 'contemporary' purposes almost beyond recognition. On the other hand, two of Chopin's Waltzes are used with great success in another and even more famous Fokine ballet, *Les Sylphides*.

Brahms and Schumann composed Waltzes which are typically German both in style and character, but with them of course Waltzes were but a small part of their output. Other composers of lesser stature made their reputation solely on the strength of the Waltz. None but the musician would today otherwise have heard of Johann Strauss, for example, much less of Joseph Lanner. These two are mostly responsible for the popularity of the Viennese Waltz and their Waltz tunes remain in favour, although not all of them are played with the same frequency as the *Blue Danube*. In his entry to the Waltz in *The*

Oxford Companion to Music Percy Scholes pithily sums up the situation:

'... it seems as likely that such a waltz as the Blue Danube, by Johann Strauss the younger, the "Waltz King" will last for ever as that Beethoven's Fifth Symphony will do.'

Franz Lehar is sometimes coupled with these two other famous composers, but he came much later; in fact in time to bring new impetus to the Waltz after the turn of the century in such works as *The Merry Widow* in 1905.

The normal pattern of the Strauss Waltzes, composed both by father and son, was to begin with a fairly slow introduction and to continue with a sixteen bar Waltz, continuing into others in related keys. For the coda the outstanding themes of these tunes were brought together. This is the form developed in the *Blue Danube*.

As he so often succeeds in doing, Curt Sachs comes up with an interesting theory, one that provokes thought, even when it does not win unanimous agreement.

'The rise of the waltz was a result of that longing for truth, simplicity, closeness to nature, and primitivism, which the last two-thirds of the eighteenth century fulfilled. The dance, too, strove for character, soul, expression, passion, "One more," we have written "the time has come when fresh blood is needed, and infusion of the imitative style from the extrovert side." Where could the new tendency have a more powerful and lasting effect than in that art from which had almost exclusively pointed Europe the way towards the imitative style, in the ballet?'

Although few if any of the dancing masters, and certainly not the dancers themselves, would have consciously been aware of such a powerful stimulus as a 'longing for truth, closeness to nature and primitivism' Sach's theory may yet be perfectly valid. Few of the participants in any expression of mass character or temperament, unless they are artists who are highly conscious of the ethos of their time, are aware that they are in fact expressing anything at all. For my own part, however, I adhere to the theory that the Waltz was the outward expression of a frenzied evolution, for during the last twenty years of the eighteenth century and a comparable distance into the nineteenth, as we have seen, more changes have taken place in Europe than in some hundreds of years before that. These changes are as markedly expressed in dress and custom as in the dance. Nevertheless, I am fully prepared

17. Le Bal Paré, Paris 1773, showing the dancers in the middle of an Allemande.

18. The British illustrator, scene painter and member of the Royal Academy, Francis Heyman (1708-1776) was best known for the decorations for the Vauxhall Gardens, which he began round about 1745. The above is a reproduction of his *Dance of the Milkmaids* in the Victoria & Albert Museum.

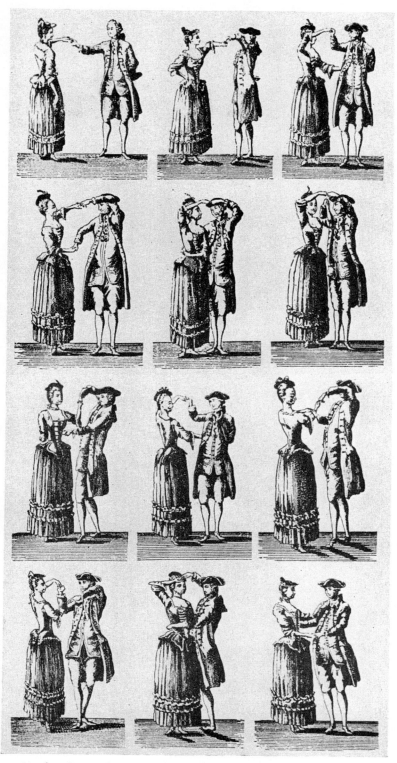

19. Twelve figures from the Allemande reproduced in a book by Simon Guillaume, published in Paris in 1770.

20. An impression of the Cotillon by a contemporary artist.

21. A ball dress featured in the *Illustrated London News* in 1844.

22. This is how the Polka was first featured in the *Illustrated London News* of March 23rd, 1844. (See appendix)

23. In its issue of May 11th, 1844, the *Illustrated London News* published a description of the Polka, including with that description the three pictures shown above.

25. The Caledonian Ball of 1844 at the Hanover Square Rooms.

26. Le Bal de l'Opéra à quatres Heures du Matin, reproduced from a drawing by Gustave Doré.

27. Le Bal du Chateau des Fleurs, another reproduction from a drawing by Gustave Doré.

29. A further drawing of a Paris dance scene, this time in the open air. This reproduction comes from *Views of Paris* and shows Le Bal Mabile.

30. A contemporary artist's impression of one of the figures from the Contredanse.

31. A reproduction from an aquatint by Isaac Roberts and George Cruikshank, showing a set of Lancers.

32. A Ball in progress at the Argylle Rooms. A reproduction from an engraving by Robert Cruckshank.

to give some credence to Sach's theory, and hope that an even more unlikely hypothesis of my own might be given some attention. Is it not possible that the rotary movement of the Waltz was a form of human obeissance, however unconscious, to the newly invented engine which harnessed the power of steam by means of rotary movement. After all, throughout history people have imitated the animals they wanted to kill or to capture. Why should not we seek unconsciously to imitate the form of movement which was transforming our mode of life, converting us from a mainly rural into a predominantly urban community?

Not until about thirty years into the century did the Waltz lose its hold on Europe and even then new developments on the dance floor were largely based on the Waltz and were certainly not reactions against it. The only entirely new rhythm and physical impetus came from the Polka. See Appendix III and IV.

Several factors contributed to the preparation of conditions which were perfect for the growth of this dance. Perhaps in the first place, although the people were now not exactly tired of the incessant Waltz rhythms and melodies, with their inevitable air of sentimentality, the need for marked contrast was becoming more and more felt; indeed, in all probability, far from robbing the Waltz of some of its popularity, I am of the opinion that after the immediate frenzy of enthusiasm with which the Polka was first greeted, the lively contrast it provided actually prolonged the life of the Waltz, leading to its development and to its adoption by the dancers of the first sixty odd years of the twentieth century.

Another reason, given by Philip Richardson in *The Social Dances of the Nineteenth Century*, is that at the coming to the throne of Victoria there existed in England a great deal of sympathy for the peoples of central Europe—peoples under foreign domination. In those countries there was at this time a powerful revival of national feeling and culture. Robbed of political freedom the people could nevertheless give expression to their nationalism and at the same time mildly vent their feelings in various art forms.

We are apt to forget, too, that France was still in a considerable state of turmoil, for few history courses pay much attention to the fact that there were between 1830 and 1848 two revolutions there, and that throughout the Continent spiritual and political oppressions were coming into conflict with a rapid growth in new ideas and the beginnings of socialistic idealism. On the dance floor, too, one saw marked contrasts: in the world of fashion it had become almost a solecism for a man to be an accomplished dancer: and those who did set foot on the floor adopted for the most part a foppish attitude, moving about with as languid an air as possible. On the other hand, and I am writing now especially of Paris, although a great number of English people were of the same attitude, the masses who now favoured the public dance halls whizzed and twirled about the floor in outbursts of robustness which matched the vulgar but vital energy of the music hall dance of this period. The Polka came just at the right moment to harness this energy and to direct it into a less uncontrolled and unseemly direction.

Largely through the great interest throughout Europe in various forms of national dance, and largely through the need for the several famous ballet dancers of the time to find new variety, a contrast to the classical ballet which sent them willy-nilly, helter-skelter, *sur les pointes*, round the capitals of Europe and beyond to make their fortunes, a number of national dances found themselves on the stage. There they were stylized and made more spectacular for public consumption and provided they gained sufficient acclaim were then tamed and simplified for use in the ballroom. Thus the dance in its original national form first went through a process to make it more complicated and difficult, and second a process of simplification. It will be readily understood that the final product sometimes differed a great deal from the dance of its origin.

Simplified though the dances of this kind may have been, however, the public in common dance halls of the time flung themselves into their execution with fervour, kicking their legs and twirling their partners into a state of near-vertigo. Hopping, skipping and even jumping steps were interspersed with rapid and continuous turns. The Waltz itself was accelerated, and all the other new dances, such as the Galop and the Can Can, were of a highly exuberant, sometimes volatile, nature. Some few years before coming into widespread favour the Polka had been danced in certain halls in Paris, but it was not until a far-seeing dancing master saw its possiblities and groomed it for the public view, that it was hailed thoughout Europe as a favourite in almost every ballroom.

It is fairly clear that the Polka originated in Czechoslavakia although the favourite story of its origin is to say the least apocryphal. This story tells of an exuberant young servant girl in the town of Kostelec on the Elbe. It appears that here on Sunday afternoons young people gathered for song and dance, and on this particular day, some time in 1830, the heroine of our tale, Anna Chadimova, sprang into movements hitherto not seen here, at the same time singing her own accompaniment.

According to some sources a Bohemian composer, and according to others a dance teacher, observing the girl dancing in this way took down the notes of her tune as well as memorizing the steps. And on the following Sunday Anna was apparently prevailed upon to teach the steps to her companions.

That observer's name is given in an exhaustive article on the origins of the Polka by Arthur Michel in *Dance Magazine of America* in January and February 1944. He was Jesep Neruda and the Polka he composed was not published until 1870. This late date of publication does not invalidate our attractive story, for there may conceivably have been a delay in publication. The oldest record of the Polka traced so far dates back to 1844, and we know the dance was widely popular some years before that, an actual description having appeared in print in 1835. It appears that the characteristic rhythm by which we recognize the music of the Polka today was the accompaniment for a number of dances which emanated each from a different town or district in East Bohemia. In some of these villages the dance accompanied by this rhythm was in fact known as the Polka.

Paul Nettl in *The Story of Dance Music* states that the word Polka derives from *pulk* which means a half, and in common with others believes that the attachment of such a word to the dance as its title can be attributed to the fact that a characteristic movement of the dance is a half step. Others claim with less plausibility that the title is attributed to the fact that the dance was originally half sung and half danced. As there appears to be no etymologicial association between polka and pulka, however, neither of these theories holds water.

From Kostelec students transferred the dance to Prague, whence it quickly found its way to a number of other capital cities. From Prague to Paris it was taken by a ballet master on tour. Once the dance was seen on stage, at the Theatre de l'Ambigu, French dancing masters soon turned it into a cult, and before long it became a rage which has not been surpassed by that for any other dance since.

First it was *les petits rats*, members of the *corps de ballet* at the Opera, who danced it at the public balls with their consorts who had waited for them at the stage door. Not slow to see the possibilities of the dance a number of excellent teachers in Paris quickly polished and refined it for the consumption of the upper classes. The dance they produced in fact bore but small resemblance to the original. For the social dance teachers were joined by the ballet masters such as Eugene Coralli, choreographer of the ballet *Giselle*, and Lucien Petipa, brother of the more famous Marius Petipa. It was in fact Coralli who set down the first fully acceptable description of the dance, giving five figures, which were a little later published, with figure drawings, in the *Illustrated London News*. There is no evidence that more figures than that were ever danced in Paris, although in London and Berlin ten were popular at one time.

But even at the outset the leading teachers, and probably others, practised and taught their own very special interpretations. Coralli employed a quiet method, whereas another great teacher, perhaps indeed the greatest actual ballroom teacher at this period, Cellarius, put into his footwork what was described by a contemporary as 'alarming passion'. It was not until 1844, that a certain amount of simplicity and discipline was brought back to the dance. By this time, however, a marked 'turn out' had become a notable feature of the dance. By 'turn out' I mean that pronounced turning out of the legs from the hip which is a feature of classical ballet.

It was inevitable that a dance which had become so much of a rage should be seen in the theatre. Professional stage dancers soon found that they could present their own versions with great success and in the Spring of 1844 Coralli himself, partnered by Mlle Maria, actually produced it on the stage of the Paris Opera; and immediately after that even more famous stage dancers, Carlotta Grisi, one of the greatest ballerinas of the time and creator of the role of *Giselle*, together with her husband and a brilliant performer in his own right, Jules Perrot, danced it at Her Majesty's Theatre, London. Other ballet dancers, with almost equal claim to fame, Fanny Cerrito and Arthur Saint-Leon, danced what must have been a different version a month later, but this was said by certain critics to bear little resemblance to the real Polka at all. Ivor Guest, in his *Victorian Ballet Girl* states that round about this time two men delighted the audience during a special show at Brighton run by the Sussex County Cricket Club, with a performance of the Polka; in fact it appears to have delighted them so much that an encore had to be given.

Back in Paris the methods of Cellarius and Coralli each had their adherents. A book entitled *La Polka Enseignée Sans Maître*, published at about this time, set out to do exactly what its title suggests, but also included some historical and background notes.

According to these notes the adherents of Cellarius and Coralli created such a controversy that arrangements were made for the two great masters to meet face to face, or rather 'Polka to Polka' to decide, although by what means remains obscure, whose method was the better. For this momentous duel, according to this book, all the votaries of the Polka in Paris were in attendance. Cellarius was accompanied by four or five of his expert pupils and when the time came for the battle to commence, took out one of his sisters 'dressed in white like a vestal virgin' and, followed by his pupils, prepared to dance for his very life. It appears that a new tune had been composed for the occasion, only the third ever to be played, but poor Cellarius and his votaries were unable to dance to it. Ignominiously they were compelled to stop the orchestra and give them the score of the original music, by now hackneyed and boring, before they could perform the steps. The tale relates:

'As the familiar strains fell on the ears the Cellarians took courage; they advanced with great spirit, bringing their heels up under the coat tails in the most daring fashion, and remained masters in the field. But their triumph was not of long duration. The crowd presently parted to make way for their terrible rivals, whose very first steps ensured the discomfiture of the Cellarians. The whole cohort dispersed, and the unhappy chief, his eyes darting flames, his heart full of fury, withdrew to swallow the affront as best he might.'

Although the narrative goes on to tell us that the Cellarians later avowed their enmity against their victors, no account is given as to why one school of thought was considered to surpass the other. In any case Cellarius, during the next forty years, succumbed to commercial attractions and resorted to what can only be referred to as inartistic methods. In short he employed *petits rats* to act as dancing partners in his classes. These badly paid members of the ballet were doubtless for the most part skilled enough for such a task, but they also felt it part of their duty to be as 'agreeable' as possible to the pupils, and this attracted many young men to whom the Polka would doubtless have been only of limited appeal.

Perhaps Cellarius was justified in this practice, but inevitably his method was copied by others less scrupulous, with the result that both manners and morals in the dance halls deteriorated to an alarming degree. Promoters took small rooms and the demeanour and general behaviour of dancers left so much to be desired that many parents forbade their children to dance at all other than in their own select circles. This employment of the *petits rats* is I believe the first recorded account of professional partners. The practice seems to have been abandoned until the advent of the great public dance halls in England a few years after the first World War.

Although, as we have seen, the Polka did not reach England until

1844 it immediately achieved fantastic popularity. At a dance given by the Duke of Wellington at Apsley House (Hyde Park Corner) a few months after the dance had made its invasion the Polka, according to a contemporary, was danced six times. Some disapproval was shown, in fact, at its undue popularity, and appeals were made in some quarters for a return to the following order: Quadrille, Waltz, Quadrille, Polka, and so on. One writer naively states:

'By observing this order, dancers would not feel so fatigued, and the Quadrille would continue to act as pleasant relief to the Waltz or Polka; leaving at the same time an opportunity for gentlemen to converse with their fair partners.'

Although such perdiodicals as *Punch* poked fun at the Polka nothing hampered its triumphal march through the ballrooms of the land and, final stamp of unqualified approval, it was soon introduced into the Court Balls, ousting in the process the Country Dance which normally concluded the programme. And it seems that it was preserved at these Court Balls some time after it had ceased to hold the public imagination, for by the end of the century there might perhaps be one or two Polkas still included in the programme. In its finally developed form the Polka can best be described as a round dance performed to two-in-a-measure music, with steps on the first three half-beats and a kind of rest on the fourth beat. In the Appendix will be found further details and the first description of the Polka to appear in England.

Today we dance the Polka only during party, and indeed chiefly during hilarious occasions; but the music has lived much longer and has exerted no mean influence on many composers. The first to develop it to any serious extent was undoubtedly Smetana who in the first place wrote a number of Polkas purely for dance orchestras. Later, however, he produced a number of melodies in which, in the words of the eminent music critic, the late Edwin Evans, 'he revealed his ambition to do for the Polka what Chopin had done for the Waltz and the Mazurka'.

After a trip to Sweden Smetana returned to Bohemia fired with a burning ambition to raise the banner of nationalism in music, and in pursuit of this ambition he understandably gave considerable prominence to the Polka. Perhaps the best known of his compositions in this rhythm is that in *The Bartered Bride*, which he composed in 1866. In spite of its rather obvious rhythm Smetana nevertheless succeeded in infusing a certain amount of subtlety into his Polka tunes, and although he naturally stylized them for operatic purposes, he nevertheless retained the quality of the rhythm.

It is the obvious and emphatic beat in the Polka which has undoubtedly prevented many composers from treating it with as much earnestness as the Waltz. Finally, to bring down the curtain on this furore of the mid-nineteenth century, I again quote Edwin Evans, who is here writing about events of the second decade of the twentieth century.

'Then there is the delightful Polka which goes by the name of Les Vendredis. Belaiev, the great Russian music patron and publisher, used to hold Friday gatherings for chamber music, and the composers who attended them often brought with them, especially on his birthdays and namedays, pieces specially composed for them, some of which were based on the musical letters of his name, B (= B flat), La (= A), F. On one occasion three composers collaborated in a Polka one continuing where the other left off. One might expect a work thus contrived to be rather a "mess", instead of which it is a real gem. The composers were Sokolov, Glazunov and Laidov. I recommended this Polka to Mme Karsavina for inclusion in a divertissement she presented at the Coliseum, and it proved a great success. I have never told her that Diaghilev made a furious scene with me for not having first brought it to him. In conclusion let us not forget the Polka which Borodin composed as an accompaniment to *Chopsticks* performed by a little girl, who thereby established her claim to be a pianist. And in Germany the theme she played, which became the germ of many ingenious variations by different composers, is known as the Cutlet Polka.'

It is thus abundantly clear that musical interest in the Polka endured long after the excitement of the dance had died, or at least until the dance remained alive only to be brought out for party occasions.

'For many years now it has been the custom in the higher grades of society to simply walk through the figures of quadrilles; but in the former times more or less difficult steps were employed by the dancers in performing them. These included not only the simple jetté (sic), Chassés, assemblé, balancé and changement de jambe; but originally expert dancers would frequently introduce such movements as the sissone, coupé dessus et dessous, and entrechat à quatre. Later on, however, when ballroom dancing began to degenerate into a mere amusement these steps were discarded, and the chassé also shared the fate of the rest, and then the pas marché, or walking step, was pressed into service, and made to do duty for all quadrille evolutions.'

That quotation opens the chapter headed Quadrilles, or Set dances in *Dancing as an Art and Pastime* by Edward Scott, published in 1892. Scott, a distinguished teacher, was also a proliferous writer both on the technique and the background of dancing. Without several of his many books our picture of the nineteenth-century dance scene would today be extremely inadequate. His literary style was at times pompous and circumlocutory, and it now appears as though he was anxious to display his erudition, for he brings in numerous classical allusions and references to works which would in his time have stamped him as a man of learning and culture. Dance teachers were often struggling to climb into a higher social level than that into which they had been born; for this purpose they associated with prosperous members of Victorian society, members whose own families had often but recently through trade risen in the world; they associated too, but with themselves on a far inferior level, with the nobility, teaching their children and the younger adults what they inevitably referred to as the social grace of dancing. Small wonder that they sought to elevate themselves, and doubtless Scott's writings helped a great deal to gain for him a place in society achieved by but few of his contemporaries. There is however no record of his ever having given himself the title of 'professor' a custom which grew increasingly popular towards the turn of the century, until at the end any teacher worth his salt laid claim to this 'honorary' title, and his wife, if she were a teacher as well, as 'madame'. The custom died hard, and even today there are still a few teachers left who employ handles. But the fault is a small one if we consider their skill as teachers. They fought all kinds of disinterest and snobbery and at the same time developed a style of dancing which still claims wide popularity.

When the English Country Dance was exported to France at the end of the seventeenth century, where it found warm favour at the court of Napoleon I, it became known naturally enough as the Contredanse Anglaise. This title, equally naturally, was soon abbreviated to Contredanse. In France this kind of dancing was subjected to certain small modifications, and one particular form of Country Dance became known as Quadrille. As may be imagined from this title the Quadrille was a square dance. The music for it had five movements in different time signatures. In 1816, Lady Jersey, a leader of society in England, saw the dance performed while she was on a visit to Paris, learned its

REVOLUTIONS AND SCANDALS—BIRTH OF A NEW STYLE

figures and brought it back to England. The first demonstration was given at Almack's by Lady Jersey herself, Lady Harriet Butler, Lady Susan Ryder, and Miss Montgomery, with Count Aldegarde, Mr. Montgomery, Mr. Harley and Mr. Montague.

At the outset a fair amount of space was required for the comfortable performance of certain figures of the Quadrille. In one figure, for example, L'Ete, the ladies had to hold out their skirts, in a manner, incidentally, taught with great meticulousness by the dancing masters of the time, point the toe and chassé from side to side. This was very well at Almack's and other smart dance resorts in the first forty years of the century, but from that time, when this kind of dancing was taken up by the middle and even lower middle classes, space was at a premiun.

After Lady Jersey's introduction the Quadrilles were taken up by almost all kinds of society. By the time Queen Victoria ascended the throne it was already a firm favourite and court balls were invariably opened with a set, the Queen herself being partnered by the most important male guest. From that point the history of the development, or rather the corruption, of the Quadrilles to the end of the century is admirably summed up in my quotation from Scott.

Our nineteenth-century teacher *cum* author is scathing in the extreme about the standard of dancing to be seen in the 1880s but attributes the decline of the Quadrilles, both in popularity and in standard, largely to the elimination of steps of a lively nature. In addition he believed that:

'... when we come to consider the fact that most of the modern votaries of Terpsichore, if such they may fairly be called, especially the males, are entirely innocent of any true conception of gracefulness, it is not a matter of wonder that they find little pleasure or profit in going through what must appear to them uncommonly like unsystematic drill formations.'

Continuing, Scott maintains that those who have really studied the art of dancing 'not with the feet only, but from the waist upwards' can make the Quadrilles attractive to the onlookers and enjoyable for for the performers in spite of the elimination of any movement. Indeed, he adds that this elimination need be no drawback at all:

'... because the Waltz, with its rotary and rapid motion, affords a stimulus of excitement that would render an alternation of dances, productive of milder emotions a positive boon, if people would only learn to regard dancing from a rational point of view.'

In common with other authorities Scott deplores the inclusion of Waltz passages in the Quadrilles. With what appears to be good reason these teachers held that enough time was devoted to the Waltz in its own right without dragging it in as a special figure in the Quadrilles. However Scott was tolerant of the practice, much though he deplored it.

'At the same time, we must allow a little for the temptation which good Waltzers feel to parade their pet step on every available occasion, especially when it happens to be the only one they know; and perhaps in those circles where it is customary for the men to take their partners by the waist, and swing them round, the Waltz step is, if anything, an improvement on the old style of pivoting. The more correct and refined way is to present both hands to the lady, as will be hereafter explained.'

Anyone who studies the figures of the Quadrilles will be puzzled by some of the names given to them: le Pantalon l'Eté, la Poule, la Pastourelle, la Finale. Le Pantalon refers simply enough to what Scott in his inimitable way describes as 'an indispensable article of wearing apparel'. This figure, the first in the Quadrille, was originally known as Chaîne Anglaise and was not rechristened more picturesquely until 1830. At that time the new king Louis Philippe permitted the wearing of breeches at official balls instead of the short culotte. This newly fashionable garment caused a certain amount of amusement and Vincent, leader of the orchestra, son of the composer of the music for this figures, renamed it.

The reason for the title of the second figure, l'Eté, is more technical. It consisted of chassés and assemblés, a combination already known in other contexts as pas d'éte. Vincent, the composer, himself, not his son this time, was responsible for la Poule for the simple reason that in his original music he had included in the introduction a sound reminiscent of that bird. La Pastourelle also owes its name to a composer, this time Colinet, who took his melody from a romance entitled Gentille-Pastourelle. La Finale speaks for itself.

There were alternatives to these figures, and the most frequently danced finale was known as the Flirtation. I can do no better than once again quote Scott on this one; here are his last words on the Quadrilles before he came to grips with a description of the movements:

'But by far the most frequently danced *Finale* is an arrangement called the *Flirtation* figure, in which as in the French Boulangère, the gentlemen dance with each lady in turn. If by any chance there should happen to be a young reader of this work who does not know the precise meaning of the English term above used, I venture to think that he or she—especially she—would indeed be a *rara avis*.'

The music for the Quadrilles was simple in form, although as will have already become obvious the melodies of various composers were frequently employed for each of the different figures. Phrases were always in eight or sixteen bars. As two steps were taken to each bar it will be seen that no complications could arise in timing and rhythm. The most famous of the Quadrille composers was Louis Antoine Jullien (1812-60) who was also a conductor of note. At his London promenade concerts he would sometimes have as many as six military bands and an orchestra playing his Quadrilles simultaneously. Through his concerts and compositions he acquired great wealth, but lost every penny and died, it is said, in lunacy as well as penury.

One particular form of Quadrille which gained fantastic popularity in the middle of the century, a popularity which did not wane for about fifty years, was the Lancers. Although this form of square dance came into being shortly after the arrival of the Quadrilles into England, it does not appear to have found much favour until about halfway through the century; in fact one or two usually reliable sources state that it did not first appear at all until that time, which is untrue. Philip Richardson carried out a great deal of research into the question, discovering an advertisement which appeared in the *Dublin Evening Post* of May 1817 which contains a reference to the Lancers. He also found two possible claimants for the credit of originating the dance.

The Dublin advertisement announces the publication of the music and figures of *New Quadrilles* and lists La Dorset, Lodoiska, La Native and The Lancers. The composition of the music is attributed to Yaniewicz and Spagnoletti and the figures to a Mr. Duval. Richardson's second claimant is Joseph Hart, whose description was published in 1820. The tunes used by both claimants were virtually the same. Richardson inclines to the belief that the Lancers had their origin in England in spite of the fact that they were to be found in France at about the same time. He bases this belief on the fact, again revealed through his own painstaking research, that the music for all the figures was either by an English composer or arranged by a foreign composer while he was in England. One theory is that the dance was based on a form originally performed by the ancient Britons at festivals held in honour of their leaders, those participating in it being armed with lances. One might just as well claim that as all the participants in the Pyrrhic dances of Greece were similarly accoutred the Lancers stems from that. Perhaps the definition given in Larousse, a masterly piece of compression, should be allowed the final word:

'Cavalier armé d'une lance; les lanciers furent supprimés en France en 1871. Le quadrille de Lanciers ou absolum, les lanciers, quadrille d'importation anglaise, où les couples se font des Visites, des saluts, défilent parallement etc.'

Musically the Lancers contributed nothing and no composer appears to have been inspired by them. In his extremely thorough book *The Story of Dance Music* Paul Nettl does not even refer to them, or for that matter to the music for any of the other set dances which followed the Quadrilles, although he has several references on the Quadrilles themselves.

Scott, in addition to the Quadrilles and Lancers, also describes The Caledonians, The Valse Cotillon and The American or Diagonal Lancers. His introductory note to this last dance is as follows:

'The figures of this dance are more animated than those of the ordinary Lancers, as all the dancers are moving at the same time. In a description kindly lent me by Mr. Woodworth Masters, it says "commence each number except the fifth by addressing partners then joining hands with partners, address the centre". With us, however, it is usual to bow to partners, and to the opposite couple only in commencing the first figure of a square dance.'

During the first half of the century the Quadrilles themselves were so popular that there was little room for variants of them. Even so it does seem a long time for the Lancers to wait for some kind of reasonable place on the programme, for not until about 1850 did this dance become really popular, much less find acceptance in society. However the dance then gained due compensation, for it grew and grew in popularity, enjoying a healthy and vigorous—at times too vigorous—life for well over sixty years. Not until the first world war, in fact, were the Lancers pushed back into obscurity, and even after that, in common with a number of other Victorian forms, the second world war again brought them into some favour.

Scott and every other leading teacher throughout the country deplored a tendency to terminate the various figures by a few bars of waltzing. Indeed, he went so far as to consult 'the best teachers in London and elsewhere, and those who are credited with having the most aristocratic connections, on certain points on which there seemed to be possiblility of disagreement'. He writes:

'The result was exactly as I anticipated. All who wrote were unanimous in deprecating the practice of waltzing in the figures. *Not one of them permitted it.* All advocate simple *walking* and balancé steps in the Quadrilles and Lancers.

Yet later, and certainly in descriptions for current revivals, the Waltz crept in as the termination of nearly every figure.

A set dance favoured at popular dances for many years was the Albert Quadrilles, more commonly known as the Alberts. It comprised the first figure of the Quadrilles, the second of the Caledonians, the third of the Lancers, the fourth of the Waltz Cotillon and the fifth of the Quadrilles. This arrangement was originated by Charles d'Albert, a Frenchman who was at one time ballet master at Covent Garden. Later he settled, of all places, in Newcastle, and composed a fair amount of dance music.

A form of Lancers much in favour right at the end of the century and into the twentieth was known as the Kitchen Lancers. In this version, which at times became extremely boisterous, the ladies were frequently swung off their feet. Presumably it acquired the 'Kitchen' in its title because of the less genteel behaviour required for its performance. Be that as it may, in more than one rich establishment, if not in noble ones, this form was at party time just as popular above as below stairs.

Wherever the Quadrille form of dancing stemmed from originally, its direct progenitor was the Cotillon. In the second quarter of the eighteenth century, as we have already seen, the Contredanse and the Cotillon began to be confused until at the close of the century they were indistinguishable one from the other. In spite of the all-conquering invasion of the Quadrilles in the nineteenth century, however, the Cotillon continued to survive wanly into the nineteenth century, and between 1825 and 1830 a new form of this dance, first introduced into the fashionable dances of Paris, found its way across the channel. This form of Cotillon continued to find favour in Paris into the early years of the twentieth century although in England its popularity seems to have waned after about fifty years.

Several albums were published giving both the music and descriptions of the many figures in this form of dance, but for one of the most handsome we are indebted to an eminent French dancing master. Here is the introduction to this album which was published in Paris in 1860:

'Il y a peu de soirées maintenant qui ne soient terminées par un Cotillon et tous les danseurs sont dans l'obligation de savoir le diriger, au moins d'en connaitre les principales figures. Je me suis conformé aux desirs de mes Eleves qui ont senti cette nécessité, et j'espère pouvoir leur être utile en leur facilitant la mission difficile et souvent délicate de conduire un Cotillon.

Je les prie d'accepter ce petit ouvrage composé tout à leur intention.
(signed) Laborde, Professeur
Paris, 30, Rue de la Victoire.'

An impression reproduced in lithograph form of the 'Salon des cours de Mr. Laborde' by an artist named A. Faivre is very imposing indeed, showing a spacious room well peopled with beautifully dressed dancers and a splendid chandelier suspended from the lofty ceiling. There are also twenty plates by the same artist, of some of the figures.

According to Monsieur Laborde the Cotillon terminated the ball. 'Quand l'orchestre a donné le signal, tout le monde doit s'asseoir et les Couples se placent à la suite les une des autre.'

Following that the first couples waltzed briefly before proceeding into one of the figures, and they were followed in that same figure by the other couples. The same procedure was adopted for each of the figures, all of them commencing 'par un tour de Valse' and ending in the same way. Altogether Monsieur Laborde briefly describes about sixty figures, some of them with various alternatives.

Although there is a great deal of actual dancing in this form of the Cotillon several of the figures are in fact parlour games. For example, few will find difficulty in identifying the following description with a parlour game popular to this day. The figure is called 'Le Colin-Maillard assis'.

'Le Cavalier Conducteur fait asseoir un Cavalier au milieu du salon et lui bande les yeux—Il place d'un côté sa Dame, de L'autre un Cavalier. Le Cavalier qui a les yeux bandés choisit à sa droite ou à sa gauche.— Il valse avec la Dame s'il la choisie, dans le cas contraire c'est le Cavalier conducteur qui valse avec elle, les deux autres Cavaliers valse ensemble.'

Another figure took the form of a kind of musical chairs, except that four ladies and one gentleman contested the possession of four chairs, the gentleman dancing with whichever lady he eventually succeeded in robbing of her seat. If the gentleman was as gallant as he should have been at this time in 'polite circles' he would have had to wait a long time for his dance. See Plates 33–5.

REVOLUTIONS AND SCANDALS—BIRTH OF A NEW STYLE

A number of balls, especially those in which high society participated, and also costume affairs, were opened by that processional dance, the Polonaise, after which opening followed Waltzes, Mazurkas and Quadrilles. The final number was often a Galop. This idea of a definite order of dances derived undoubtedly in the first place from the fourteenth century, in which a set order was laid down. From that early beginning the movements of music gradually developed their order in the musical suite, music taking up, as it were, where dancing left off. With the passing of the years the dance has abandoned any idea of a definite set order except to contrast one rhythm with another.

The Galop was undoubtedly one of the simplest dances ever to take the floor. With a hold in which the gentleman placed his right arm lightly round his partner's waist and with the other held her right hand, the couples faced out towards their line of direction round the room and proceeded by means of chassés and turns. As the title of the dance suggests the Galop was lively in its movement and the music was in 2/4 time. At one time a figure akin to the Galop was introduced as the final figure of the Quadrilles.

When the Prince Consort died in 1861 the Court in England no longer set any sort of example in the lighter social activities. As a result the tremendous enthusiasm for dancing gradually diminished in society, although there was still a great deal of it among the middle classes. For some years now in various circles it had been considered right and proper for 'gentlemen' to dance badly. Because of this, many dances deteriorated in standards and crowds of people on the floor were to be seen doing little more than 'walking through' dance after dance. With this decline in interest among the upper classes and a growing interest among the less inhibited section of the community the time was ripe for a new impetus. The Waltz had lost much of its excitement and had become, as it were, a part of the Establishment. In order to infuse it with new vitality the orchestras gradually increased the speed of Waltz music until towards the end of the century everyone was flying round at a great pace—everyone, that is, who had the energy and who wanted to dance rather than walk round. Another kind of novelty had been introduced in the form of the Waltz *à deux temps*. This introduction of a new kind of timing into a dance in which two steps instead of three were danced to each bar, represented an attempt to add liveliness and variety to a dance which, unless performed by skilled and rhythmic dancers, did set up in itself a very definite monotony. This style, however, with its sideways glide and chassé, although certainly investing the dance with a new liveliness, at the same time robbed it of its dignity.

Nevertheless eventually it was instrumental in bringing about a most desirable improvement in the construction of Waltz timing; for instead of a flat, even three steps all of equal length and duration, the dance now developed a less monotonous rhythm. Scott again admirably explains this style, and its development from what had gone before:

'Space does not permit of my entering into details concerning the evolution of the modern waltz, but very briefly I may point out that in it the more pleasing qualities of various former movements have been blended. These movements were imperfect in themselves, but whatever was worthless has been discarded, while whatever was found to be best has been retained. Thus the old *trois temps*, in which three steps, each of equal duration, were taken to a bar, was found to be exceedingly monotonous, although not wanting in a certain degree of stateliness; while the *Deux temps*—very erroneously so-called—in which two movements only were taken to a bar, was more lively and exhilarating, but altogether wanting in dignity. This however was owing to the fact that the glide and chassé constituting the step were taken sideways, a proceeding which rendered impossible the graceful twinkling, playing in and out movement of the feet, which properly belongs to the Waltz. The great improvement in the general style of waltzing which the introduction of the two-step waltz eventually effected, was the substitution of the pleasing dactylic rhythm for the old molossus (a metrical foot of three equal beats), in which the partners appeared to be continually running round one another, without any reciprocal action whatever.

'If to the six steps of the *trois temps* we add a slight rearward sliding action of the left foot in the turning, accompanied by the proper muscular action of the limb, and prolong the first step, as regards duration of time, to occupy half the second interval of the bar, we shall have a waltz movement which combines the sprightliness of the *deux temps chassé* with the more correct action of the feet in the original waltz. And if we dance this improved and indeed perfect waltz with due regard to those unalterable dynamical laws which regulate the motions of all bodies, sentient as well as inert, we shall reach the perfection of *terre à terre*, rotary movement. But before the pupil can arrive at this state there is much for him to learn besides the mere sequence of steps, which in reality are to waltzing just what the notes are to a musical composition. These, like the waltz step, must of course be correct; but you may play them in a variety of ways. You may put stress on one or other of them, or the time and accent may be correct, and yet the right feeling and expression may be wanting. But in waltzing there is more than step, time accent, and expression to consider. It is not only necessary that every part of the individual body should move in the most perfect accord one with the other, but in waltzing with a partner it is essential that the movements of one dancer should be in perfect harmony and coincidence with the corresponding movements with the other dancer; that they should become as one body for the time being, and as such be affected by the action of gravitation and other physical forces.'

It is not always possible to determine whether the temperament of a particular time creates a dance for the expression of this temperament, or whether the arrival of a new dance creates its own demand. Usually a combination of both conditions is necessary for the success of any powerful new development in the ballroom. I have no doubt whatever that various dances and dance styles have died simply because the climate was not right for them at that time, whereas had they come into existence at some other time they would have won popularity and longevity. Time and time again one finds that a dance born into an age sympathetic to it will enjoy repeated popularity in subsequent periods when the climate of that time would not have tolerated it.

One of the national dances of Poland, as we have already remarked is the Polonaise, although its original spelling gave it a more masculine air, the final 'e' not appearing for many years after the advent of the dance some time in the sixteenth century. Although the dance changed in character to a certain extent during the next 250 years, it nevertheless retained its fundamental processional form.

As we have seen no more suitable processional music can be imagined than that of the Polonaise. In a stately three-in-a-measure time, it is clearly marked rhythmically and provides just the right amount of variety to avoid the boredom of a straightforward march. A quaver, two semi-quavers and four more quavers in each bar form the basic rhythm and no matter what variations are imposed on this basis, the six quavers to the bar rhythm is always to be felt if not heard.

Bach and Handel included the Polonaise in some of their suites, although these are not typical of the music as it finally developed. Various Polish composers experimented with the form. Chopin wrote thirteen examples, in each of which he expressed his own frustration as an exile from a troubled homeland. Indeed, from his earliest days Chopin must have been familiar with the singing and dancing of his country's people and his first published composition was probably influenced by this national form, for it was in fact a Polonaise. In one of his later efforts he expressed with considerable force the gallantry as well as the oppression of his nation.

The Polonaise also has a place in the divertissements in classical ballet, perhaps the best known being that in the last act of *Coppelia* for which Delibes composed the music, although Tchaikovsky also included them in *Swan Lake* and *The Sleeping Beauty*. Nicholas Legat, an exile from Russia and famous teacher of classical ballet, was deeply interested in the theatrical presentation of the Polonaise. In *The Dancing Times* of April 1928 he wrote an article which would greatly help present day dancers in ballet when they are called upon to perform the dance. Rarely is it executed with any real feeling today. He writes:

'He should regard her with a smile expressive of dignified greeting, the while she returns his look with one of tenderness, yet reserved and proud. Each link of the chain should present an enraptured pair of the stronger and weaker sex.'

His description of the actual movement of the dance is so graphic that it gives not only a vivid picture of the pattern, but recreates the actual feeling set up by the movement:

'At every third step all the couples simultaneously make a slight bend of the knee. At the conclusion of the first circuit of the hall the couples divide, the gentlemen and ladies, with a slight bow towards each other, taking different directions, but continuing to follow one another with their eyes. Thus completing half the circuit of the hall, they rejoin, greeting each other with another bow. The gentleman takes the lady's hand as before and the procession proceeds embellished with all manner of figures of movement dependent upon the imagination and phantasy of the director of the dance. The procession ends with a mutual bow, each gentleman then conducting his lady to her seat.'

During the seventeenth and eighteenth centuries the Polonaise was widely practised on the continent of Europe but does not appear to have found particular popularity in England. Towards the end of the eighteenth century, however, it began to find occasional favour, being appropriately employed as the opening dance at costume balls. In fact a ball of this kind given by Queen Victoria at the newly enlarged Buckingham Palace in 1846 began with a Polonaise which, of course, was led by the Queen herself and her Prince Consort.

In 1866 Theophile Gautier described the opening Polonaise at a great court ball in the Winter Palace at St. Petersburg. The dance is led by the Emperor, who is followed by the rest of the court in order of precedence. What a headache, incidentally, this sort of thing must have given those responsible for protocol, especially when visiting dignitaries were present.

'The *cortege* of brilliant uniform goes on increasing—a nobleman leaves the hedge (Gautier uses this word for the spectators who form a passage for the dancers) and takes a lady by the hand, and this new couple take their place in the procession, keeping step by step with the leader. It must be very difficult to walk thus under the fire of a thousand eyes, possibly ironical. Military habits do much for the men, but how different for the women. Most of them walk to perfection, and it is a very rare art, that of walking gracefully and simply while being watched; more than one great actress has never understood it. What adds to the originality of the Russian Court is that from time to time a young Circassian prince in his fastidious Oriental dress, or a Mongolian officer, will join the cortege. Mahommedan prince or duke—are they not both subjects of the Emperor of all the Russias?'

Another dance which originated in Poland and which won a great deal of popularity on the continent of Europe was the Mazurka. It does not however appear to have been greatly in favour in England at any time, although it was included in the programmes of some dances. It seems to have gained a place on the floor in Britain chiefly as a figure in the Cotillon.

In this dance the lady is given the privilege of choosing her partner. In the words of Liszt:

'As if in the pride of defiance, the cavalier accentuates his steps, quits his partner for a moment, as if to contemplate her with renewed delight, rejoins her with passionate eagerness, or whirls himself rapidly round as though overcome with sudden joy and yielding to the delicious giddiness of rapture.'

The Mazurka found its way to Germany during the eighteenth century and a little later to Paris. In its issue of April 25th, 1830 *The Observer* stated that dance was just 'introduced or intended to be introduced into this country'.

Like the Polonaise the Mazurka is also in three-in-a-measure time, but its basic rhythm is quite different, its basis being two quavers and two crotchets in each bar, with an occasional modification of the timing of the quavers, the first being lengthened and the other shortened. The step which accompanies this rhythm is a combination of foot-stamping and heel-clicking, together with a turning movement.

In Poland in the eighteenth and nineteenth centuries many Mazurkas were composed but again it was left to Chopin to crystallize this music into a form of national expression. In the process he departed far from the original concept of the music. Usually he used for his opening of each section a popular folk melody and then proceeded to develop the theme with all the subtlety of which he was capable. It is perhaps of interest that while his first published composition was a Polonaise, his last was a Mazurka.

Normally the Mazurka took the form in the ballroom of a round dance for four or eight couples. Although the dance comprises only one definite set figure, a certain amount of invention was indulged in by those who became skilled in the dance. One writer claimed that the Mazurka was introduced into England by the Duke of Devonshire when he returned from Russia after being our Ambassador in that country for some years. In common with the Polonaise the Mazurka too has found its way into ballet, largely I think because of the music rather than the dance. Chopin's Mazurka, which has been employed in the suite of *Les Sylphides* provided Fokine, the choreographer, for example, with an opportunity not to present a Mazurka as such, but a neo-classical dance based loosely on the characteristic rhythm of the Mazurka. A Mazurka also appears in the last act of *Coppelia*, in close proximity to the Polonaise, and in *Swan Lake*.

With the continued vitality of the Waltz and the impetus of the Polka, combined with the variety of the set dances, and other forms the century could easily have come to a close with no new excitements or novelties, especially as the court was no longer much concerned with the gayer aspects of social life. Yet in 1888 a new dance crossed the Atlantic to capture our imagination and to enjoy tremendous favour in almost every dance hall for nearly twenty years, well into the next century. This was the Barn Dance, which required energy rather than skill for its enjoyment. In fact it was perhaps a boisterous expression of communal *joie de vivre* in which lay its great appeal. Its high skipping action and quick turning chassé, to highly individual music in 4/4 time, are perfect for this kind of expression, and style in performance never counted for as much as the jollity with which it was performed. Even middle-aged folk could briefly enjoy a turn at it, and then drop out to take vicarious pleasure in watching the younger generations vying with one another in energy and a not indecorous abandon.

The origin of the dance is obscure, although Richardson must surely

REVOLUTIONS AND SCANDALS—BIRTH OF A NEW STYLE

be right when he states that the title emanated from the music, as the dance first appears to have been performed to a piece called 'Dancing in the Barn'. The dance can be traced back to rural America, and Scholes considers that it may have originated in the festivities by which rural communities must have celebrated the completion of a new barn. As Scholes puts it: 'consecration by jollity.' Certainly in England to this day, although the custom is no longer very widely practised, there are barn dances to celebrate various important events. The barn is swept and cleaned, sacks of wheat are piled into the corners, the floor of wide panels is brushed, French chalk applied to it and the orchestra sometimes put in the loft in order to give the dancers more room. Beer and ample food supplies appear on trestle tables at the ends, and the farm community congregates to watch or participate in the dances. Doubtless it would be possible to associate this kind of festivity with those of ancient times in which the sowing and the harvest were celebrated by festivals of various kinds. As Scholes says, however:

'. . . it is perhaps, hardly necessary to find an ancestral religious motive when the mere existence of a new large room, momentarily unoccupied, or perhaps the wish to reward neighbours who have helped in the building, will sufficiently account for the practice.'

Almack's undoubtedly governed fashionable dancing from 1765, when these rooms were first opened, until about 1840—a long time for one establishment, however powerful at any given time, to hold such sway. At the outset it was possible for members of society to attend a supper ball once a week for twelve weeks for a subscription of ten guineas. But that modest fee was not the important consideration. First the hopeful aspirant to this social *cachet* had to be approved by what must have been a formidable committee. In 1814 Lady Jersey was chairman of this committee, and this is when the dances at Almack's were seemingly without parallel. The Honourable Mrs. Armytage contributing to the Badminton Library volume on *Dancing* published in 1895, writes, although not of course at first-hand, of those early years in the century. She is quoted in full in the Appendix, as is the Countess of Ancaster on 'Balls: Hostesses and Guests'.

Gradually the assemblies which had been so popular during the first two-thirds of the century grew less and less fashionable. Society retired more or less from the public scene and lavish private parties became increasingly in vogue. In fact hostesses ready to organize balls in large town residences were perhaps the chief reason for the demise of the famous assemblies. A later effort to revive them was a failure, although for a number of years Almack's magnificent rooms (by this time known as Willis's rooms) and other assembly halls were employed frequently for charity balls.

The many buildings given the title of assembly rooms which sprang up towards the end of the century were of quite a different nature, being erected to satisfy the demands of more and more people. Mostly these buildings were of a by no means noble architecture, their sole purpose being to house a large number of dancers. In many of them the floors were simply of polished boards, although others did possess parquet flooring and a few even boasted sprung floors. The rooms subsidiary to that containing the dance floor were kept to a minimum size. Gracious living had given way to the demand for the dance shorn of airs and graces. From that time on the dance, in fact, began to express the life and new vitality of the people and no longer the artificiality of a dying society. Where the aristocracy regarded it more and more as bad form to dance well, the people now began to put dancing England once more on the map, until we were to become in the early years of the next century the best dancers in Europe.

There is nevertheless some irony in the realization that the *palais de danse* of today, a potent symbol of the power of youth and democracy, has its roots firmly in Almack's, that most aristocratic and exclusive badge of early nineteenth-century society. For Almack's led to the less exclusive assembly rooms of the later nineteenth century, and they in turn were to lead directly to the first palais in London in 1920.

Within the span of the nineteenth century America transformed itself from an agricultural country, with very few large cities, and poor means of transportation, into a great industrial power. At the same time it also began to develop a culture of its own, no longer depending so strongly upon the influence of Europe.

Religion naturally remained an important factor in the life of this still pioneering nation, but no longer did it dominate man's life. Nevertheless, in the puritanical atmosphere which still governed much of American religious life at this time dancing remained in some areas one of the seven deadly sins. On the other hand certain religious sects and movements actually included the dance as part of their rituals. A number of preachers went even further than this and urged that the dance should became a part of the life of the people, believing that it was an innocent pleasure and that it helped to improve manners. Not that the preachers were chiefly concerned with innocent pleasure and good manners, but they believed that these two elements were both invaluable allies against intemperance, an evil which was fought by the church in America with undying energy.

One minister at the end of the century contemplated the organization of a dance school under the direction of the church officials. In a *New York Times* report it was stated that this preacher had already permitted a church gymnasium to be employed for dancing; apparently he believed that young people would dance anyway, and it was therefore advisable to give them the most propitious spiritual enviroment for it.

The main weight of the attack by the church against dancing was directed at the upper classes. I quote from Joseph E. Marks III *America Learns to Dance*:

'The main reason given against dancing by the ministers and the host of anti-dance books that issued from the presses was directed against the upper classes: that great expense in both time and money was spent on the preparation for a ball, either public or private. The preparation included expensive dress and jewellery, the service, and even the furniture; and the expense grew greater as each tried to outdo the other in giving the most lavish ball. Another reason given was the harmful effects upon health of those who danced: the late hours; entering the cool night air before becoming sufficiently cooled; the using up of the oxygen in the room and thereby breathing foul air; and also the mental and physical excitement caused by a ball. Its evil influences upon intellectual improvement and its moral and religious aspects were other reasons given against dance as practised among the upper classes. Among the lower classes, dance was associated in the minds of the ministers and reformers with the cheap dance halls that sold liquor and had gambling rooms and prostitutes.'

But the story is very similar to that elsewhere. These attacks on the dance appear at this distance in time to have exerted very little if any effect on its development. No outcry or action can suppress a genuine movement which springs spontaneously from the desire for self-expression of the people in the mass, if not actually in the whole. What effect did the vigorous protests of the powerful members of the church exert on Jitterbug at the outbreak of the last war? And to what extent did similar, and perhaps even more passionate protests from others as well as members of the Church, exert on the Twist. It may be claimed that the voice of the church, perhaps the voice of public morality, is less clear, less resonant than it was a hundred years ago, but the comparison remains. A strong demand from a large body of the people for freedom to express themselves in a particular way can rarely be suppressed.

In any case a tendency to exaggerate the extent of the protests is difficult to overcome, for in all periods scandal and attack on public morality have always been given their full value in publicity. The fact is that in America, as elsewhere, social dancing of various kinds continued to gain ground as a pleasant form of relaxation fit even for the daughters of highly respectable families. In women's journals with substantial circulations instruction was offered in the dances in vogue. *Godey's Lady's Book*, for example, published detailed descriptions, pictures and music. Its editress was also the headmistress of a girls' boarding school in Philadelphia, where social dancing was included in the curriculum.

As in England the Waltz created a great storm, offering the puritans and others who detested dancing a wonderful opportunity for censure. Again, as a number of American and British teachers in the early 1960's protested vehemently against the Twist, so in the 1820's did American dance teachers seek to reprobate the Waltz.

This extract from the *Gentleman and Lady's Book of Politeness* published in 1833, typifies the more liberal attitude which soon began to prevail:

'The waltz is a dance of quite too loose a character and unmarried ladies should refrain from it in public and private; very young married ladies, however, may be allowed to waltz in private balls, if it is very seldom and with persons of their acquaintance. It is indispensable for them to acquit themselves with dignity and decency.'

In what contrast that stands against the following, taken from the *Boston Weekly Magazine* dated August 30th 1817:

'. . . They rise, they twirl, they swing, they fly,
Puffing, blowing, jostling, squeezing,
Very odd, but very pleasing—
'Till every Lady plainly shows
(whatever else she may disclose)
Reserve is not among her faults
Reader this is to the Waltz.'

One of the outstanding teachers in New York throughout a large part of the century was Allen Dodworth, who opened an academy round about 1835 and taught for over fifty years. In 1885 his book entitled *Dancing and Its Relation to Education and Social Life* was published. This perhaps more than any other single work, summarizes the development of the social dance in the capital. The following is what he has to say about the influence of the round dances:

'With the introduction of the waltz, galop and other round dances, a complete revolution in social dancing took place. These were so easily learned that the education in motion was deemed unnecessary; simply to make the motion required was quite sufficient, manner becoming entirely secondary. Many learned from one to the other, frequently transmitting their own mistakes . . . (The new dance teachers) not having had the advantage of the teachings and associations of the older ones, they were aware of the proper nature of their duties; but they were able to waltz expertly, and the teaching of the waltz and a few other dances was all they believed to be required of them; they were, therefore, simply dance teachers, not teachers of motion and manner, which is the definition of dancing master as the term was formerly understood.'

One of the greatest social events in New York halfway through the century—perhaps the most important single social occasion in the lives of New York's *élite*—was what *Ballroom Dance Magazine* of America in its December 1961 issue described as:

'. . . the fabulous subscription ball given 101 years ago in honor of His Royal Highness Albert Edward, Prince of Wales, the first royal personage ever to pay a visit to the New World metropolis.'

The reason for this reference is the fact that in 1961 a great New York Ball was organized at $50 a ticket, the theme being the representation of New York of 1860 including shop and street scenes. Naturally it became appropriate for the ball itself to be modelled on the 1860 original. Although no programme of dances is given, items such as the Oriental Lancers, the French Circle, the Varsoviana and the Polka were features. An account of the ball is included in the appendix.

The Polka appears to have attracted just as much denigration in America as had the Waltz before it. In fact all the round dances were subjected to this kind of censure. The reason is not difficult to find. Many of the set dances possessed figures which required an equal expenditure of energy, but they did not depend for their performance upon the close hold which had now come into fashion. It was this, as in Europe, which was the cause of the scandal. Although that kind of close hold would today be considered an 'open hold', it was then too much for the parents, never mind the church, who had never before seen such intimacies among polite people in public. Even after this new style of dancing had been established for a number of years there were still sporadic attempts to quell it. But by this time as we have seen there were many enlightened teachers throughout the great country, both in the country as well as the town districts. Basing their instruction on a sound basis of the dances that had travelled across the Atlantic from Europe, they now began to graft into their instruction certain movements, rhythms, and styles which developed from the national or regional character of the people. Although the diehards continued to protest right through to the close of the century, by that time the inborn desire of the people to dance, coupled with the pioneering spirit of the teachers, and a number of educationalists who saw the benefits of dance, although some of them had never actually experienced any desire to dance themselves, had ensured that the dance was thoroughly and firmly established. It was this combination of training, natural desire, and the new outlook of the people which would in the next century provide fertile ground for the development of entirely new rhythms. In fact it was mostly the rhythmic impact of its native forms which were for the first time to reverse the flow of traffic in dance trends between Europe and the U.S.A., converting the importing country almost overnight into an exporter of vital importance.

CHAPTER VII

The Twentieth Century

JAZZ AND AFTER

> Dancing is a manner of being.
> HONORÉ DE BALZAC

IN a century of two world-embracing wars during which the speed of man's travel has accelerated to such an extent that the journey to New York now takes about as long as a trip to Paris fifty years ago; when the devices which we today regard as commonplace would at the beginning of the century have struck terror into men's hearts; in such a period man's customs, habits and outlooks must inevitably undergo radical change. Thus by the end of the nineteenth century, very little indeed remained of rural England. The severe agricultural depression of the last thirty years of that century had dealt heavy blows both to the aristocracy and the labourer. The significance of this depression on the changing way of life is perhaps best demonstrated by the fact that in 1911 eighty per cent of the 45,000,000 inhabitants of the United Kingdom already dwelt in urban districts.

Perhaps the one safe generalization that can be made to apply to the entire century so far is that the tension between man the individual and man as part of the community has grown to such proportions as to create its own mass neurosis. On the one hand the rights and powers of the individual are stressed and exaggerated, mostly it is true by advertisers who are anxious to sell more goods of so called status value; while on the other hand work for all but the limited few becomes more and more of a less responsible nature. Men and women in the economic empires of our time are diminishing into infinitesimal cogs in an ever-growing machine. As individuality is stressed, often by the vast impersonal organizations for which we work, so the outlet for this expression of individuality is more and more denied us. Small wonder that all but the super-ambitious few drop out of the struggle and seek to express themselves outside their work and often in a such way as to abolish the savage element of competition which bestrides the century.

These two factors, the growth of urban life and the increasingly mechanical nature of work, with its constant decrease in responsibility, have directly brought about the growth in our hobbies. Right from the end of the last century a large proportion of the growing spending powers of the public has been channelled into leisure pursuits. But even in such pursuits the need for uniformity remains a testimony to the strength of the community. What we need most of all is to feel like individuals, free and untrammelled, yet at the same time to have behind us the support and cohesion of a community.

In the social dance this dichotomy has expressed itself with utmost clarity. Up to 1910 our form of dancing was the same, naturally with minor modifications, as it had been for many years past. The sequence and set dances put everyone firmly into a communal activity; everyone did the same thing at the same time so that a vital element of the pleasure derived from dancing was this feeling of participation in a group. But after that the dance kept pace with the shift in moral and spiritual outlook, with a tug of war between the growing sense of individualism and the absorption of the individual into the automatism and irresponsibility of cogs in industry.

In the dance we still continued to do the same steps as one another, except that the new kinds of dancing gave just a little more room for individual interpretation than the sequence dances of the immediate past. The mere fact of our doing the same steps at different times in our own sequences, rather than in an order laid down for us, gave a new feeling of individuality while retaining the security of group activity.

The Edwardian period continued to support the authoritarian way of private life which had flourished with Victoria. The family was a close-knit unit under the supreme governance of the master of the house. The family's affairs, whether social, economic or moral, were of an essentially private nature. Chaperons were in full employment; any man of substance would have been appalled at the information we are called upon today to supply to the Inspector of Taxes; and divorce was still regarded as a foul stigma which could bring down in one blow any man dependent upon the goodwill of the people.

The gradual breakdown of that pattern of society, and the growth of public responsibility for the welfare of the people, led at the beginning to a great deal of perplexity and there were many who declaimed against Lloyd George's first parliamentary bill to develop public responsibility for at least some of our welfare, as a price of gross immorality. Such perplexity naturally found its expression in many activities, dancing being by no means the least of them.

During this period too, with the growth of the urban population, dancing became more and more the activity of all classes of society. At this time dance functions could be divided into several broad classifications. First came the State Balls, followed by the private dances of society, often held in the great houses of the nobility or the new rich. County balls, including those of the various hunts, came next, these being held in assembly rooms, hotels and any suitable rooms available for the purpose. On much the same level as these were the subscription dances, at which in many districts throughout the country clubs and groups of various kinds, sometimes formed for the sole purpose of running dances, one paid a subscription to cover admission for a number of dances to be run during the season. Lower in the social scale were the popular dances, or assemblies as they were still frequently called at this time. These grew rapidly in number during the next few years to keep pace with the growing popularity of dancing among the lower middle classes.

Apart from the first and last of these groups the dances included in the programmes of these various kinds of dance did not vary a great deal. State Balls continued to favour Quadrilles and Polkas, but the Waltz dominated the programme, with a Galop to conclude each ball. The other groups, apart from the popular assemblies, favoured the Waltz even more determinedly, with one or two set dances, usually the Lancers, and a few Two-Steps, to vary the programme. The popular functions, however, favoured a great many sequence dances, the Veleta being a firm favourite, set dances such as the Lancers, Quadrilles, d'Alberts and Valse Cotillons, and a few Waltzes sharing the rest of the programme. These Waltzes, incidentally, were played more slowly than for those in the higher social brackets.

Although at this time there were a number of assembly rooms dotted about the country, there were few public dance halls run exclusively for dancing in the nature of the great chains of halls at the present time. In the seaside resorts halls were used for dancing several nights a week, sometimes every night during the holiday season, but apart from those facilities there was nothing of a permanent and regular nature. For the growing number of people anxious to dance, therefore, the dance teacher came to the rescue. In his own school, usually at that time known as an 'academy', he ran dances every week in addition to his normal classes and, provided his practice was substantial enough, would at regular intervals, varying from a week to a month, organize public dances in the town halls, assembly rooms, village halls or other suitable places. The cost of admittance to these dances before the first world war rarely exceeded one shilling. In fact several halls in London continued to charge this modest price until into the early 'twenties.

The biggest dance halls were in Lancashire, in that biggest of all seaside resorts, Blackpool. There the Empress Ballroom, looking then much as it does now, flourished throughout the summer, holding some three thousand dancers. In addition there were in that same resort the Palace and the Tower Ballrooms, the last named being situated in the building beneath the famous Blackpool landmark. In those halls the standard of dancing was high and teachers were employed every year to act as M.C.s and to popularize any new dances considered of sufficient merit.

In London, with space even then at a premium in comparison with the conditions prevailing elsewhere, the halls could not compete in size with those at Blackpool and a few other resorts. One must remember too that the seaside halls were catering for people on holiday; more would have the time and wherewithal to go dancing while on holiday than during the rest of the year. Although of course holidays with pay were still many years distant, the wakes still brought thousands of people to the north-west resorts every year. Nevertheless, there were some excellent halls in London at this time, three of them being owned and run by Mr. G. F. Hurndale, a notable teacher. One was the Arlington at Peckham, which held about four hundred dancers, another was the King's Hall, also in south-east London, and a third in Shepherds Bush, the Carlton. The first and last of these halls remained in operation as dance halls until quite recently. In its issue of April 1918 *The Dancing Times* contained the following:

'The floor of the "Arlington" is of pitch-pine, with a centre of walnut and oak, and five nights a week it is crowded with dancers, a modest shilling being charged for admission. At the moment the dances principally in vogue are the one-step, fox-trot, the valse, the quadrille, the lancers, the alberts and variations of the tango. The old round valse still finds favour, and it is taken rather slowly (seventy to eighty), but several of Mr. Hurndall's own inventions are very popular, notably the 'Maxina' which won the first prize of the B.A.T.D. Conference.'

One interesting innovation at the Arlington was an outdoor marble floor, surrounded by garden seats, tables, chairs, flower covered trellis and trees for dancing during the summer. This was certainly one of the first, if not the first, of the twentieth-century outdoor dance rendezvous, which led a few years later to a number of such haunts. In south-east London, in particular, this *al fresco* dancing enjoyed a considerable vogue.

Early in the century came faint stirrings of a revolt against the style so well established at the end of the nineteenth century. A conventional pattern of sober sequence dances, with a small leavening of variety and frivolity were not suited to the youth among the common people. Dancing, if towards the end of the previous century no longer remaining the prerogative of the upper and middle classes, was still dictated as to its form by those classes. But now, with the greatly increased urban population, the growing restlessness of the people and the real democracy which was beginning to germinate, the people themselves were prepared to take over the pleasures of those who in the last century they had still regarded as their superiors, Keir Hardie and his followers notwithstanding.

By 1910 social dancing became a round-the-year pastime. Hitherto it had been seasonal, although during the previous century the London season had been followed for the upper classes by the holiday seasons in the watering places and seaside resorts. Not until several years into the twentieth century were British working people able to contemplate the kind of holiday which has now changed the nature of the British coastline. Young people who went frequently to dances wanted something more than set steps and patterns for their entertainment.

The first important revolt came against the artificial turned out position of the feet. Until this time the basic posture for all dances consisted of the five positions, which the social dance had in the first place given to the ballet. In 1910 the Waltz remained the indisputable favourite, dominating every programme in the ratio of something like eighteen waltzes to six other dances. But although both master and servant danced this same dance their styles began to diverge further and further from each other. At the smart dances the speed of Waltz music was maintained at about fifty bars a minute whereas at the popular dances, many sons of the aristocracy incidentally finding more pleasure here than at their own select affairs, the speed was brought down to about thirty-two bars a minute. But the conflict was not chiefly one of speed, but of style.

The fast Waltz of this time was almost completely rotary in its pattern, with a simple pas de valse between each series of turns to right and to left. This was admirably suited to the turned out positions of the feet, and gave really skilled dancers a perfect opportunity to show the excellence of their footwork. But younger dancers were finding a more lateral pattern more to their liking, a pattern in which the amount of turn was not so great. This led to the widespread adoption of the Boston, a dance which had in fact been adopted both in Britain and the U.S.A. some years earlier, but without the favour which now came to be bestowed upon it. According to Curt Sachs the Americans developed the Boston, with its slow and gliding steps, round about 1874, but nowhere else is this date supported. In several instances in fact Sachs gives dates for various innovations which he does not back up with any substantial evidence. As other authorities who differ from him in these instances have given more weight of evidence one must reluctantly come to the conclusion that Sachs is wrong. I say reluctantly because owing to these small unsupported statements, which one must assume to be lapses, a few teachers and students of dance history have condemned his great work. This is a lamentable state of affairs because there is no doubt whatever that his *World History of the Dance* is the most exhaustive general study yet to be produced over this enormously wide field.

To return to the Boston, Richardson, the most reliable source on dates of this period, states: 'It is said to have made its first appearance in this country about 1903 at the K. D. S. dances. . . .'

It appears to be generally accepted that the Boston came to England from the U.S.A. as the hold was the same as that adopted for most close dances across the Atlantic, right hip to right hip rather than directly in front of each other and therefore with the man's feet outside those of his partner. In view of this presumed American origin it may at first seem strange that the Vernon Castles make no reference to the Boston in their *Modern Dancing*, especially as its smooth movement and languorous steps would seem to be tailor-made for their own style. But the Boston had by then enjoyed its short period of intense popularity and had faded from the scene in England by 1914. In the U.S.A. it must surely have died even earlier, and the Castles in their writing were concerned with popularizing the dances and style which were popular at that time, not with the promotion of a dance that had lost favour. Further, they had by then developed other dances which perhaps owed something to the influence of the Boston, dances which began where the Boston left off. But despite this sudden decline of the Boston there is no doubt whatever that its style and movement were largely responsible for the early growth of what we now know as the English Style.

33. Two drawings from Laborde's book on the Cotillon published in 1860. *Above*, Les Ronds No. 3, *below*, Le Chapeau.

34. Two more drawings from Laborde's book on the Cotillon. *Above*, Le Moulinet, *below*, Le Rond Déployé.

35. Another reproduction from Laborde's book on Le Cotillon, this time showing his Salon des Cours.

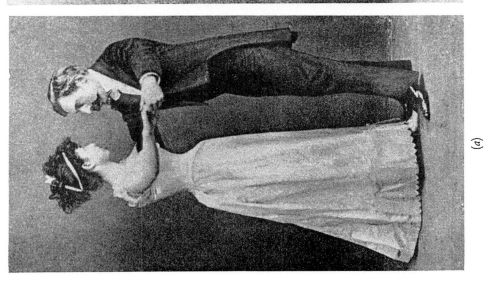

36. Three reproductions from Edward Scott's book *Dancing as an Art and Pastime*, published in 1892. (*a*) high-class style, (*b*) low-class style and (*c*) no style.

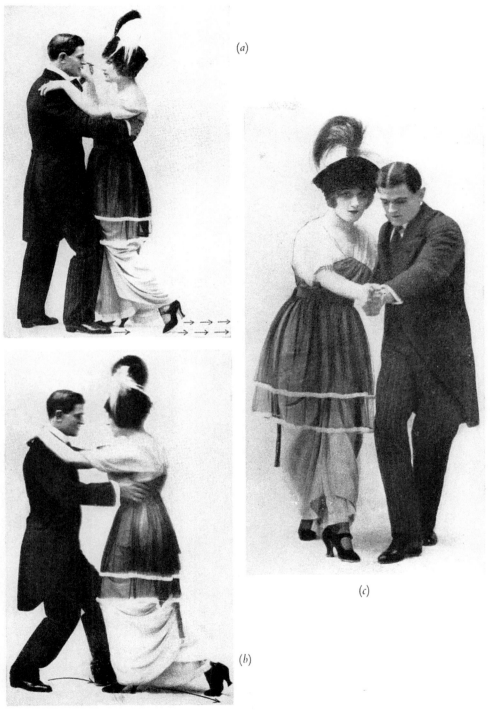

37. Three reproductions from *The Tango and How to Dance It* by Gladys Beattie Crozier. (*a*) La Promenade, a quite different figure from the Promenade in the twentieth century Tango. This Promenade is in fact a walking step, which is a nearer approach to the meaning of 'Promenade' than our definition today. (*b*) The Dip at the end of the Promenade. (*c*) The Pas oriental à Gauche. This figure is obviously the forerunner of the present day Promenade.

Specially designed "Lucile" "Thé Dansant" Gown, which bears the piquant title "You'd better ask me!"

Grey-blue chiffon velvet, with silver, lace embroidered, net bodice, and deep tunic, edged with soft grey fur, and belt of Chinese embroidery.

By special permission of Lucile, Ltd.

Specially designed "Lucile" "Tango Ball Gown," known by the title, "Bébé d'Amour."

Of soft blue crêpe chameuse, draped to show flounced underdress of silver lace. The bodice is of silver lace, with sleeves and vest of white chiffon, and the girdle is of a curious and most attractive shade of green.

By special permission of Lucile, Ltd.

38. Two more reproductions from Crozier's *The Tango and How to Dance It.*

39. This and the next pictures are of the Vernon Castles, the most famous ballroom exhibition dancers in the teenage of the twentieth century. This picture shows the actual 'hesitation' in the Hesitation Waltz.

40. A figure in the one step, described by Vernon Castle thus: 'The man stands still for a second while the lady continues for two steps to the side.' This was the entire description. How much more detail would be given today!

41. The Tango. Note that Castle actually has his hand in his pocket. It is interesting to observe that the weight is held back just as at the present time.

42 and 43. These two pictures show clearly the diversity of holds still permitted

in ballrooms during the reign of the Castles. They are dancing the Maxixe.

44. The Castle Walk.

45. The final of the International Professional Championship in progress at the Royal Albert Hall, London.

46. Sonny Binick and Sally Brock, two of our most successful professional ballroom champions in the '

47. A formation team at the end of its performance.

48. At the Winter Gardens, Blackpool, every year the most important championships, known as the British, are held. The 'modern' events and the 'old time' events each occupy a full week. This picture shows the first round of an 'old time' championship.

JAZZ AND AFTER

In the 1947 edition of the *Encyclopaedia Britannica* a section on modern ballroom dancing opens:

'Until 1912 modern dancing was a decadent phase of 18th and 19th century forms. In that year began a new era of popular dancing, in which 20th century industrialized society finaly broke away from the courtly steps which had expressed the emotions and social attitudes of another civilization and found new steps to fit a new cultural situation. America led the way in this renaissance.'

Omission of a reference to the Boston here is stranger than in the case of the Castles, for in England the dance began to find favour well before that time. Is it possible, after all, that this important early development in the social dance revolution was made in England? I should like to believe that this was the case, not from any outworn patriotism, but because the conception of the Boston seems to me to be an early example of the style in which the dance of today, the English style, has grown up. The Boston, surely, was the first true example of the smooth flow and natural walking movement of this from. It could be argued perhaps that the One Step and Two step were earlier examples but although they were based on a flowing, walking movement, they did not demand the natural walk of the Boston.

Be all that as it may, the popularity of the Boston in England at the turn of the first decade of the twentieth century shows how ready we were for the American invasion which was to burst upon the ballrooms of this country during the remaining years before the first world war. The timing of the dance to the music allowed a leisurely movement to fast music, for a full turn occupied four bars of music instead of the two required for the Waltz. Six steps comprised this turn, each one being kept as flat as possible. But apart from the turn there was a great deal of direct forward and backward movement that called for the natural walk which was such a distinctive feature of the dance. Perhaps of equal importance to this movement was the growing attitude to the interpretation of the music, the best dancers, as it were, feeling the music and expressing themselves to it rather than merely performing to a set time and tempo in which the melody played but a small part.

After enjoying great favour in Britain for a few years, and having played its part in the formation of our style, the Boston virtually faded away before the outbreak of war in 1914, although here and there it was still occasionally and sporadically enjoyed in isolated pockets after that. According to Richardson:

THE TWENTIETH CENTURY

'The crowded floors at such smart "dance clubs" as the Lotus, Ciro's and the '400' where the rag was the popular dance of the day, did a great deal to kill it. It wanted more space as, like the Slow Foxtrot, it, it was essentially a "travelling" dance.'

Coincident with this new style in movement came the revolution in dance music: ragtime. Before proceeding any further with an historical survey of this element of dance music it is obviously desirable to discover what is meant by the term; and to define jazz. Briefly ragtime is the syncopation of music throughout its duration, so that this syncopation becomes the main rhythmic pulse rather than a device for varying the pulse. Invariably music in ragtime contains two, four or even six beats to the bar. Without syncopation the main stress would fall on the first beat of the bar, with a subsidiary accent on the third beat. In ragtime, however, the accents fall on the second or fourth beats. The commonest way of achieving this is by tying the second note to the third. This means that the second note is lengthened and that no stress can be put on the third beat. Similarly the fourth beat of one bar can be tied to the first beat of the next bar, thus eliminating the accent from the first beat.

This principle of syncopation can be applied in a number of ways, but the result is always the same. Although the duration of each bar remains constant, the rhythm becomes irregular, jumping here, hesitating there, and constantly displacing the normal beat.

The argument may today appear to revolve around mere semantics, but jazz in its true meaning has nothing whatever to do with rhythm at all, much less with syncopation. Indeed, it is possible to have jazz music which contains no element of syncopation. Jazz in fact refers to the instruments on which the music is played. At the outset the original negro jazz bands employed a few wind instruments and a drum. Then, when this style of music was embraced by a wider community, including the white races, the combination developed into a mixture of orthodox and unorthodox instruments: drums, banjo, pianoforte, violin and often a saxophone on the one hand and on the other klaxon horns, rattles, whistles and an ever growing variety of noise-making devices. It did not take long for those who had to listen to such cacophony, and for the players themselves, to sicken of this kind of din, with the result that after a short time it became more and more of a rarity, until these unorthodox instruments were used for little more than an occasional shock, or for humorous affects. Orchestration grew more and more sophisticated and developed after a while into the kind of music produced by such famous orchestras as that of Paul Whiteman. From then on the development was more one of finesse and variety rather than outstandingly new ideas. Styles of orchestration change and one combination stresses a different kind of sound from another, but the basic fabric remains the same.

One highly important element of jazz is that of extemporization. Its most usual form is the 'break' in which a certain performer fills the gap between one series of eight or sixteen bar phrases and the next with music of his own spontaneous devising. This element has played an important part in the growth of jazz music, and was in the first place possibly responsible for the name jazz itself. It has been suggested that the word stems from the French jaser, to gossip, the French language being common usage among early white inhabitants of the southern states of the U.S.A. What more descriptive word could there be for the conversation, the gossip, that went on between the various instruments in a jazz band?

In the U.S.A. at this time the finale in vaudeville consisted of an item in which all the performers came together. This was known as the jazzbo. This too could have derived from the same French verb and could have been the intermediate term from which the jazz was formed. Another theory, not in my opinion so likely as the others, is that jazz stems from Jas, an abbreviation of James Brown, one of the very earliest exponents of this kind of music.

Not until jazz music had been established for a number of years was an attempt made to obtain any kind of laid down orchestration, and it is widely believed that Paul Whiteman was the first to demand from his musicians adherence to what was written on the score. Leaders before him had provided orchestral parts, but jazz musicians were not content to conform to such discipline. Even with Whiteman's development of jazz orchestration little attempt was made for some years to merge the instruments into a true orchestral score, but rather to make them stand out in contrast one with another. In fact, some of the leading bands of this time frequently played music more in the style of a concerto, with all of the instruments taking a solo part from time to time.

Quite early in the growth of this kind of music the saxophone became the dominant instrument. With its plantive sound, seeming always to be slightly off key, its somewhat treacly melancholy was highly appropriate for the expression of sadness and nostalgia which is the badge of all negro music. With its release into the white population the emotional impetus of such music was inevitably exaggerated and corrupted, for the white people had no conceivable idea of the innermost emotions of the negros. By the time, in fact, that Whiteman and others elevated the music they had wrought out of jazz on to the concert platform, its original motive had become almost lost in obscurity. *Rhapsody in Blue* pays only lip service to the form, exquisite though it may be, and led only to yet more rarified compositions which, instead of marrying the classical and jazz elements of music, simply took the classical form and imposed jazz elements upon it. At one time before the last war we had in super-cinemas enormous orchestras playing 'concert' arrangements of dance music in a style which appealed to all the superficial sentimentality of a vast cinema audience. This phase demonstrated to what depths of corruption a genuine art form can sink and at the same time the brilliance of the instrumentalists in many American and some British bands.

The music played so excellently in the palais de danse today consists of jazz orchestration mounted on ragtime, thus producing what is best described as modern syncopated dance music.

Frequently a development in the style of music initiates a comparable development in the dance. On the other hand, until well into the seventeenth century the dance itself unquestionably led the way, the dance suite having begun purely through the demands of the dancers. Only rarely today does the dance exert a strong influence on dance music, although the detestable tendency of competition dancers immediately after the last war to distort the movements of the Tango until the dance became almost a burlesque of itself did cause dance bands, against the inclination of at least some of the leaders, to speed up the music. In the late 'twenties dancers had exerted a more beneficial influence on dance music. With the emergence of the Foxtrot as a quite separate dance from the Quickstep bands gradually, with persuasion and sometimes even coercion, divided their common-time music into two different tempi: slow and quick. This in turn led to the composition of special music for this slower speed, music which was to play an ever-growing part in the musical scene. These, however, are isolated instances, and for the most part the music now calls the tune in a double sense.

Even so, I do not think that this new musical development, ragtime and jazz (the two terms are today usually regarded as synonymous) was responsible for the dance revolution which took place in the first quarter of the twentieth century. As so often happens, a number of forms of self-expression were affected at roughly the same time by a new outlook, a new morality, which came in with the century and which was strengthened by the first world war in particular, and by other social upheavals such as the great slump and the new conception of social security.

Following their separate lives into the first ten years of the twentieth century, the new dance music and the new style of dancing came together round about the end of the first decade. Berlin's music played by Alexander's Ragtime Band, the first of the outfits from the U.S.A. to invade Europe, and especially Britain, put its collective foot heavily down on the accelerator pedal of dance development; and the dance led to more and more musical experimentation and popularity. Not until the late 'twenties, in fact, were the great combinations built up by such leaders as Herman Darewski and Jack Hylton to make any extensive appeals to passive audiences as distinct from dancers actually moving about on the floor.

But in 1911 jazz and Alexander's new noises had not yet appeared on the British horizon. In its March issue of 1911 *The Dancing Times* published a description of the Boston by one of the best known teachers in London at that time, Mr. Walter Humphrey. In this description only the principal movements were given; Zig Zag (this figure bore no resemblance whatever to the Zig Zag which is one of the basic figures in today's Quickstep), the Turn, The Crab Step and the Run. In an introductory note the editor stated that he was publishing this description because he had been informed by a number of country readers that the dance was not so well known in the provinces as in London; at that time this was by no means unusual, for there was a great deal more dancing in the metropolis, where expert dancers might besport themselves at a number of different functions several times a week. In the provinces dances were far fewer, and an expert from Town was often regarded with awe and admiration.

Towards the end of the previous year (1910) the same magazine had conducted an enquiry which it entitled 'Will the Boston Live?' Here it was stated unequivocally that this dance was easier to learn than the genuine Waltz, although at the same time 'to dance it correctly it is essential that one be taught by a thoroughly competent instructor'. It was urged that it was only because so many had tried to 'pick it up' that the dance had become in so many places a degenerate exhibition. The 'investigator' who was conducting the enquiry for *The Dancing Times* here quotes a dancer who he claims to be both a perfect Bostonian and a perfect old time Waltzer:

'I learned the Boston three years ago because I found that there were so very few good Waltzers, and that unless one's partner *was* a good waltzer, it was impossible to dance in comfort at the terrific speed insisted upon by fashionable bands. I found that partners who had been indifferent waltzers became excellent Bostonians, and that by using that step I got round the room at the pace required by the band, but with only one half the exertion. My wind is not so good as it used to be, and for the introduction of this new step, 1 should have had to have given up dancing. But I will candidly admit that even now, if I know my partner to be a perfect waltzer, I prefer to do the old-fashioned waltz with her.'

Asked to express an opinion on the life of the Boston Edward Scott felt that the 'true' Boston, by which he meant the American version with a prolonged slide and rapid twist on each foot alternatively, would be likely to live 'because, although absurdly simple, and even imperfect, if regarded as a waltz, it does not in any way violate established rules of dancing'.

Commenting on the style of Boston as illustrated in a Baumer drawing from *Punch*, which accompanied this first section of the enquiry, Scott had this to say:

'Being, as it is, merely the outcome of foolishness, and a desire to attract notice, on the part of those who affect it, the ridiculous movement will soon be relegated to the limbo of forgotten things. Foolishness is, of course, a permanent quality of human nature, but its shapes are various as those of Proteus, and this, its latest Terpsichorean presentment will quickly take a fresh form.'

'Investigator' himself, concluding this first article hoped for an early death of a form of Boston in which a couple apparently hovered in one place for a few bars, and then suddenly shot across the room 'like a tongue of flame'. This eccentricity was said to bring great pleasure to its executants, but not surprisingly brought discomfiture, and even physical pain, to those who were unfortunate enough to be in the line of flight of a couple enthusiastically following this style

Subscription dances remained at this time popular in various strata of society, from the great balls run in London hotels and famous houses, to the local tennis and cricket and football club affairs, sometimes held in the club house or at best at the local assembly rooms. A well known but not the most exclusive London hotel charged 4s. 6d. a head for one hundred and fifty people, this sum including in addition to the dance room, a hot supper, light refreshments during the evening and soup at the end. It was at this time, incidentally quite common to drink hot soup at the end of many social occasions, whether private or public, before starting the homeward journey. Perhaps we shall in the 'sixties return to this pleasant custom if the law concerning motorists and drink is tightened up. Tickets for a London dance of this kind rarely cost more than 7s. 6d. and for this sum, besides the supper, an excellent band could be provided, pleasant floral decorations and even prizes for novelty competitions.

Another type of subscription dance was run in various parts of London and elsewhere by more or less professional organizers and at times these seriously menaced the success of the 'amateur' functions. By 1910 there were many more who danced reasonably well than there were at the turn of the century, and these skilled enthusiasts were attracted to these regular series of dances in the knowledge that they would there find many dancers of their own standard. At cricket and rugger dances the standard was no higher then than it is today. Further, qualified teachers were now beginning to grow in number, for the first of the examining bodies, the British Association of Teachers of Dancing had by now been in existence several years. Already, through its methods of instruction, and through the dissemination of collective knowledge by means of annual conferences, this association, and others who followed it, were laying down a new path. The Imperial Society of Teachers of Dancing, founded in 1904, was within the next twenty-five years to become the most powerful of these teachers' organizations, and the first to establish London headquarters. The president for many years was Cecil H. Taylor, a Leeds dancing master whose family had been in the same profession for over 150 years. Between the two wars the ballroom activities of the 'Imperial' were to dominate the professional scene and serve as a prime factor in the establishment of the technique of the new style of dancing which emerged in the 'twenties.

The dances of court and society had become boring through constant repetition and lack of variety, for they consisted of little more than an interminable succession of Waltzes and Two Steps, with perhaps a Quadrille or two and a Cotillon to enliven only the most exclusive affairs. Occasionally, too, society would briefly adopt an American or European novelty, but beyond that its standard was dropping as that of the middle classes, and particularly of the lower middle classes, began to ascend.

These associations of dance teachers ran annual competitions to find a new sequence dance, with the result that a number of such dances were promoted in large areas of the country. One of the first, and certainly the most successful of these dances was the Veleta, which still remains in favour today with thousands of dancers throughout the country. This dance was typical of the best in this kind of sequence dancing, with pleasant and not too difficult figures performed sometimes side by side, and at others facing each other, with a felicitous gliding movement and a few bars of waltzing to terminate each sequence. These dances grew and grew in number until there were hundreds of them. Some, extremely popular in one area, were completely unknown in another, but the most successful of them took the whole country by storm.

In addition one or two new set, or square, dances were brought in during the first few years of the century. The Lancers may have virtually disappeared from society, but among the people this boisterous affair was taken up at all levels. It was therefore inevitable that other dances of a similar nature should be introduced. The first of these to bedeck the twentieth-century dance scene appears to have been Le Carnival, with passages of Barn Dance, Polka and Waltz intermingled with attractive set patterns. In common with the Lancers and other dances of this type each set comprised four couples.

But in spite of these innovations the Waltz continued its supremacy in all kinds of ballrooms, from Buckingham Palace to the sixpenny hop in the Old Kent Road. Eminent teachers could express fears for its future through the abuses it suffered at the hands of those who sought constant novelty and sensation; and others could complain that standards were constantly failing. It all made no difference; the Waltz dominated every programme, although of course this one word meant various things to various sections of dancers. In one set the idea of the Boston innovations was anathema, and in another Waltz music was the signal for the Boston rather than the Waltz.

In the U.S.A. much the same strata of society existed, with similar divisions except of course for the Court. At this time there was the same degree of class distinction in New York as in London, and the same occasional 'condescension' of the upper classes to the lower. In Britain the mingling of the classes took place mostly during public holidays, when the squire might well dance with his kitchen maids. Rarely did the British make such self-conscious efforts as in the U.S.A. where occasions for the temporary crossing of class barriers were created more frequently. Nevertheless such events as the following in Chicago in 1910 were rare even across the Atlantic. This report comes from the Chicago correspondent of the *Daily Chronicle*:

'At Milwaukee a Ball was recently given by the Socialist Mayor Seidel and the City Council which is unique in the annals of civic functions in this country. Over 2,000 people were present and never before has there been such a mingling of the rich and poor on a similar occasion.

'The function was carried out on strictly Socialistic lines. Mayor Seidel opening the ball by leading in the grand march with one of the richest Society dames in Milwaukee. The Mayor wore a frock-coat and light trousers, while his partner was dressed in a gorgeous evening robe and glittering with diamonds.

'The same disparity of dress was noticed in hundreds of guests, Society ladies in the height of style dancing with working men and street car conductors in their best suits, known here as "store clothes" owing to their being bought ready made.

'Despite this, the Ball was a great success, young Society men dancing with working girls, and all mingling with the greatest friendliness.'

Before 1914 fancy dress balls were a colourful feature of social life in a number of cities, although naturally the largest and most extravagant spectacles of this nature were to be found in London. Some of these in fact, still continue today although in very different form from that in which they began. The first of the Chelsea Arts Balls, for example, was held in 1911 when four thousand people attended, and it was believed at that time to have been the largest fancy dress ball ever to have been given. So great was the demand for tickets, which at fifteen shillings each were fairly expensive, that a black market exchange developed in which many tickets were resold at £5 each. At ten o'clock, when the dancing was to begin, the large floor of Royal Albert Hall was packed. As there was a set period or motif for the disguises the mixture was remarkable, with cavaliers and cardinals jostling against beefeaters and Red Indians. One gentleman disguised as Charles II was carried round the floor in a Sedan chair borne by beefeaters, and another as Don Quixote was mounted on a Rosinante consisting of two of his friends.

But probably the greatest costume ball of the century, some say for all time in Britain, was the Shakespeare Ball, held in June of that same year. The proceeds of this great affair were to be devoted to the project of a Shakespeare National Theatre to which the London County Council had already given an option for a site in Spring Gardens. Writing in the national press in order to explain that the high price of the tickets (four guineas) was due to a desire of the committee to obtain a large sum, one of the organizers, Mrs. J. Cornwallis West, said:

'I hope that it (the theatre) will be permanently endowed, and that a school and a pension fund for actors will complete a British institution which, in the interest of one of the greatest of the arts, is seriously needed.'

As for the Chelsea Arts Ball four thousand people again filled the Albert Hall in the Shakespeare Ball, but beyond that there was not much similarity. Far from the floor being packed throughout the evening it appears, if one writer can be believed:

'... that except during the Elizabethan Quadrille there were never more than three or four hundred actually dancing at once ... and one could dance at one's heart's content on an excellent floor to the best dance band which it has ever been my fortune to hear.'

The music which inspired the last comment came from the Corelli-Windeatt Band, which was famous throughout the country, although not of course nearly as famous as bands were to become with the advent of broadcasting. It is fair to add, here, however, that the best known of all dance music makers of this time was Herr Gottlieb's Viennese Orchestra, a combination which played at the State Balls at Buckingham Palace and a large number of the smartest society functions. Despite its foreign name, and the Austrian nationality of its conductor, a number of the instrumentalists were British.

To return to the Shakespeare Ball. Here the costumes followed the obvious set theme. The vast hall had itself been transformed into a Tudor garden complete with lawns and yew hedges and cypress trees. The main entertainment on the floor came from a procession in which was presented the Court of the Virgin Queen, as it existed in 1598, with Lord Burghley, Francis Bacon, Walter Raleigh, Francis Drake and many others together with their dames and maidens. These characters were impersonated by revellers richly but accurately disguised. Some of the plays were also represented by various groups in the procession, the most wildly applauded being that of *Much Ado about Nothing* in which Beatrice was impersonated by Ellen Terry. Although the King and Queen were unable to be present the reports stated that 'practically everybody who is anybody was present'. The Duke of Connaught acted as host in the Royal Box, where there were to be seen all the Royal guests who had come to London for the coronation. The conclusion of this ball is perhaps best summed up by a dancer who was present:

'Shortly after the Elizabethan Quadrille the Royal Party, who had been keen and interested spectators, departed and a little later long streamers of confetti bearing Shakespearean mottoes fluttered down from the boxes and entwined round the dancers.

Until this point in the evening everyone seemed to be overweighted with the importance of the occasion, but from now things became a trifle more lively. The Americans left staring at *the* box and began to think about enjoying themselves, and my word, what a lot of Americans there were! There was one amusing group of eight girls from the States all dressed as nuns, who, to their huge enjoyment, were solemnly saluted by every Cardinal present.

'The programmes were a splendid inspiration, Henry the Eighth with an ordinary ballroom programme really is unthinkable, but with an imposing roll of parchment, tied with green ribbon and fastened with a red seal, he is bang in the picture.

'And so this wonderful dance went on to its appointed end, when the whole Corelli-Windeatt band of 130 musicians were playing for six couples to dance to. These had seen the affair right through, and had assisted in the gathering in of £10,000 for the Shakespeare Memorial Fund. How they must have slept on Wednesday night.

'To sum up: As a dance the Shakespeare Ball was great—for those who took the trouble to dance, as a carnival it was not to be compared (it was never meant to be) with the Chelsea Arts affair; as a spectacle it was so magnificent that very few of us will ever see its like again.'

The Boston heralded the reverse of the traffic across the Atlantic. With the invasion of ragtime Europe was for a number of years to be transformed from an exporter to an importer, with very little trade in the reverse direction. In fact although in England in particular during the first ten years of the twentieth century there was a sizable crop of new dances and movements these innovations never found their way into the new world. The Veleta, for example, popular though it became here, never caused even the mildest stir outside our shores—at least until well after the second world war when a few visiting teachers from various countries attempted with varying success to take what was by then a quite successful revival of this and other similar forms into their own countries. One such dance was the Military Two Step, founded on a salute and march. Another later effort, in 1914, was the Maxina, based on the Maxixe and this also had a tremendous though short-lived appeal. But these ideas did nothing to stem the tide of the irresistible invasion.

After the Boston came the One Step which in 1914 was claimed by Vernon Castle to be 'by far the most popular of all dances . . .' One reason for this acclaim was that, again to quote Vernon Castle, '... it can be learned in a very little time by anyone, young or old, who is able to walk in time with the music—and, I might say, by many who cannot'. But an equally important reason lay in the fact that the dance was inspired by rag-time music. Yet again to quote Castle:

'The Waltz is beautiful, the Tango is graceful, the Brazilian Maxixe is unique. One can sit quietly and listen with pleasure to them all; but when a good orchestra plays a "rag" one has simply *got* to move. The One Step is the dance for rag-time music.'

Here indeed lies the fundamental difference between what might well be referred to as the pre-1910 and the post-1910 styles. In the former, no matter what the dance, the main attraction lay in the actual steps, and in some cases the exhilarating movement. After 1910 the main impetus came unquestionably from the rhythm rather than the movement, although frequently the two were now combined as never before. In the earlier form the bodily rhythm which remains the driving force of all modern dance forms was hardly known. In fact it was probably the influence of this actual rhythmic force, stemming from the African jungle, which injected our dance forms with this entirely new force.

As Castle has said, the actual steps of the dance were as simple as could be desired. The couple stood directly in front of each other, the lady's right hand in the gentleman's left, in the kind of hold which approximates to that in use today except that the dancers were not actually in bodily contact with each other. Novices in the dance invariably demand of their teachers some instruction as to which foot should be the first to move when they commence a dance. In fact at certain times throughout the century various 'authorities' have sought to lay down that either this or that foot must move first if we wish to be *de rigueur*. Today the skilled dancer scorns such advice, for with close contact between the man and his partner there is no difficulty for the woman to follow, no matter which foot is used, for the bodily movement of the man provides sufficient indication. At the beginning of the second decade of the century, however, although in certain circles the so-called close hold of the time was looked at askance as being too intimate, this kind of indication was not possible. 'Don't stand too close together,' admonished Castle 'or too far apart; be comfortable, and you stand a good chance of looking graceful.'

Because of this lack of physical communication between the man and his partner a definite rule had to be laid down, for it simply was not done by experienced dancers to inform their partner as to their intention by word of mouth. At this time in the One Step and other dances the gentleman used his left foot first.

Doubtless it will have been observed that in the foregoing paragraph I have referred once to the 'man' and once to the 'gentleman'. No subtle distinction is implied by this: for the purposes of the dance the two words, and those of 'lady' and 'woman' are synonymous. In books of instruction at this time it was not considered genteel to use the correctly paired words, man and woman, with the result that lady and gentleman have remained in common usage in books of instruction to this day. In an age when the vast majority of those who learn to dance correctly are in the younger age groups, many of them adolescents, such a form of address seems ridiculous. Some teachers, conscious of the absurdity, commit an even more unpardonable blunder by retaining the lady and attempting to minimize the effect of gentility by the compromise 'man and lady'. One writer who used man and woman was condemned so harshly and by so great a number that he has never again had the courage to assert the correctness of these terms.

To return to the One Step. Castle is explicit and positive as to how the dance should be begun and as to the style of movement:

'The gentleman usually starts forward and the lady backward—the reason being that the lady is generally more graceful and can go backward with greater ease, and a man can also see where he is going, and thus prevent a collision with other couples.

'Now to begin the dance: the gentleman starts forward with his left foot, and the lady steps backward with her right, walking in time to the music. Bear in mind this important point: when I say *walk*, that is all it is. Do not shuffle, do not bob up and down or trot. Simply *walk* as softly and smoothly as possible, taking a step to every count of the music.

Castle then proceeds to describe the various figures of the One Step; the Castle Walk, the Eight Step, the Spin, the Step Out, One Step Cortez, the Outer Edge, Zig Zag, Polka Step and the Wind-Up.

The Castle Walk (for further reference to this and other Castle dances see the Appendix), which for a time was practised by everyone who sought some skill on the floor, whether in New York, London, Paris or Berlin, consisted of raising oneself on to the balls of the feet at each step, the legs rather stiff, and, again to use Castle's own words:

'... breeze along happily and easily and you know all there is to know about the Castle Walk. To turn a corner you do not turn your partner round, but keep her walking backward in the same direction, leaning over slightly—just enough to make a graceful turn and keep the balance well—a little like a bicycle rounding a corner. If you like, instead of walking along in a straight line, after you have rounded your corner, you can continue in the same slanting position, which will naturally cause you to go round in a circle. Now continue, and get your circle smaller and smaller until you are walking around almost in one spot, and then straighten up and start off down the room again. It sounds silly and is silly. That is the explanation of its popularity!'

Castle certainly knew the public taste. Almost every novelty dance which has swept the western world momentarily off its feet—almost literally sometimes—has been silly. If vulgarity and sensationalism can be added to this silliness the success is multiplied. Fortunately, on both sides of the Atlantic today there are enough skilled and honest teachers who are able to exploit these elements while at the same time modifying them. In this way, through the ridiculous publicity accorded these novelties in the popular press, more people become interested in dancing, and at least a few of them remain interested long after the novelty which first attracted them on to the floor is forgotten.

Other dances described by the Castles in their book were various kinds of the Tango and the Hesitation Waltz. Of these the Tango unquestionably created the greatest sensation. For several years right up to the outbreak of war in 1914, and even beyond, it retained a tremendous popularity, at various times dominating the programme to the same extent as the Waltz was all powerful when the Tango first began to make its impact. In 1913 the poet Jean Richepin, invited to lecture to the 'immortal forty' of the Academie des Beaux-Arts, chose the Tango as his subject. Both by his choice and by his treatment of the subject he created no small stir in Paris, tracing the origin of the dance back to the war dances of the ancient Thebans. The poet did not however quote his sources and we must therefore regard his theory as imaginative rather than scientific. An Argentine writer, Eros Nicola Siri, more recently carried out an extremely painstaking investigation into the origin of the dance and came to the conclusion that it derived its name from the Tangano, a negro dance transported from Africa by the slaves into certain parts of Central America, particularly Cuba and Haiti, where they practised it during the beginning of the eighteenth century. Later, it seems, the negroes were again responsible for a further transfer of the dance, for those who migrated transplanted it in the River Plate area where it became known as the Candombe. There it was quickly adulterated by the movements of other dances, some of them of European origin, but gradually developed a rhythm and style of its own, in which form it became known as the Argentine Tango. At first a dance of the riff-raff, it was not long before it was tamed sufficiently to gain wider approval. Indeed, at one time it appears to have ousted all the other dances from the floor. From the River Plate the Tango successfully invaded the U.S.A. and Europe, where it remains popular, although in a very different form, to the present day. In Scholes' *The Oxford Companion to Music* the article on the Tango concludes:

'Its cadenced and rhythmic music expresses the melancholy which is an underlying characteristic of the Argentine people, and which is perhaps a nostalgic legacy from the various exiled races which have gone into the formation of the Argentine nation.'

In the years immediately before the first world war the Tango took people of all classes by the throat. Not a day passed without some reference to it in the popular press. Perhaps the most lasting tribute to its influence at that time, however, is the fact that a forty-thousand-word book was devoted to it. Neither before nor since has a book of this length concentrated on any one dance other than the Waltz. This book, *The Tango and How to Dance It* (see Appendix), by a well-known dance teacher, Gladys Beattie Crozier, dealt briefly with the history of the dance, and then proceeded to describe the 'Parisian Tango'. Its figures differ considerably from that described by the Castles in their book published some months later. The English description does not include the kind of Promenade which was already a distinctive feature of the American version, although it does make use of the word 'promenade' in connexion with the basic walking figures. Miss Crozier's description of the style required is enlightening:

'The essential basic movements of the Tango are the rhythmic smoothness of the Walk, the Glide and the Sway, dancers transferring their weight from one foot to the other without the slightest movement from the shoulders. The gentleman should rather bear down his partner, to accentuate this smoothness, throughout the dance, until the last step of each figure, or of the Corte, is reached, when the lady slides her right foot forward, with her right knee straight, leaving the left foot pointing behind, and comes to rest stretched to her full height upwards.

'The knees of the dancers throughout the general progress of the dance are alternately straightened and relaxed, but seldom bent. "Imitate the sinuous grace of the tiger, mademoiselle," said Les Almanos, when describing how to dance the Tango, and embryonic tangoists cannot do better than bear that graceful animal in mind when attempting to follow their advice.

'To begin the dance, the partners stand facing one another, and, as has already been said, hold one another in the ordinary position, as for waltzing, but as far apart as is compatible with grace, to allow space for the sudden turns introduced into certain figures of the dance.'

'Les Almanos' referred to by her were brilliant exhibition dancers who took a large part of London society by storm demonstrating a number of the figures which they claimed to be the mode in Paris. In addition to appearing in hotel and restaurant ballrooms this distinguished couple also presented a more sensational version of Tango for the stage and fulfilled a highly successful season at the Coliseum.

Skilled dancers of today will immediately realize how much the Tango has changed in the fifty years of its variegated career. Although the Castle version is still a long way from today's version, or even from that which became standardized in the mid-twenties, it is apparent that it is from this Castle version that the English development of the dance owes most allegiance. Those same skilled dancers will also be amused by the admonition in the extract from the Crozier book that the partners stand as far apart from each other as is compatible with grace, for today any 'daylight' between partners in a competition would militate seriously against their chances of victory.

London hotels and restaurants were in 1913–14 featuring the Tango more prominently than any other dance. Indeed, the Princes' Restaurant ran 'The Tango Club' and both the Waldorf and the Cecil in London ran special Tango Tea dances, as did the Metropole in Brighton, the Queen's Hotel Westgate, and the Grand, Scarborough. These afternoon sessions were most publicised as 'Thé Tangos'.

The custom of the tea dance had already been popular in several Riviera resorts for a number of years. From there in the spring of 1913 they became extremely successful in Paris society. French teachers of the Tango, as well as the restaurants, made small fortunes, and a few months later, the social dance in London at that time still being in the main a winter occupation, the metropolis opened its arms wide to receive the great Tango invasion. Miss Crozier is illuminating on this fashion:

'What could be pleasanter, for instance, on a dull wintry afternoon, at five o'clock or so, when calls or shopping are over, than to drop in to one of the cheery little "Thé Dansant" clubs, which have sprung up all over the West End during the last month or two, to take one's place at a tiny table—one of the many which surround the dancing floor—set forth with the prettiest of gold and white china; to enjoy a most elaborate and delicious tea, served within a moment of one's arrival, while listening to an excellent string band playing delicious haunting Tango airs, with an occasional Waltz—for those who prefer Bostoning—or lively rag-time melody, introduced from time to time?'

At this time a number of dance clubs came into being, some of them of an extremely exclusive nature, One, for example, confined its members to a hundred, with a high subscription and election stringently administered through a committee. At this same club no young girl was admitted as a guest unless accompanied by a chaperone—an unusual rule this at a time when young girls were experiencing greater freedom than ever before and when votes for women were already being discussed on all sides.

At the Savoy Hotel the Public Schools and Universities Dance Club ran one of the best organized dances of their kind, and often, in the two ballrooms available, about 700 people were present twice a week. These dances started at nine o'clock, at 11.15 supper was taken by many in one of the Savoy restaurants (table d'hote supper 6s.) and then more dancing until the early hours. The best dancers, however, frequented the Saturday Supper Club at the Grafton Galleries in Grafton Street, a club which opened at the beginning of the century. A new dance was usually first demonstrated there and if the members approved that dance would stand a very good chance of achieving at least temporary fame. The Boston was for example danced there in its early days and the Tango featured prominently while still comparatively unknown.

In 1914 the Maxixe was rapidly gaining favour. This dance had some years earlier been a feature of various musical comedies, but had not gained favour in the ballroom. The Tango atmosphere and style promoted a more propitious reception, with the result that the Maxixe had an intense although short lived period of popularity. Stemming in the first place from Brazil, the dance had by the time it reached the U.S.A. and Europe tamed its excessive body movement into a series of gentle sways and dipping motions. But the Maxixe had to contend with a great deal of competition, some sensational and some said to be sensational but in fact being nothing but a bore. The unsettled times during the last few months before the war led to a spate of novelties from various parts of Europe. None of them survived, or if they did they were dead on their feet by August 3rd 1914.

Prospects for the dance season after the outbreak of war could certainly not have been very bright. Although civilization had not yet reached the stage of total war it was already evident that the people, as distinct from members of the regular armed services, would be more involved in this war than in any which had preceded it. However, after a couple of months confidence began to return. I quote 'Sitter Out' in *The Dancing Times* of October 1914:

'It is very evident that the present season is to be utterly different from anything that has ever gone before. Three months ago its prospects could not have been brighter, now all that is altered. At one time I thought that we were to have no ballroom dancing at all. But that is not to be, and in a few days a commencement will be made in a quiet and unobstrusive way. We may take it as a fact that an enormously high percentage of young dancing men of this country have joined the forces. But remember that during the past few seasons dancing has by no means been confined to the young bloods. We still have among us those who are on the wrong side of thirty-five, and also a very large number of young men, who though they have joined the forces, are still stationed at home.

'There will be many who say that they do not feel in the mood for dancing in the present circumstances. That, of course, is a matter which the individual must decide for himself. On the other hand, there will be a great number who will welcome an opportunity of a little healthy relaxation from the stress of the times. These will also feel that they are helping a profession that has been very hard hit by the war. Large public balls are, I think, at any rate for the moment, quite out of the question, but I am sure that small, inexpensive and informal dances will be welcomed by many.'

Europe, however, continued to have its influence, and many leading teachers in the States, especially on the West Coast, liked to boast that they were teaching the latest styles after having returned from a tour of Europe and New York. Across the Atlantic the portents of war had not of course in 1914 even begun to reach the people at all. An enormous boom was taking place on the dance floor, and most of the new trends were at this time being born in the States, many of them undergoing some purification before appearing on the highly respectable social scene of New York. Undoubtedly the most important of the new developments in the summer and early autumn in New York was the advent of the Foxtrot. By the opening of the winter season it had already established itself so firmly that not only had it gained its own place on every programme, but frequently it was used as an encore to the then extremely popular One Step. Even so do not suppose for a moment that the Foxtrot of this period bore much resemblance to that which was to become the main vehicle of the English Style. It was described by a contemporary as 'very rollicking, and has a tendency to put everyone in good humour'. Some of its popular steps are described in the Appendix to this volume.

It might have been thought a fairly simple matter to trace the origins of a dance which was not born until 1914, but the Foxtrot, in common with so many of its predecessors, defies this kind of simple detective work. Possibly the most convincing story of its origin is that a comedian named Harry Fox, who worked in the Ziegfield Follies, introduced in 1913 a number of trotting steps accompanied by rag-time music into his act, and that this strange kind of movement became known as Fox's Trot. On the roof garden of the New Amsterdam theatre a well-known dancer and dancing master, Oscar Duryea, was engaged to lead the pony-ballet girls through the audience, using trotting steps in dance position to an accompaniment of lively 4/4 music. This proved to be a popular innovation, and the patrons were invited to join the procession, which was introduced each evening intermittently from midnight until the early hours of the morning—every time, in fact, when Harry Fox's Trot was playing. This constant trotting motion, however, proved quite tiring, with the result that a less strenuous variation was interpolated, consisting of a few walking steps. This was enough to convert the novelty into a real dance and soon a group of New York dance teachers established a definite form of the dance, as follows:

> 'Four slow steps forward (in closed position).
> Four quick steps forward.
> Four quick steps, turning right.
> One slow step forward.
> One slow step, crossing in back.
> Four quick steps forward.
> Four slow steps forward, turning right.'

In the same year, 1914, Mr. Duryea demonstrated and taught this Foxtrot to members of the Imperial Society of Teachers of Dancing in

London. A Scottish teacher, Mr. D. G. MacLennan also promoted the dance in Britain after learning it during a lecture tour of the United States.

In *The History of English Ballroom Dancing*, Richardson, while agreeing with the year and country of origin, states that the Foxtrot was the 'direct offspring of the One Step and the Rag, and the tendency then very much in fashion on the other side of the Atlantic to introduce "canters" and "trots". Its immediate forerunners were the "Horse Trot" and the "Fishwalk" of the preceding year.' This theory in no way conflicts with that which credits Harry Fox with the origin, but simply complements it, for Fox could have taken his innovation from a common trend of the period and adapted it to his own use, following which Duryea too could have naturally made his own modifications for the pony-ballet girls and the audience participation. Since that time the English version of the Foxtrot has departed far from the original, and there remains little trace of any relationship. It is nevertheless true that the dance which has come to represent twentieth-century English Style dancing at its best did in fact originate in the United States, where the dance is enjoyed in a different form, retaining the chassé movement where the British have developed the long, smooth strides and gliding motion.

By 1915 the Foxtrot had firmly established itself in British ballrooms and its form became to a certain extent stabilized, although from time to time it underwent a number of revisions, and not for about ten years was it to approach the style in which we know it today. Hops, kicks and other bizarre figures were interpolated into it, for at this time it still depended upon its actual steps rather than its stylistic movement for its attractions. Further, when in 1917 the Americans came into the War, American servicemen brought some varieties of figures with them.

During the war the Waltz had suffered a period of stagnation and was in 1918 almost extinct. Jazz did nothing to revive it, for this kind of music had seemingly nothing to gain from a relationship with the flowing, romantic shape of the typical Waltz melody and its rhythm. In addition the war had seen the end of those German and Austrian orchestras which had specialized in this kind of music. However, soon after the war a slower, rotary Waltz—that is one in which the turn was of a circular rather than an elliptical shape—came into some favour. By this time the Boston style had disappeared and the need was felt for a rhythm in strong contrast with that contained in all the music in common, 2/4 and 6/8 time. It was round about this time that the closed third step became a definite feature of the Waltz, although it would yet be a few years before this closing movement was generally accepted by any but teachers and skilled performers. In the Foxtrot the feet were passed during the turning movements, but in the Waltz each bar was felt rhythmically to be more of an entity, so that rhythmic dancers gradually came to feel that the right movement at the end of each bar was a firm closing of the feet before moving off with a long, flowing step into the first strong beat of the next bar.

Although she does not throw any light upon dancing itself, Loelia Ponsonby, later the Duchess of Westminster, after spending her early years at St. James's Palace, grew up in the bottle party epoch of the Bright Young Things in the 'twenties. The following summarizes the attitude of her set in the immediate post-war years. It is taken from her book, *Grace and Favour*, published in 1961.

'When "The Great Interruption" was over, the hostesses of London naturally tried to put the clocks back to 1914. Wounded soldiers in their blue suits and red ties disappeared from the square gardens and hospital wards became ballrooms again. London was dancing mad—the aftermath of the short-leave-from-France frenzy.

'It seemed we couldn't have enough of it. We still had *thés dansants*, a custom which had grown up during the War. One was asked for four o'clock and arrived about five with a partner. We wore hats pulled well down over our noses and our skirts were trimmed with heavy silk fringes which swung out as we whirled around; and supported by nothing but tea or coffe (a glass of sherry would have turned it into an orgy) we fox-trotted tirelessly till it was time to dash home and change into evening dress for a real dance.

'The parties themselves varied in size and formality, from what we scornfully called a "gramapont"—that is a gramophone dance in Pont Street a district we despised—to the big ball in a house standing in its own grounds. The majority were in medium-sized houses, which were so plentiful that one hardly ever had to dance in a hired public room or in the same room twice.'

There was still a great deal of flux and uncertainty as the new styles of dancing either established themselves or faded from existence. One of these new influences came to us from Paris, although never again was that great continental capital to exert the strong influence it had once possessed. At first, in such holiday resorts as Deauville and Le Touquet, the new Tango had found favour among cosmopolitan crowds, and soon penetrated into Paris. A transformation in the nature of the music was chiefly responsible, the beat now being more subdued than in the pre-war version. As a result the steps of the dance were for the next few years to be invested with a more exotic—a more sinuous—movement than hitherto. In France this kind of Tango soon won great popularity, so that it featured so frequently as to be played once in every fourth dance. In Britain its progress was slower, although within a few years such well-known teachers and dance hostesses as Belle Harding and Madame Vandyck were able to organize special Tango teas to which the whole of West End society flocked with regularity.

During 1920–21 the first three of the so-called 'informal conferences' of dance teachers were held in Britain. At the last of these conferences a committee was set up which was able to make certain minimum recommendations for the basic figures of Foxtrot, Waltz, and Tango. Perhaps the 'general' recommendation as to style, however, is the most illustrative comment on the trend of style at this time.

'In modern dancing the committee suggest that the knees must be kept together in passing and the feet parallel. They also repeat their suggestions that all eccentric steps be abolished and that dancers should do their best to progress always round the room.'

This same committee found that a wide divergence of opinion still existed about the Waltz, but strongly urged the step, step, together pattern of steps which, as we can now see, was the birth of the Waltz as we know it today.

With this gradual emergence of a definite harnessing of the new trends into some kind of disciplined technique and patterns, the way was cleared for the growth of competition dancing. From the beginning of the century competitions had in various parts of the country gained some popularity, but now they were to grow far beyond the scope of anything of this nature to be held in the past. At this time competitions were staged mostly at fairly exclusive rendezvous such as Murrays, the Grafton Galleries and the London hotel ballrooms, but already there was a sign of what was to follow. In 1919 London saw the opening of the first palais de danse, at Hammersmith. During the first twenty years of the century there had of course been a number of public halls dotted about the country, but these were mostly in the nature of assemblies, with various dances being run by clubs, groups and by dance teachers themselves for the benefit of their pupils and friends. At these functions the programme consisted chiefly of the sequence and set dances against which the new trends were hotly opposed. Many teachers were seeking desperately at this time to retain the popularity of the form of dancing at which they had made their reputation, and it is to their efforts undoubtedly, small success though they gained in the third decade of the century, that we owe the continued life of sequence and set forms today.

But in the meantime there were thousands of young men and women who could not afford to patronize the west-end hotels and restaurants, but who were as keen to exploit the new trends as their contemporaries higher up the financial and social ladder. For them the palais de danse was the answer to a prayer. Here was the perfectly sprung and spacious floor, together with the modern orchestra with its new sound and rhythm which had grown out of the early triumphs of rag-time and jazz. Soon Hammersmith was followed by other palais, and in 1925 the Royal Opera House, Covent Garden, became a palais in all but name, for under the control of Bertram Mills, of circus fame, a floor was constructed to cover the whole of the stalls and the stage, leaving the circle, boxes and further reaches for sitting out. Although it continued to enjoy spells of duty for the purpose for which it was built, dancing held sway there for a number of years, and during the last war it became a rendezvous for forces on leave and workers in search of relaxation. Not until February 1946 was it, in fact, to be permanently returned to its rightful function, at which time it was reopened by the Sadler's Wells Ballet, now of course the Royal Ballet.

At Covent Garden during its first spell as a dance hall one member of the firm contracted to supply the catering was named C. L. Heimann. Seeing the potentiality of the public dance hall he was able to persuade his firm to obtain other dance halls. The organization grew rapidly until today the Mecca Organization, of which C. L. Heimann is the joint chairman, controls the biggest chain and best equipped of well run public dance halls in the world. Hiemann can in fact justly claim to have been a chief pioneer in providing the twentieth century with its magnificent dance facilities. Others have followed Mecca and the next largest chain is that controlled by the Rank Organization, which in the last few years, since the decline in cinema attendances, has converted a number of cinemas into dance halls. This same concern has also developed a large chain of dance studios which are conducted in the joint names of the organization and Victor Silvester.

Victor Silvester himself is a living symbol of the growth of the popularity of ballroom dancing for the masses. When he began to make records there was a serious dearth of recorded music played at the correct tempo. Although he started with modest sales, these built up to such an extent during and after the war that today Silvester records are in greater demand than those of any other modern dance band.

By the end of the 1920's dance teachers in Britain had created several examining bodies. Some of them were of a national character, with members all over the kingdom, and others were regional, confining their membership to certain highly popular centres of dancing. The first of these organizations had been created just before the turn of the century, and others followed in the next decade. Most of them covered several kinds of dancing, including such branches as ballet and tap, but the majority carried out the bulk of their examining work in the various kinds of social dance. All these bodies now found the need for a central organization by means of which they could co-operate and work for the common good, and the Official Board of Ballroom Dancing came into being for this purpose. Its function has until recently been almost entirely concerned with the control of competition dancing, and a complex book of rules governing amateur status and other matters has come into existence. Today, however, this Board is beginning to concern itself more actively with the development of social dance, while still maintaining vigilant control of competitions. Shortly after the war the need was felt for an international body of a similar character, leading to the birth in 1950 of the International Council of Ballroom Dancing, in which all the countries concerned with competition dancing and the development of an international style of dance, based firmly on the English Style, are able to co-operate. Through the agency of this Council international championships have been created, starting with European events, and in 1959 to World Championships.

In the early 1930's there were far fewer teachers of dancing than there are today. An important stimulus was administered in 1934, when one of the examining bodies inaugurated what are known as medal tests. These tests were arranged to fix a certain standard for pupils and proved an almost inmediate success. Soon all the examining bodies included bronze, silver and gold medals in their syllabuses. For a modest charge pupils can after undergoing a short course of classes take a test, the passing of which ensures the achievement of this standard. These tests have unquestionably brought a great deal of business into the dance schools, and have also built up the financial strength of the examining bodies themselves.

In spite of these efficient organizations, however, the vast majority of people continue to ignore instruction, but simply teach themselves by observing others and by venturing on to the floor. Although the numbers of dancers who have actually taken instruction grows each year, it is still an infinitesimal proportion of the dancing public as a whole. Whether they are patrons of Hammersmith Palais or the exclusive Embassy Club in London, the enormous Roseland Ballroom or the Rainbow Room in New York, dancers are mostly self taught. From time to time a new rhythm or a new movement, sometimes both in unison, brings a tremendous new impetus to social dance. Suddenly such a movement as Jitterbug with its vulgar and uninhibited movements sweeps the ballrooms of all kinds and wins headline after headline in the world press. Invariably many are shocked, just as La Volta, caused scandal in the days of Elizabeth the First, and the Waltz when he first saw it horrified Byron, so Jitterbug appalled parents of the immediate pre-second world war years. But in common with all such movements as far back as can be traced, Jitterbug was tamed into Jive, which is today accepted everywhere, the skilled exponent being regarded with envy by his contemporaries and amused admiration by those too old to dance it, although the elderly adherents of this form are surprisingly large in number. Cha Cha Cha is a development of Jive which has already enjoyed a few years of intense popularity. As I write another exotic innovation, The Twist, has just begun to live down the scandalous reputation it was at first given, and teachers of the highest possible reputation are, perhaps with some reluctance, teaching it. In time its movements will doubtless be tamed almost beyond recognition, and the form itself will become an indiscernable influence upon the whole structure of social dance. Thus the dance changes and fluctuates with the temper and climate of each period. No matter to what degree we refine and sublimate the dance forms of any period, however, we are unwise if we fail to remember that most social dance, in common with much art and the vast bulk of great literature, has its firm foundation in the sexual impulse. When we are able to direct this impulse into mentally and emotionally creative channels we shall obtain dance forms which are both satisfying in their physical movement and rhythm and which are even, perhaps, potent forms of self-expression. It is only in periods of prudery and false modesty that dance forms decline into artificiality and motiveless movement. Most forms of self-expression reflect the advanced trends of a few creators who lead public taste, rather than reflect it, for great creative artists are usually some years ahead of their time. Social dance, on the other hand, is one of the few arts of the people and is always a true reflection, if only we can read the signs, of the outlook of the time, not only the outlook of those who practise it, but of the time itself.

Immediately after the 1939-45 war dance teachers and promoters in Europe and U.S.A. settled down to harness this great new popularity of the social dance. Between the wars the dance had become essentially the pastime of the people. While a fair proportion of the working classes—but by no means such a large proportion as some dance teachers would have us believe—had acquired some skill on the floor, the middle and upper classes, particularly in Britain, had given it up. As a result the standard of dancing diminishes in proportion to the price of admission. At Hammersmith Palais, for example, one sees possibly the best general standard in the world, whereas in the ballroom of the Savoy hotel one sees little but a formless, rhythmless, unco-ordinated shuffle.

A number of dance teachers, especially certain groups in the North of England, continued through all the vicissitudes of the century to keep tenuously alive that kind of dancing which had been so popular at the beginning of the century: the sequence dances such as the Veleta, The Military Two Step, Barn Dance, and set dances including the Lancers. As this style of dancing also makes a great deal of use of a special kind of Waltz this dance too had been nurtured by those groups of teachers and enthusiasts. Whereas the Waltz developed during the last thirty-five years is based on a diagonally turning movement, with the feet closed at every third step, this older style is founded on a more rotary movement, with the feet turned out and crossing instead of closing.

Towards the end of the war, after six years of rationing, air raids, blackouts, fear and long working hours, the mothers and fathers of the young men and women in the fighting services naturally felt the need for some kind of relaxation. What more natural than that many of them should seek the same kind of pleasure which they had enjoyed in their youth? And this they did in great numbers. Clubs sprang up all over the country, with teachers to jog rusty memories as to how the sequences of forgotten dances must be done. These dancers used the palais de danse only when it had been especially engaged for their occasions, with their own bands, quite different from modern outfits, and with the doors closed to the young modern dancers. Many village halls, restaurants and town halls were engaged from time to time and one well-known promoter was able after taking his orchestra round the country to play for dances in city after city, to run a great ball at London's biggest rendezvous, the Empress Hall, to bring five thousand enthusiastic dancers from all round the United Kingdom to the climax of his season. Coaches and special trains were taken by groups and clubs to enable their members to attend this great occasion.

Unfortunately this style of dancing had somewhere along the line acquired the ridiculous title of 'old time'. Not content with this absurdity a number of teachers and club secretaries went to yet further lengths and printed on their posters in large gothic type the words 'Olde tyme'. This alone was enough to cause the younger generation to shy away from such a form, and in addition they were put off by the more fundamental reason that the style of movement and the music were completely out of date. Today the young people who take up 'old time' are as a general rule members of an extremely united family, or friends of a family who practise this kind of dancing. For it is an essentially family affair. In fact it is perhaps the only kind of dancing practised in the ballroom today which can really claim to be social dancing; all the other kinds, when one has acquired any marked skill, are to a large extent anti-social, for the tendency is to dance with only one partner and to exclude all others from your own world of movement.

Old time dancers on the other hand form themselves into a community. Throughout the country there are hundreds of clubs—some say there are thousands, but no definite figures are available. To these clubs come the families who really enjoy this kind of dancing—or rather this kind of communal activity, for old time dancing is essentially a communal pursuit. One of its most pleasing features lies in the performance of the same steps at the same time by everyone on the floor. This sort of thing provides individual satisfaction to many as well as producing a by no means unsatisfying spectacle.

In common with many others I thought that after the mothers and fathers had taken their fill of fun and of going out after the discomforts and deprivation of the war years this kind of dancing would quietly return to the moribundity in which it had spent the period between the wars. Instead it reached a tremendous climax of popularity in the early 'fifties, and has since undergone only a small decline, so that today there remain a large number of organizations which promote no other kind of dancing.

The sequence dances which feature so largely in this form number several hundreds; and every years several more are added. Most of the various teachers' examining bodies—there are nine represented on the Official Board of Ballroom Dancing—continue to organize an annual competition for the best sequence dance, and the Board itself also promotes a similar event. Even at the great Blackpool Dance Festival there is a competition for the best original sequence dance. In some years there are produced in this way perhaps a couple of dances which make an immediate appeal to a large section of the 'old time' public and a few of these dances insinuate themselves into the permanent repertory. But these are very few in number; the backbone of the programme remains with the Waltz, Veleta, Boston Two Step, Military Two Step and other well-tried favourites, interspersed with set dances such as the Lancers and Caledonians.

In spite of the 'old time' form, however, British teachers are justly most proud of their development of what is appropriately named the English Style, although other countries understandably employ other titles. In Europe it is usually known as the 'standard dances' and in North America and even Australia as 'International Style'. This style is concerned chiefly with the modern Waltz, Foxtrot, Tango and Quickstep. Generally speaking it is built up on that smooth walking step which came to Britain from U.S.A. and of which the Vernon Castles were the first great exponents and, by their demonstrations both on the ballroom floor and on the stage, the greatest promoters and advocates.

Since the last war competition dancing has increased in popularity a great deal. Although in the 'thirties there was certainly a great deal of this kind of competition, it was not until after the war that it grew almost into a disease. Great championships such as those promoted by a newspaper in London and at the Winter Gardens in Blackpool, both of which have been running for about thirty years, continue to play important parts, and indeed the two British Championships, amateur and professional, at Blackpool remain today the best organized events of their kind and the most coveted titles. Indeed, leading couples would prefer to be able to style themselves British Champions than World Champions, so great is the reputation of this event. But today there are in all about three hundred championships ranking from county and area events to national championships organized by big commercial enterprises.

In addition to this, television in Britain has played an important part. Throughout the winter a weekly programme is put on featuring nothing but ballroom dancing at its best. One of these programmes, the B.B.C. Television Dancing Club, for which Victor Silvester provides the music, has been running for twelve years and is claimed to have the longest continuity of any television programme with the exception of the news. Here once a fortnight one can see the cream of amateur and professional dancers in demonstrations and competitions. Here too one finds the kind of 'uniform' which has been developed especially for this kind of dancing. The girls pay no heed to fashion trends from outside their tightly enclosed world, but continue to favour skirts of tulle with as many as a hundred yards of material, so that these skirts flow and flounce in sympathy with the dancers' movements. The bodice receives less attention than the rest of the dress, for it is little in evidence during the dance, On the other hand thousands of sequins are stuck on the skirt, for this gives a certain kind of scintillation. Occasionally there comes a shift of fashion when the length of the skirt is either increased or diminished, and perhaps a new idea about an overskirt is soon copied with variations by almost everyone, but by and large the 'uniform' remains basically unchanged. The men too, although they wear the 'tails' which are fast disappearing from the normal masculine wardrobe, can also be said to sport a uniform since the cut and pattern of their tails differ considerably from any design likely to gain the approval of a Savile Row tailor. The tails themselves are long and swallowlike, coming well below the knee, again to harmonize with the flow of movement, and the lapels are often loosely joined by a cord in order to prevent the coat from opening out and exposing the waistcoat during rapid turns.

But all this activity in competition dancing consists largely of a shop window with very little stock inside. Through television and to a lesser extent through the great championships, a mistaken impression has sprung up as to the extent and strength of this kind of dancing. In fact it is very small. Registered with the Official Board are fewer than three thousand dancers, fifteen hundred couples, yet every dancer who wishes to enter any championship must be so registered. There are many other competitions not carrying the status of championships which non-registered competitiors can enter, but these too are limited in number, and it is doubtful whether there exists throughout Britain today more than five thousand dancers who regularly enter competitions. Probably not as many.

Another variant of the English Style popularized by television is known as formation dancing. In this form a number of couples, frequently eight, make variegated patterns, and teachers who specialize in this kind of work have developed an ingenuity which perhaps justifies the title sometimes given to them of 'choreographers of the ballroom'. But here again television has misled the public as to the ramifications of this form. Today there are certainly not more than fifty formation teams throughout the country, and the majority of these have sprung up only since television began to make its demands for such teams. It seems that the height of ambition of the members of these teams is to appear on the little screen.

In spite of all the spectacle it provides for public entertainment, therefore, this highly organized style of dancing is in truth only a fringe activity. The vast bulk of people who go dancing do not wish to learn this style. The main objection to it is that it is too difficult; yet another, scarcely less important, is that it requires space, and space today is becoming more and more at a premium. The vast crowds who go dancing night after night, then, dance the forms of the moment. During the last ten years there is no doubt that the trend in this kind of spontaneous dancing is to cover less and less floor space, but to indulge in rhythmic movements of the body. Thus we have Cha Cha Cha, Twist and a number of ephemeral variants of these forms, each one springing, it seems, from a slight difference in the musical beat, innovations which spring naturally from musicians from time to time. Once again, returning to the years before and after the first world war, these trends are stemming from North America. Just as rag-time was developed there, with the white influence to tame the original negroid impulse, the same thing seems to be happening all over again, except that the negroid impulse, itself now adulterated since its long exile from its native land, comes direct to the people.

Thus in Britain until recently, but not in America, we have had the anomaly of pupils in schools of dancing being taught one style and the people who go dancing in the hundreds of public dance halls dancing something not only different but alien to that style. As a result many schools become the social centre of their pupils, who practise what they have learnt only in the school and but rarely in a dance hall. This was an absurd state of affairs which could not continue. In North American schools pupils are taught simple rhythmic figures in each dance, the idea being to enable them to get on to the floor with a minimum of difficulty after the very first lesson, not to develop a great deal of skill in them. The only trouble there has been that one could learn one basic figure in one school and go to another school round the corner and find that the system was quite different. In Britain we have had the uniformity but too much complexity, and certainly too little regard for public taste; whereas in America there has been little uniformity but an acute awareness of the public pulse. In Europe there was for a time in some areas an uneasy compromise between the two methods. In France the English Style has barely percolated, whereas in Holland, Germany and Denmark teachers in large number have long admired and practised the English Style. On the other hand, being of a more realistic nature than our own teachers, they have in those countries during the last ten years developed a form which on the face of it owes practically nothing to the English Style. Simple rhythmic movements which can be danced comfortably within a confined space have been worked out and exploited with considerable success.

Now, at last, British teachers have become increasingly aware of the need for a closer awareness of what the public wants, with the result that many teachers have already adopted a style, and worked out a syllabus, more on the same lines as the other countries I have named. At the same time, just as has been done elsewhere, the English Style will be retained for the benefit of those who possess more than ordinary ability and who wish to go further than what is little more, when viewed dispassionately, than a kind of ordered, civilized, shuffling round. Another factor too is that the physical discipline and flow of movement of the English Style, like classical ballet for the highly trained stage dancer, is an absolute necessity if one wishes to excel on the floor.

Until the end of 1961 the International Council of Ballroom Dancing, which includes members in Japan and Australia, South Africa and America as well as Europe, concerned itself almost exclusively with competition matters, and among other things founded world championships. But here too the wind of change was keenly felt and early in 1962 a determined effort was made to develop an international form of social dance for complete beginners, so that one could walk into a ballroom in Munich or Manchester, London or Ludveck, New York or Naples and perform the same simple basic figures. Members of the council are already fired with enthusiasm for this idea, and it is hoped that in a few years' time all the difficulties will be overcome, so that teachers of social dancing throughout the world will be able to develop a true form of social dance and no longer in certain countries remain isolated from the dance which is springing from the people. For social dancing cannot be imposed upon the people; it must spring from the climate of the time although as has occurred regularly throughout history, teachers must be able to harness the forces and rhythms themselves in order to make them both palatable and easily sensed by unmusical but perhaps rhythmical ears.

Appendix I

SOME BOOKS FOR FURTHER STUDY

THE following list is by no means exhaustive, but is intended as a fair cross section of reliable literature which will prove of value to those who wish to study particular aspects of the dance scene, whether from a historical, social or technical angle.

REFERENCE BOOKS

The Dance Encyclopedia edited by Anatole Chujoy. New York. A. S. Barnes & Co. 1949.

Although concentrating chiefly on ballet, this encyclopedia nevertheless carries numerous references to the social dance, as well as some authoritative articles on the same subject.

The Oxford Companion to Music by Percy Scholes. London. Oxford University Press. 6th Edition, 1945.

An indispensable work for anyone studying dance music, whether its background or its structure.

Dictionary of English Costume by C. Willett Cunnington, Phyllis Cunnington and Charles Beard. London. Charles and Adam Black. 1960.

A Pictorial History of Costume by Wolfgang Bruhn and Max Pilke. London. A. Zwemmer Ltd. 1955.

Both these works are invaluable as guides to the costumes of all periods. Although the *Pictorial History* is not by any means comprehensive its hundreds of plates, in colour, provide a vivid picture of various costumes used on dance occasions.

GENERAL

World History of the Dance by Curt Sachs. Goerge Allen & Unwin Ltd. 1938.

The most exhaustive and profound study of the dances of many regions throughout history. A few small errors have surprisingly misled some into questioning the undoubted authority of its author. It is indispensable to every serious student of the history and ethnology of dance.

APPENDIX I

Dance by Lincoln Kirstein. New York. G. B. Putnam's Sons. 1935.

From the end of the seventeenth century this book, by one who has financially sponsored the New York City Ballet for several years, deals almost exclusively with ballet. The earlier chapters, however, discuss in interesting style the social dance, at the same time showing signs of endless research and containing illuminating theories.

Religious Dances by Louis Backman. London. George Allen & Unwin Ltd. 1952.

A great deal of religious dancing is very emphatically social dance. This is a comprehensive study of the religious aspects of the subject.

Dancing (in the Badminton Library Series), edited by His Grace the Duke of Beaufort, K.G. London. Longmans, Green & Co. 1895.

This volume was for many years regarded as a standard work. Although much of it has now been superseded by twentieth-century research, it continues to provide an insight into many angles.

Memorable Balls edited by James Laver. London. Derek Verschoyle. 1954.

Well informed and colourful, in some cases highly imaginative accounts by various writers of several famous occasions in history, such as Le Bal des Ardents in 1393, the notorious Eve of the Massacre of St. Batholomew in 1572, the Jubilee Masquerade at Ranelagh in 1749, to the Poiret Ball of 1910. The setting and the intrigue are treated with consumate skill by all the contributors, but there is not a great deal about the actual dancing.

America Learns to Dance by Joseph E. Marks III. New York Exposition Press. 1957.

A short but remarkably well-informed study which contains many quotations from contemporary sources.

The Dance by Troy and Margaret West Kinney. New York. Tudor Publishing Company. 1936.

This book deals with many kinds of dance in many different lands: from the dances of ancient Rome to twentieth-century ballet. Much invaluable information.

The Story of Dance Music by Paul Nettl. New York Philosophical Library. 1947.

A fascinating study of the development of dance music from early times.

The Social Dances of the Nineteenth Century by P. J. S. Richardson. London. Herbert Jenkins Ltd. 1960.

The History of English Ballroom Dancing (1910–1945) by P. J. S. Richardson. London. Herbert Jenkins Ltd. 1948.

These two short works are the only ones devoted exclusively to these two periods of dance history. Both are thorough and meticulously accurate.

APPENDIX I

Gateway to the Dance by Ruby Ginner. Newman Neame. London 1960.

Although the author, the founder of the Greek Dance Association, is chiefly concerned with the form of revived Greek dances, she nevertheless provides an absorbing account of the dances and dance customs of the Greeks of antiquity.

Pre-classic Dance Forms by Louis Horst. New York. The Dance Observer. 1940.

A well-known musician in America, the author deals historically with the Pavane, Galliard, Allemande, Courante, Sarabande, Gigue, Minuet, Gavotte, Bourrée, Rigaudon, Passepied, Chaconne, Pasacaglia, and other lesser forms. The book is invaluable to students of the history of these forms and particularly of their music. In an appendix technical descriptions are quoted from various contemporary works.

Dances of Spain and Italy (from 1400 to 1600) by Mabel Dolmetsch. London. Routledge and Kegan Paul Ltd. 1954.

Dances of England and France (1450 to 1600) by Mabel Dolmetsch. London. Routledge and Kegan Paul Ltd. 1949.

Historical Dances (12th to the 19th Century) by Melusine Wood. London. C. W. Beaumont for the Imperial Society of Teachers of Dancing. 1952.

More Historical Dances by Melusine Wood. London. C. W. Beaumont for the Imperial Society of Teachers of Dancing Incorporated. 1956.

Advanced Historical Dances by Melusine Wood. London. C. W. Beaumont for the Imperial Society of Teachers of Dancing Incorporated. 1960.

All these five works are essential to students who seek to master the figures and style of the dances of the renaissance and later. Those by Melusine Wood, founder of the Historical Dance Branch of the Imperial Society of Teachers of Dancing, are more thorough from a technical point of view, whereas those by Mabel Dolmetsch, although also dealing with the figures and style, provide a greater insight into the history and background.

A Jewish Dancing Master of the Renaissance. (Gugliemo Ebreo) Otto Kinkeldey —reprinted from the A. S. Freidus Memorial Volume. New York. 1929.

This brilliant study discusses and compares the work of Guglielmo with that of Cornazano and that of both of them with the work of their teacher, Domenico of Ferrara.

Apologie de la Danse by F. de Lauze. London. Frederick Muller Ltd. 1952.

This work, in both English and its original French, is a 'Treatise of Instruction' by a distinguished authority of the first part of the seventeenth century. The translation is by an eminent authority on the dancing of that time, Joan Wildeblood, who also provides an absorbing introduction as well as most useful notes.

APPENDIX I

Dancing: As an Art and Pastime by Edward Scott. London. George Bell & Sons. 1892.

No better or more comprehensive work on the dances of the nineteenth century exists, nor a more colourful, if at times pompous, discussion on their background. Scott was a prolific writter on the dance as well as a well-known teacher.

The Tango and How to Dance It by Gladys Beattie Crozier. London. Andrew Melrose Ltd. 1913.

A whole book devoted to one of the greatest dance crazes of all time.

Modern Dancing by Mr. and Mrs. Vernon Castle. New York. Harper & Brothers. 1914.

The most famous of all dancers and teachers of the twentieth century, up to and during the first world war, describe the dances in vogue at the time in New York.

Ballroom Dancing by Alex Moore. London. Sir Isaac Pitman & Sons Ltd. (Constantly revised).

This is the most lucid and comprehensive book on the technique of the English style of ballroom dancing as it is practised at the present time.

For a fairly complete picture of the twentieth-century social dance scene *The Dancing Times* (since 1956 *The Ballroom Dancing Times* has become a separate publication, leaving *The Dancing Times* to concentrate on theatrical forms) is invaluable. The first issue of this monthly periodical appeared in 1910.

Students who wish to examine contemporary material of before the nineteenth century are under some difficulty, as original works of the fifteenth, sixteenth, seventeenth and eighteenth centuries are extremely rare. Indeed, most of such works are in the hands of private collectors. A study of Bibliographical Descriptions of Forty Dance Books in the collection of P. J. S. Richardson (London. The Dancing Times Ltd. 1954) will repay study. A copy of this catalogue is obtainable from most reference libraries. Some of the key works in this catalogue are listed below. Microfilm copies of several of them are available, together with a reading machine, in the Westminster Central Reference Library. Some of them are also in the possession of the New York Public Library and various libraries in Europe.

Livre Des Basses Danses	c.1450
Zuccollo's La Pazzia Del Ballo	1549
Arena's Bassas Dansas	1572
Caroso's Il Ballarino	1581
Belgioso's Ballet Comique de la Royne	1582
Thoinot-Arbeau's Orchesographie	1588
Feuillet's Choregraphie	1701

APPENDIX I

Feuillet's Recueil de Dances	1704
Feuillet's For the Further Improvement of Dancing	1710
Weaver's History of Dancing	1712
Feuillet's Orchesography	c.1722
Rameau's Le Maitre a Danser	1725
Playford's The Dancing Master	c.1728
Tomlinson's The Art of Dancing	1735
Dubois's Principles D'Allemandes	c.1790

Appendix II

DANCE OF SAVAGES, 1393

An extract from *The Chronicles of Froissart*

Chapter CLXXXVIII (CXCII)

Of the adventure of a dance that was made at Paris in likeness of wodehouses, wherein the French king was in peril of death.

It fortuned that soon after the retaining of this foresaid knight a marriage was made in the king's house between a young knight of Vermandois and one of the queen's gentlewomen; and because they were both of the king's house, the king's uncles and other lords, ladies and damosels made great triumph. There was the dukes of Olreans, Berry and Burgoyne and their wives, dancing and making great joy. The king made a great supper to the lords and ladies, and the queen kept her estate, desiring every man to be merry. And there was a squire of Normandy called Ilugonin of Guisay, he advised to make some pastime. The day of the marriage, which was on a Tuesday before Candlemas, he provided for a mummery against night: he devised six coats made of linen cloth covered with pitch and thereon flax like hair, and had them ready in a chamber: the king put on one of them, and the earl of Joigny, a young lusty knight, another, and sir Charles of Poitiers the third, who was son to the earl of Valentinois, and to sir Yvain of Foix another, and the son of the lord Nantouillet had on the fifth, and the squire himself had on the sixth: and when they were thus arrayed in these said coats and sewed fast in them, they seemed like wild wodehouses full of hair from the top of the head to the sole of the foot. This devise pleased well the French king, and was well content with the squire for it. They were apparelled in these coats secretly in a chamber, that no man knew thereof but such as holp them. When sir Yvain of Foix had well advised these coats, he said to the king: 'Sir, command straitly that no man approach near us with any torches or fire; for if the fire fasten in any of these coats, we shall all be brent without remedy.' The king answered and said: 'Yvain, ye speak well and wisely: it shall be done as ye have devised': and incontinent

APPENDIX II

sent for an usher of his chamber, commanding him to go into the chamber where the ladies danced and to command all the varlets holding torches to stand up by the walls, and none of them to approach near to the wodehouses that should come thither to dance. The usher did the king's commandment, which was fulfilled. Soon after the duke of Orleans entered into the hall, accompanied with four knights and six torches, and knew nothing of the king's commandment for the torches nor of the mummery that was coming thither, but thought to behold the dancing and began himself to dance. Therewith the king with the five other came in: they were so disguised in flax, that no man knew them: five of them were fastened to another; the king was loose and went before and led the device.

When they entered into the hall, every man took so great heed to them that they forgat the torches. The king departed from his company and went to the ladies to sport with them, as youth required, and so passed by the queen and came to the duchess of Berry, who took and held him by the arm to know what he was, but the king would not shew his name. Then the duchess said: 'Ye shall not escape me till I know your name.' In this mean season great mischief fell on the other, and by reason of the duke of Orleans; howbeit, it was by ignorance and against his will, for if he had considered before the mischief that fell, he would not have done as he did for all the good in the world: but he was so desirous to know what personages the five were that danced, he put one of the torches that his servants held so near, that the heat of the fire entered into the flax (wherein if fire take there is no remedy) and suddenly was a bright flame, and so each of them set fire on other. The pitch was so fastened to the linen cloth, and their shirts so dry and fine and so joining to their flesh, that they began to bren and cry for help. None durst come near them; they that did, brent their hands by reason of the heat of the pitch. One of them, called Nantouillet, advised him how the buttery was thereby: he fled thither and cast himself into a vessel full of water, wherein they rinsed pots, which saved him or else he had been dead as the other were, yet he was sore hurt with the fire.

When the queen heard the cry that they made, she doubted her of the king, for she knew well that he should be one of the six, wherewith she fell in a swoon, and knights and ladies came and comforted her. A piteous noise there was in the hall. The duchess of Berry delivered the king from that peril, for she did cast over him the train of her gown and covered him from the fire. The king would have gone from her. 'Whither will ye go?' quoth she. 'Ye see well how your company brens. What are ye?' 'I am the king,' quoth he. 'Haste you,' quoth she, 'and get you into other apparel, that the queen may see you for she is in great fear of you.' Therewith the king departed out of the hall and in all haste changed his apparel and came to the queen; and the duchess of Berry had somewhat comforted her and had shewed her how she should see the king shortly: therewith the king came to the queen, and so soon as she saw him, for joy she embraced him and fell

APPENDIX II

in a swoon: then she was borne into her chamber and the king went with her. And the bastard of Foix, and the earl of Joigny, borne to their lodgings and died within two days after in great misery and pain. Thus the feast of this marriage brake up in heaviness; howbeit, there was no remedy: the fault was only in the duke of Orleans, and yet he thought none evil when he put down the torch. Then the duke said: 'Sirs, let every man know there is no man to blame for this cause, but all only myself: I am sorry thereof: if I had thought as much before, it should not have happened.' Then the duke of Orleans went to the king to excuse him, and the king took his excuse. This case fell in the year of our Lord God a thousand three hundred fourscore and twelve, the Tuesday before the feast of Candlemas; of which fortune great bruit spread in the realm of France and in other countries. The dukes of Burgoyne and of Berry were not there present at that season: they had taken their leave before of the king and were gone to their lodgings.

The next day these news spread abroad in the city, and every man had marvel thereof; and some said how God had sent that token for an ensample, and that it was wisdom for the king to regard it and to withdraw himself from such young idle wantonness, which he had used overmuch, being a king. The commons of the city of Paris murmured and said: 'Behold the great mishap and mischief that was likely to have fallen on the king: he might as well have been brent, as other were. What should have fallen then of the king's uncles and of his brother? They might have been sure none of them should have scaped the death; yea, and all the knights that might have been found in Paris.'

As soon as the dukes of Berry and of Burgoyne heard of that adventure, they were abashed and marvelled greatly. They leapt on their horses and rode to the king and comforted and counselled him; which was necessary, for he was sore troubled, and the peril that he was in was still in his imagination. He shewed his uncles how his aunt of Berry had saved him; but he said he was sorry for the death of the earl of Joigny, of sir Yvain of Foix and sir Charles of Poitiers. His uncles recomforted him and said: 'Sir, that is lost cannot be recovered: ye must forget the death of them and thank God of the fair adventure that is fallen to your own person; for all the realm of France by this incident might have been in greater danger of losing: for ye may think well that these people of Paris will never be still; for God knoweth, if the misfortune had fallen on you, they would have slain us all. Therefore, sir, apparel you in estate royal and leap on your horse and ride to Our Lady in pilgrimage, and we shall accompany you, and shew yourself to the people, for they desire sore to see you.' The king said he would do so. Then the king's uncles took apart the duke of Orleans and in courteous manner somewhat blamed him of his young deed that he had done. He answered and said how he thought to have done none evil. Then anon after the king and his company leapt on their horses and rode through the city to appease the people, and came to Our Lady church and there heard mass and offered, and

APPENDIX II

then returned again to the house of Saint-Pol; and little by little this matter was forgotten, and the obsequies done for the dead bodies.

Ah, earl Gaston of Foix, if this had fortuned in thy life days, thou shouldest have had great displeasure and it had been hard to have peased thee, for thou lovedst him entirely. All lords and ladies through the realm of France and elsewhere, that heard of this chance, had great marvel thereof.

Appendix III

THE POLKA

THE following text accompanied the publication in *The Illustrated London News* of March 23rd, 1844 of the music of the Polka and the two drawings which are reproduced on plate 22.

We have received from Paris, by the last post, the accompanying sketch of the new dance recently imported from Bohemia into the French metropolis, entitled the Polka, and which, to the exclusion of all other considerations—Legitimacy, Tahiti and the Right of Search not excepted—has seized this volatile and light-hearted people universally by the heels. With all respect for the lore of our learned neighbours, we think that St. Vitus, and not St. Denis, must have been the patron saint of France; but, be that as it may, there can be no doubt that that saint is their guardian angel, who, by infusing into them this lively elixir, withdraws them from the morbid contemplation of fancied and imaginary wrongs, and the long train of fatal and inglorious consequences which generally follow. The English are an imitative people, and we may reasonably expect to find the Polka amongst the other west-end importations during the season. Our daily contemporary *The Times*, thus alludes to the rage which prevails in Paris with regard to this most recent innovation.

'The Paris papers are destitute of news. Our private letters state, that "politics are for the moment suspended in public regard by the new and all-absorbing pursuit—the Polka—a dance recently imported from Bohemia, and which embraces in its qualities the intimacy of the waltz with the vivacity of the Irish jig. You may conceive how completely is 'the Polka' the rage from the fact that the lady of a celebrated ex-minister, desiring to figure in it at a soirée dansante, monopolized the professor par excellence of that specialité for three hours on Wednesday morning last, at 200f. the hour. This is an unfortunate diversion for the war party, whose subscriptions for the sword of honour for Admiral Dupetit Thouars will be put hors de combat by this fascinating novelty".'

The Polka is an original Bohemian Peasant Dance, and was first introduced into the fashionable saloons of Berlin and St. Petersburg about eight years since. Last season it was the great favourite at Baden-Baden. The Polka is

APPENDIX III

written in 2-4 time. The gentleman holds his partner in the manner shown in the engraving: each lift first the right leg, strike twice the left heel with the right heel, and then turn, as in the waltz.

The Bohemians accompany this movement with characteristic gestures but the action is rather rude. The Berlin Polka combines grace with elegance.

The Polka we now publish has been composed expressly for the *Illustrated London News* by a celebrated French artiste; and we feel great pleasure in being the first to introduce it to our subscribers.

And the following appeared in *The Illustrated London News* of May 11th, 1844. See also Plate 23.

THE DRAWING-ROOM POLKA

We are much gratified in being enabled to lay before our readers an accurate description of the véritable, or Drawing-room Polka, as danced at Almack's and at the balls of the nobility and gentry in this country.

La Polka having appeared amongst us under so many different guises, we determined to spare no pains to procure a true description of its danse; for which we are indebted to Mrs. James Rae, who has been fortunate enough to secure the details from M. Coralli, Fils, the instructor of the young noblesse and gentry in Paris.

La Polka, like its predecessors, the waltz and galop, is a danse à deux, couples following each other in the salle de danse, commencing at pleasure, and adopting, of the following figures, that which pleases them most at the moment. All those anxious to shine in La Polka will dance the whole of them, returning from time to time, by way of rest, to the first figure.

The measure, or time, is 2-4; but to facilitate our definition we subdivide each measure or bar into one-two-three-four-; the accent on the two, &c.: to be played not so fast as the galop.

The steps are two, and the following description may, in some measure, convey them to our readers; we commence with the first and most general. At the one, hop on the right leg, lifting or doubling up your left leg at the same moment; at the two, put your left leg boldly forward on the ground; at the three, bring your right toe up to your left heel; at the four, advance your left foot a short step forward; now at the one in the next measure or bar of the tune, hop on the left leg, doubling or lifting up your right leg, and so on—proceeding in this step with your arm circling your partner's waist round the room, as shown in our sketch. This may be termed the first figure.

As the change of figures and duration of each in this dance is left entirely to the cavaliers, as also the most careful guidance of his lady round the room, we must be supposed to be addressing ourselves to them in these remarks, though, at the same time, our definition will be equally understood by their fair partners.

Figure 2. Still adopting the same step, with your right arm round your partner's waist, and her right hand in your left, you place your lady exactly before you, and back all round the room, your lady pursuing you (as shown

APPENDIX III

in our sketch); you then reverse this figure, and let your partner do the back step whilst you pursue her, and at the same time carefully guide her round the room.

In backing, the leg which in figure 1 you put boldly forward on the ground, you now fling boldly backward, and are thus enabled to effect your progress round the room.

Figure 3.—With the same step you waltz round the room—in other words, you perform the galop waltz, substituting the Polka step just described.

Figure 4. This also is a waltz with the second step, which we will now describe as the 'Heel and Toe step'. At the one, make a little hop on the right leg, dropping your left heel close to the right foot; at the two, another little hop on the right leg, pointing your left toe (not forward, but as close to the right foot as possible); at the three, another little hop on the right leg, advancing one step forward with the left foot; at the four, bring up the right foot, turning at the same instant, and passing yout partner over to your left arm from your right arm; in the next measure return your lady to the left arm, and so on.

Figure 5.—This is termed the back waltz. The step adopted in it by yourself and partner is the back step described in figure 2; and you turn in this waltz exactly the contrary way to that in which you turn in all other waltzes —hence its name.

In *La Polka*, before commencing the figures we have just described, there is a short introduction (of which we give a sketch), consisting of four measures, danced thus: leading your partner from her seat, and giving her her place in the circle, and placing yorselves vis-à-vis, you take her left hand in your right, and make the first step four times—first forward, then backward, forward again, and then backward, taking care to gain ground in the forward steps; you then start with the first figure.

In conclusion we would observe that La Polka is a noiseless dance; there is no stamping of heels or toes, or kicking of legs in sharp angles forward. This may do very well at the threshold of a Bohemian *auberge*, but is inadmissible into the *salons* of London or Paris. La Polka, as danced in Paris, and now adopted by us, is elegant, graceful, and fascinating in the extreme; it is replete with opportunities of showing care and attention to your partner in assisting her through its performance. To our fair readers, however, we would say one word, for careful as their cavaliers may be, the front of many dresses, particularly in executing figure 2, will have much chance of being trodden upon and torn, unless the usual length is considerably shortened. This we have seen done with much grace on one or two occasions by the transplanting of a bunch of artificial violets, with a long pin attached thereto. from the waist to the lower part of the dress, which serves to loop up to the desired shortness, and which contributes greatly to the elegance of this dance, as the feet are thus shown, which is indispensable.

Appendix IV

Two extracts from the volume on *Dancing*, published in 1895, in the Badminton Library.

CHAPTER XV

A RETROSPECT

by the Honourable Mrs. Armytage

Dancing as it was practised in 1845 differs greatly from dancing as it is carried on in 1895 in the ballrooms of London society. Some few of those who now look on at the entertainments and amusements of this generation from the vantage post of the chaperon's bench can recall their own experience of the earlier period of Queen Victoria's reign. The balls at Almack's certainly made and ruled the fashion in dances from the date of their first existence in 1765 until their final extinction about the year 1840-1. These assemblies were held at the rooms in King Street, St. James's, known at the present time as Willis's Rooms, which, however, took their first name from the original proprietor, Mr. Almack. The opening of these rooms is alluded to by Horace Walpole and also by Guy Williams, another gossiping letter-writer of that time. The former writes on February 14, 1765, to Lord Hertford, that the rooms were open in such an unseasoned state that the ceilings were dripping wet, but the Duke of Cumberland was among the company. Williams wrote to Selwyn that there were three elegant, new-built rooms, and that for a ten-guinea subscription you may enjoy a ball and a ball and a supper once a week for twelve weeks; and in writing again he pictures 'Almack's Scotch face in a bag wig. Waiting at supper would divert you as would his Lady in a sack making Tea and curtseying to the Duchesses.'

The lady patronesses of this social institution were absolute in their rule, and an admission or refusal to the sacred portals stamped a novice's position at once. In 1814 the famous Lady Jersey was at the head of the Council, and the balls at Almack's were the ne plus ultra of fashionable entertainments. In those days a voucher for Almack's only obtained from one of the six lady patronesses, was the aim and object of all who wished to shine in the mystic circle of the ultra-fashionable clique of London society; and an intro-

APPENDIX IV

duction to one of these great ladies was a matter of most anxious importance. The very stringent code of rules which guarded these gatherings from the intrusion of anyone outside the privileged circle was drawn up by Lady Jersey and her co-patronesses, and an admission was fraught with great difficulties. Each lady could only give a certain number of vouchers, and only the quintessence of aristocracy were present, while it was said three-fourths of the nobility knocked in vain at the portals of Almack's. Colonel Gronow states that, though there were three hundred Guardsmen going about town, not more than half a dozen ever succeeded in obtaining a voucher. Lady Jersey is described as a theatrical tragedy queen, presiding over these reunions, 'into whose sanctum sons of commerce never intrude'. A stern rule also forbade the admittance of anyone after midnight had struck, and when the Duke of Wellington appeared at the door a few minutes after the prescribed hour he was refused admittance.

These two facts speak for themselves of the different state of things in reference to balls then and now. The idea of refusing admittance at such a comparatively early hour will strike the present generation as quaint. In addition to Lady Jersey, the leaders of fashion who supported her included Ladies Sefton, Cowper, Castlereagh, Princess Esterhazy, Countess Lieven, and the late Lady Willoughby De Eresby; and they met in solemn conclave to consider the petitions for admission. In 1815 the contredanse, Scotch reels and jigs (said to have been introduced into London by Jane, Duchess of Gordon, when in the zenith of her youth and beauty she came down from Scotland after her marriage), were the established dances then in fashion; but in that year Lady Jersey ventured to introduce the quadrille from France, where it was so popular, and its reception at Almack's put the cachet of approval upon the new dance. The first night on which it was danced, Lady Jersey, Lady Harriet Butler, Lady Susan Ryder, and Miss Montgomery, with Count Aldergarde, Mr. Montgomery, Mr. Harley, and Mr. Montague for their partners, made up the first set that was ever seen in London. The figures were intricate; the steps, positively essential to their correct interpretation, were manifold; and it was quite as necessary to master the difficulties of Pas de basque, Chassez-croisez, with the regulation Balancé and Poussette, as it had been in the past century to grapple with the minute etiquette of the Menuet de la Cour or Gavotte; nor was it till long after the writer's own début that the lazy, nonchalant fashion of walking through the figures was at all tolerated. Queen Victoria and the Prince Consort, with Prince George (now Duke of Cambridge) and his sister Princess Augusta, Duchess of Mecklenburg-Sterlitz, were particularly graceful dancers; but few people will now believe that, as the ladies started to dance 'LEté' figure of the quadrille, it was absolutely necessary to hold out their skirts, with hands placed in the exact position taught by the dancing-master of the time, point the toe and chassé across from side to side, each figure in its turn being danced with the same careful attention to regulation steps; all of which required far more

APPENDIX IV

room than can usually be found in most London ballrooms at the present time.

Having now established a new dance from across the Channel, we next hear of the 'mazy waltz' coming in from Vienna, and find that as early as 1816 it was danced at Almack's by a few very bold spirits; among these were mentioned, as being very expert, the names of Lord Palmerston and Madame de Lieven, Princess Esterhazy and Baron de Neumann, who were constantly dancing together. One or two old prints represent these leaders of fashion starting to waltz in Willis's Rooms. By degrees these assemblies became gradually less fashionable and less popular, Society was content to meet at friends' houses, the number of ball-giving hostesses increased so rapidly that subscription balls were no longer patronised, and thus, after an existence of ninety years, Almack's died away. A late attempt to resuscitate similar gatherings was a distinct failure; still, for many years the fine suite of rooms was in requisition for some special entertainment got up for charity, which was often patronised and attended by royalty. When one recalls the rank and beauty of English society that from time to time have met within the walls of Willis's Rooms, the spot may be called almost historical. The famous Caledonian Ball was always held here up to the last ten years, but this annual 'gathering of the clans' was at length transferred to the New Club, Covent Garden, and more recently to the Whitehall Room, Hotel Métropole.

The waltz, when first introduced in London, was a slow movement in trois temps, and very different from that which we recognise in this latter part of the century.

The first appearance of the polka in 1844 created no little excitement, and some of the newspapers of the day, in alluding to it, said that 'its introduction into fashionable society may be regarded as the commencement of a new style in the art of dancing. Russia and Bohemia are said to be responsible for its origin. The style of dancing the polka varies considerably as the most graceful persons dance it in a quiet easy manner, but the movement of this elegant and fashionable dance still continues, and will most likely increase in time.'[1] Directions for dancing it describe it as three steps and a rest, which would hardly insure anyone's mastering its intricacies. At a fancy ball the original dancers appeared in costume which were picturesque, but perhaps rather startling to the ideas of 1844. Short skirts of scarlet cloth edged with white fur were worn by the ladies under Polish jackets, and showed high scarlet boots with clattering heels, while coquettish little caps completed their dress, the whole eliciting much comment at the time; but the polka was accepted, and has held its popularity up to now, though danced at its advent in a very different style, the step being elaborate, while such music as the Annen Polka, by Strauss, inspired the dancers.

[1] The dance is treated in its proper place, and it will be perceived that the writer quoted was incorrect in attributing responsibility for its origin to Russia.

APPENDIX IV

Who changes the order of things in dancing is quite as great a mystery as who is the priestess that presides over the creation of new fancies and fashions in dress, and demands the sacrifice at her shrine of so many fond ideas of what was once the ideal in dress or custom; but steadily and surely the alterations creeep in, by slow degrees the old trois-temps waltz died out, and the deux temps usurped its place and reigned in triumph, until pushed aside again by that which has since been adopted.

While these gradual changes in round dances went on, another new dance sprang into life during the season of 1850. Madame Sacre, the fashionable dancing mistress of that time, held her classes for instruction in the Hanover Square Rooms, and as her elder pupils made their appearances in London society she often persuaded them to look in occasionally, while the younger generation were under her instruction, and to join in some of the fanciful or novel dances which she delighted to teach; thus the lancers was first thought of and suggested as a welcome addition to the ball programme. Four young ladies who were popular in London set to work in earnest to learn and to practise the very elaborate figures, while they also induced the necessary number of young men to join them. How one smiles to think of such energy, and to picture the young men of today taking such trouble over a dance! Impossible; but it was not so in 1850, when Lady Georgina Lygon, Lady Jane Fielding, Mdlle. Olga de Lechner (daughter of Baroness Brunnow, our Russian Ambassadress in England), and Miss Berkeley danced the first set of the lancers in a London ballroom. It was danced at the Turkish Embassy, at Bath House, at Lady Caroline Townley's and many other balls during that season by the four couples who knew it, whilst others looked on. The lancers was then considered particularly pretty and graceful, and was very different from the lively friskiness of the fin de siècle dance as we know it; there was indeed a certain stately grace about it which is entirely lost. Steps and figures were most carefully gone through; it soon became most popular, but, as the number of those who attempted it increased, the rigid observance of the original figures was soon dispensed with, and the alterations have certainly changed its whole style. It is amusing to read over the published directions given in 1850, in a fashionable newspaper, as to the 'etiquette of dancing the lancers'.

'This elegant dance, denominated as "Hart's set," when well executed, is one in which the dancer can display his skill to great advantage,' the critic says. 'It consists of four couples arranged vis-à-vis, and the figures were thus danced:—1st figure, "La Chaîne." The leading lady and opposite gentleman advance and retire, re-advance, turn with both hands and retire; the leading couple pass between the opposite couple and return outside to their places; all four couples set to corners; repeat four times.' Then come directions for the other figures—'Zodorska,' 'D'Orset,' 'L'Etoile,' and 'Finale des Lancers.' Though thoroughly established in popularity, and regularly danced for some years at private houses, it was quite ten years before the lancers was included

APPENDIX IV

in the programme at Her Majesty's State balls, where now it is never omitted; but one doubts if the original arrangers of this dance would recognise some of the figures as performed with the lively additions of modern hilarity, or would quite appreciate the change.

The orchestras of years gone by were led by Weippart, Jullien and Koenig, Labitzky, Coote and Tinney; whilst a Strauss was then, as now, considered the master of the art of composing waltzes and polkas, as well as of leading the orchestra for dancing. 'Strauss's band' is still with us, and yet, at the time of the Queen's coronation in 1837, we know that his band was engaged to play at Almack's, and that the waltz music of this talented artist created a perfect furore. The elder Strauss must have long ceased to wield the baton, but the prophet's mantle surely fell on his successor, for the Strauss of today is in no way inferior to him who ruled the orchestra in 1839.

While recalling the balls and dances of other times, one contrasts the arrangements of the royal entertainments at Buckingham Palace with those given by Her Majesty soon after her accession, in what was then the new royal residence. Prior to that time Court balls, as well as Drawing Rooms and Levées, were held at St. James's Palace, but the entrée to these receptions was strictly limited to the Court circle and the most important and illustrious members of the aristocracy. Very quaint old records and pictures of some of these entertainments are still extant. The reception rooms at Buckingham Palace have been greatly enlarged by the addition of the magnificent ballroom and corridors, an alteration quite essential for the increased and increasing number of guests who are now honoured with a royal invitation. In 1838, and until the extension of the palace in 1853 was completed and the new rooms opened, two of the State apartments were set apart for dancing; a band was stationed in each room so that the dancers were divided; and the fine picture gallery separated the ballrooms. Weippart and Strauss, Jullien and Coote, were among those who played in the palace. Her Majesty and her Court entered the ballroom before ten o'clock, when, choosing a partner, the Queen opened the ball with the first quadrille, and also joined in other dances; later in the evening a move was made to the second ballroom, where Her Majesty finished the ball by leading off a country dance, sometimes as late as three o'clock. The names of Lord Uxbridge and Lord Torrington appear among some of the Court circle who had the honour of being the Queen's partners in the old English dance. Quadrilles and waltzes, with an occasional galop, were danced throughout the evening, until after Her Majesty's marriage in 1840, when the polka appears to have been introduced, and the concluding country dance was omitted. In 1849 a Scotch reel was danced before the Queen, with the bagpipes in attendance, Lord Breadalbane, Lord Douglas, Cluny Macpherson, Dr. Dundas, Lady Charlotte Eliot, Lady Rachel Russell, Miss Kerr, and Miss Baillie forming the set, and the gentleman who took part in it were nearly always those who attended Court in full Highland dress. Reels continued for some years to be danced

APPENDIX IV

at the old palace by those who by virtue of their Scotch blood could really do them justice. A distinctive feature in the Court balls of years gone by was that once or twice during the evening a pause was made in the dancing, and the guests passed by the Queen, as Her Majesty sat on the dais in the Throne Room. Independently of the fact that our Sovereign has been unable for many years to appear at the balls, never having been present since the days of her sad widowhood, the enormous increase in the number of invited guests would make this impossible.

Reference to some old records reveals the fact that a so-called cotillon was known in the reign of George IV. A public breakfast was given by the Prince Regent at Carlton House when 600 guests were present. Nine marquees were erected, and various amusements provided; four bands played during the afternoon; comic entertainments were performed by the best actors of the day, and after refreshment the company danced on a beautiful lawn, his Royal Higness the Prince leading out Lady Waldegrave, and 'all frequently changed partners and grouped into cotillons, all being over by six o'clock'. This is certainly not a cotillon as now understood, though the change of partners tells of some sort of similarity. A good cotillon is often considered a very popular and excellent wide-up dance at a ball. Perhaps one of the most noticeable cotillons ever danced was at the famous ball given by the Brigade of Guards to the Prince and Princess of Wales on June 26, 1863, a ball scarcely ever equalled in magnificence. The second great International Exhibition was over, and the vast building standing empty in Cromwell Road was secured for the entertainment. The decorations and general arrangement were carried out by the committee of officers chosen for the purpose, and with a most brilliantly successful result. The immense galleries were transformed into a series of magnificent reception rooms, one of the largest was devoted to dancing, and on this occasion Mr. Godfrey, the well-known bandmaster, composed his most popular waltz, 'The Guards' Waltz', which was the delight of ball-goers for some years. Notwithstanding the size of the ballroom, it was densely crowded till a very late (or early) hour and a cotillon begun after two o'clock had not finished till the clock had struck five. The numbers who had stayed to join it may be estimated by the fact that chairs all round this enormous room were required to seat the dancers. Like everything else, the cotillon of thirty years ago was very different from that which is now given, where entertaining is on a lavish and extravagant scale. The figures were simple, they could be danced without all the accessories now considered essential, and flowers were almost the only necessary addition. Now all sorts of fanciful figures are introduced from Paris, and on some occasions very expensive presents are provided.

With the immense increase of society and the crowds which fill most London houses, dancing has certainly undergone great changes; it would be quite impossible to dance quadrilles or lancers as was once imperative in good society, and they are now walked through in lazy fashion, even at

APPENDIX IV

Court balls. Waltzing still holds its own; it is quite as popular as when first introduced at Almack's, and it is always a pleasure to watch those who excel in the art when, to the fascinating music written by the best composers, the well-matched couple float by with all the poetry of motion.

One can hardly write of dancing as it was without a few words on what must always be one of the accessories of a dance, now frequently considered as the first necessity—a good supper! Thirty and forty years ago, the mysterious invitation to a 'Thé Dansant' informed the invited guests that only light refreshments would be provided, and it also suggested that the music would not comprise an orchestral band, but the more modest piano and cornet; still, the invitations were accepted, and those who went to dances for dancing's sake were satisfied, which would hardly be the case now that such elaborate suppers are considered the crucial test of a good or bad ball. Whether the art of dancing has deteriorated or the enjoyment of dances has decreased is an open question, and beyond the province of one who only recalls the past and contrasts it with the present, having shared the past and being still an interested spectator.

Chapter XVI

by the Countess of Ancaster

There can be no question that the balls now given in London far excel those of former days in many important particulars. Modern taste and appliances enable hostesses to make a far more picturesque display than was formerly possible. Every detail is considered, and the most is made of the house to conduce to the pleasure and enjoyment of the guests. The use of flowers in the adornment of ballrooms, especially of the beautiful palms which are to be had at a very moderate expense, is quite a modern feature, and a very charming one. Though no light can compare with myriads of wax candles when well protected and well diffused throughout the ballroom, still the electric light of these days has added greatly to the brilliancy and effect, particularly of large halls. Again, the instrumental bands which supply the very music simply vie with one another in the excellence of their performance, and far surpass anything known earlier in the century. Another very important detail contributing to the success of a ball is the supper and wine; and it is the rarest exception when both these are not of the very best, served at round tables in the greatest comfort, instead of there being a scramble for food at a buffet, as often happened in less luxurious days.

Balls given in country houses are quite as well done as in London. The 'stately homes of England' are perhaps even better adapted for the purposes of entertaining than London houses, excepting of course the great establishments, such as Stafford House, Devonshire House, Montagu House, Grosvenor House, and a few others. The public balls in the county towns form a

APPENDIX IV

special part of our county social life, and vary so much that it would be impossible to speak of them as a whole; but when there are parties formed in country houses round about a populous centre, and the lady patronesses and the stewards take pains to make the gatherings a success, this they hardly ever fail to be, and they are looked forward to by the young people of the neighbourhood as the great event of the year. One of the best public balls is the Royal Caledonian Ball, which takes place annually in London for the benefit of Scottish charities. The Duke of Atholl has been treasurer now for many years, and with the assistance of the Lady Patronesses, who get up parties for a reel and fancy quadrille, it has become most popular. It is well done in every way, and the tickets are moderate in price. Vouchers are issued for this ball, a circumstance which recalls the days of Almack's. The Lady Patronesses were so very exclusive when Almack's was the vogue that many stories are told of the methods employed to obtain the longed-for tickets, and of the heart-burnings that arose from the refusal to grant them to one and their bestowal on another. Nothing of this kind happens now. 'Autres temps, autres moeurs.' It would be impossible in these days to go back to the small and select society of the past. Neither, happily, is it necessary to do so, as it would be an extraordinary thing now should any real breach of good manners or decorum occur. We live in an age when there is a general 'levelling up'. All are fairly well mannered, but there is less courtesy than there used to be. People are not sociable, they think too much of their own individual amusement, and for that reason there is a lack of spirit or 'go' at many modern dances.

In spite of all that goes to make balls so delightful, it is doubtful if they are enjoyed by the majority of those present as they used to be, or certainly as much as they might be. Balls may be considered from two points of view—from that of the entertainers and the entertained. It has been stated that no pains are spared by modern hostesses. Never was there more hospitality shown than there is now; indeed the fault is that givers of balls are sometimes too lavish in their invitations, and thus sacrifice the pleasure and comfort of their guests by overcrowding their rooms. Their kind desire is to afford pleasure to a larger number; but it is distinctly a mistake to invite more guests than the rooms will hold. It prevents any dancing that can be called a pleasure; it changes the beauty of the scene to a heated, struggling crush. Dresses are torn, tempers are spoilt. There is a general look of boredom and disappointment where all ought to look bright and cheerful, and what with fewer people might have been a great success becomes a failure. One of the reasons why rooms are so often crowded is that the proportion of ladies and gentlemen is so unequal. It is supposed to be necessary to ask three or even four times as many men as ladies. The reason for inviting a large proportion of gentlemen is very much owing to the constant 'round' dances, so called, and the absence of 'squares'. A propos of this, a very great lady said one evening to a Royal Duchess—both ladies are dead, but they were well known to many still living—'Do you not think, madam, that the manners of the present day have very much deteriorated? The young men come forward, and, instead of asking for the honour of a dance, they say, "Have a square? Dance the next round?"' This offhand style is not perhaps so common as it was a few years back, still the deterioration of manners is very much animadverted upon by those who remember the past generation.

In considering the reason for this overcrowding of rooms, the solid phalanx of black coats to be seen drawn up across the ball-room or filling up the doors is partly the cause of it. This, of course, refers to the average-sized London house, as in the great London palaces the question of numbers hardly matters at all. It people crowd together, it is their own fault; but clearly, when a house is of ordinarily moderate size, the number of guests invited is of the greatest importance; and, though it is necessary to issue a larger proportion of invitations to gentlemen than to ladies, this is overdone. Since quadrilles and lancers have been given up, so also has any regular introducing of partners. It is tiresome to the onlooker to see this phalanx of black coats, mostly composed of quite young men, who naturally know hardly anyone, and then to glance round the room where stand numbers of nice, bright, pretty girls, in front of their chaperons. It is not 'the thing' to introduce. Everyone allows that the introducing of poeple in society is a matter requiring tact and good judgment, and there are many different ways in which it should be done. But that the débutants and débutantes are to be left to a sort of fate or good luck till they get to know a few partners is a stupid and unnecessary custom which ought to be altered. It is well enough for the families who lead in London society, and who can entertain and so make acquaintances as they please; but it makes it very uphill work for those who are not in this fortunate position, and is one of the causes of the dullness of balls and the lack of enjoyment.

At those balls where, besides the host and hostess, there are other members of the family who can introduce partners, make up sets for a quadrille or lancers (not that ugly romp called Margate or Kitchen Lancers, utterly unsuited to a London ballroom), see that those who wish it are taken to supper, and who perform other kind and gracious little acts of the sort, the affair is as cheery and pleasant again as at those melancholy reunions where it seems that everyone is only thinking of his or her own amusement.

Thus far, balls have been considered from the point of view of the 'entertainers', and there is now the side of the 'entertained.' Though to make a ball agreeable there should be people of mature age as well as young, balls are mainly intended for the young people, and for the unmarried members of both sexes. Delightful as it is, and greatly as it enhances the smartness of a ball to see the married ladies taking their turn in the dance, still it is not the business of their lives. Besides the dancing, it is, or ought to be, through the medium of balls that young people become acquainted easily and pleasantly, and, moreover, are introduced to friends of their parents. Balls, particularly in London, are as much wanted for this agreeable side of our social life as they are for the delightful pastime of dancing. It is for this reason that the complete extinction of square dances is so much to be regretted. If there is a quadrille played now, it is with the greatest difficulty that the set is made up. Perhaps eight or ten couples dance it. This makes the ballroom very dull, and quadrilles cannot be introduced with any chance of success unless the young people, more particularly the men, will take the trouble to learn the figures.

Probably square dances were abandoned a few years back because of the great crowd which prevented movement, and there was a disposition to stand instead of joining in the different figures. Unless, therefore, people will take the pains to acquire the knowledge of these very simple figures, so that they may easily, courteously, and pleasantly set through the measure, it would be of no advantage to society to dance them again. If at the Court balls and at the great houses in London it was an understood thing that four or five square dances would be given during the evening, and that it was the wish of the ballgivers that all should join in when possible, they would soon become popular again, and would assist enormously to break up the exclusiveness of the dancing of these days, making the guests feel they have occasionally to join in helping to make it all 'go'. Introductions would be more easily accomplished. Again, numbers of men and a certain number of girls are incapable of waltzing, and it is a great pity they attempt it. The men who do not dance round dances now keep away from balls altogether, or go to swell the black array of lookers-on, and very soon disappear. Those girls who are not good waltzers have little enjoyment, and soon get tired of balls. It would be impossible in writing about balls not to mention the modern custom of sitting-out, which has come into fashion entirely since there have been nothing but constant round dances. Up to a certain point it is good and restful, but it is not very sociable. What would the courtly lords and ladies of old think of us if they saw the manners of these times? No sooner does the music of the waltz or polka come to a conclusion than the man makes a rush for the door, with his partner following behind as best she may, so that a seat may be gained in the balcony on or the most convenient chair in the drawing-room adjoining! The offering of an arm seems to have fallen entirely into disuse, and many of the pretty, though perhaps formal, courtesies of life are passing away. We can hardly be surprised when there is so much competition in all kinds of sport and athletics between ladies and gentlemen. By all means let the ladies enjoy to the full measure of their powers all healthy and health-giving exercise, but there never should be competition between the sexes. It is owing to this that the deference which used to be paid to the weaker by the stronger is no longer given, because no longer demanded. It may be that in some respects there is much now in general intercourse which is better than probably it ever was before; but in writing upon the balls and dancing of the present day it is necessary to review the past, and to compare it with the present time. There is no time and there

APPENDIX IV

can be no age when it will be possible to do without courtesy, or even without ceremony, and, therefore, the ladies should set the fashion, and the manliness and the chivalry of the present age will soon adopt the courtly bow, the courteous deferential ways, which many now living remember in their fathers and grandfathers.

Quiet, stately dancing is the only kind suited to such an occasion as a Court ball. The young generation care for nothing but the wildest waltz or polka. There are at every ball good dancers, but, on the other hand, how many who cannot dance at all! They can hop and jump and make a great display of physical force, but this is not consistent with good taste, and is certainly not dancing. A proper amount of genuine vigour is suitable to such lively dances as Scotch reels; but even in these the steps should be clearly defined and not merely stamped out anyhow. The attempt to introduce theatrical effects into drawing-room dancing is also a great mistake. Movements, airs, and graces which are effective on the stage, when executed by well-trained, naturally graceful performers, are wholly out of place on the polished floor of the ballroom, and certainly not suited to the general requirements of drawing-room dancing, which should be, above all, an amusement in which the many can take part, and not merely an opportunity for the few to show off. Of course the study of fancy or stage dancing, as a study, is sometimes useful, and is now very generally taught as a means of acquiring grace and deportment; but it will be admitted that the due appreciation and feeling for art which enable us to give to every style its own peculiar and legitimate character should also teach us to make the proper and necessary distinction between stage and drawing-room dancing.

'Lookers-on', the proverb says, 'see most of the game.' The perpetual dancers are hardly aware how very unbecoming it is to get hot and overdone. There is so much of beauty and of dignity in quiet, graceful movement, that if the stately old-fashioned dances could be reintroduced it would give great pleasure to those who sit by and watch with interest, even if they no longer take much share in the active business of a ball.

There can be no question that some of the simple square dances, even if only walked through with due regard to time and measure, would be a great social improvement, and would enable many to take part in balls who are now left out in the cold. Why are those people who cannot waltz, who dislike it—which is by no means uncommon among many of the most charming of both sexes—to be debarred from (actively) participating in balls? Some of them try to waltz when quite incapable of the art, and become a terror to their companions. Then there are those who, no longer so young and active as they once were, still, for the sake of good-fellowship, like to take a share in the gay, bright scene in the ballroom, and help to make it pleasant. The 'sitting-out' does not by any means fill up the place which the more sober kind of dancing should occupy. Before closing the subject of square dances it should be added that, to make these a perfect success in a

APPENDIX IV

ballroom, there ought always to be one or two gentlemen at every ball who would help to make up the sets and do other little acts of kindliness. It is impossible for the hostess to be everywhere at once, and a little assistance from members of the family or friends does much to make things pass off well.

With regard to 'round' dancing, there can be but one opinion as to the delight of a waltz danced by a well-matched couple to the strains of one of Strauss's or Waldteufel's or Linka's beautiful tunes. No other dance can be compared to this, and the description of the valse à trois temps by Mr. d'Egville will bring back the recollection of many a happy hour to those who have the gift, and with that the necessary training, to enter thoroughly into it.

With the technical description of dances which completes this chapter my brief essay may conclude, after just one word more has been said as to the manners and style of the present day. It is for us who are taking our part in the world around us to watch that, with all our modern advantages, with the happy state of improved social intercourse that has done so much to raise the moral standard of society, we do not let the good old forms and ceremonies slip away from us altogether. They are the means by which the young are taught most valuable lessons, and, above all, a proper and courteous way of behaving towards those older than themselves.

Dance well if you do it at all; go out into the world; enjoy yourself as best as you can, and all the better because you must remember you have a share in helping towards the enjoyment of others. It seems now to be taken for granted that everyone can dance, and that no teaching is necessary. This book upon dancing will prove the fallacy of this idea. Again, people talk of old-fashioned manners as if good manners ought ever to be out of fashion. There is simply not enough reflection given to these things nowadays, and less care is taken every year in teaching the young numberless thoughtful, courteous acts which go so far to make life better and happier. Are we any the better for letting these things go and taking our lives in such a rush that there is no time for civility? It is in the drawing-rooms of the leaders of society that these things must be found time for, and must be taught and acquired. There still remains much that is pleasant and courteous. Let the present generation keep it up, and leave it as a precious inheritance to those who must succeed them.

On the subject of the tempi to be observed in dance music, I am enabled to add an authoritative word, as it is dictated by that most distinguished composer, Herr Eduard Strauss. In a letter now before me the Austrian musician (after commenting on the untrustworthiness of the metronome because of its tendency to slow down) gives the following scale:—

Valse	.	.	.	76	
Polka	.	.	.	116	Maelzel metronome
Polka-mazurka	.		.	58	
Galop	.	.	.	144	

Appendix V

THE greatest single influence on the style of social dancing after the 1914–1918 war came from the famous American dancers, Irene and Vernon Castle. The following extract from their book, *Modern Dancing*, published in April 1914, describes the style, and movement, and some of the figures which they popularised and developed in the U.S.A. Before long this kind of dancing was enthusiastically adopted in Britain, developing gradually into the style which had become popular in dance schools throughout the world. See also plates 39–44.

III

The One Step — The Castle Walk — The Eight Step — The Spin — The Step Out — The More Difficult Step Out — The One Step Cortez — The Outer Edge — Zig Zag — The Polka Skip — The Wind-Up

Up to the present moment by far the most popular of all dances is the One Step. There are many reasons for its popularity, the chief being that it can be learned in a very little time by any one, old or young, who is able to walk in time to music—and, I might say, by many who cannot. Another reason is because the music is rag-time. People can say what they like about rag-time. The Waltz is beautiful, the Tango is graceful, the Brazilian Maxixe is unique. One can sit quietly and listen with pleasure to them all; but when a good orchestra plays a 'rag' one has simply got to move. The One Step is the dance for rag-time music.

THE ONE STEP

This is the way to dance it: The dancers stand directly in front of each other, the lady's right hand in the gentleman's left. The elbows should be slightly bent, not held out stiffly, like the bowsprit of a boat, as this not only looks awkward, but is uncomfortable and often dangerous to the other dancers. The gentleman's right hand should be a little above the lady's waist-line, more or less over her left shoulder-blade; but this, of course, depends upon the size of the lady. All I would say is: Don't stand too close together or too far apart; be comfortable, and you stand a good chance of

APPENDIX V

looking graceful. The lady's left hand should rest lightly on the gentleman's right shoulder. She should not curl her arm tightly around his. The gentleman usually starts forward and the lady backward—the reason being that the lady is generally more graceful and can go backward with greater ease, and a man can also see where he is going and thus prevent a collision with other couples.

Now to begin with the dance: the gentleman starts forward with his left foot, and the lady steps backward with her right, walking in time to the music. Bear in mind this one important point: When I say walk, that is all it is. Do not shufflle, do not bob up and down or trot. Simply walk as softly and smoothly as possible, taking a step to every count of the music.

This is the One Step, and this is all there is to it. There are very many different figures, but they are in this same strict tempo. It is simply one step—hence its name. I am going to try to explain the different figures, more or less in the order in which they should be learned. This will make the dance comparatively simple even for those who have never tried it—if there are any.

THE CASTLE WALK

First of all, walk as I have already explained in the One Step. Now, raise yourself up slightly on your toes at each step, with the legs a trifle stiff, and breeze along happily and easily, and you know all there is to know about the Castle Walk. To turn a corner you do not turn your partner round, but keep walking her backward in the same direction, leaning over slightly—just enough to make graceful turn and keep the balance well—a little like a bicycle rounding a corner. If you like, instead of walking along in a straight line, after you have rounded your corner, you can continue in the same slanting position, which will naturally cause you do go round in a circle. Now continue, and get your circle smaller and smaller until you are walking around almost in one spot, and then straighten up and start off down the room again. It sounds silly and is silly. That is the explanation of its popularity!

THE EIGHT STEP

The Eight Step is really a Tango step. From the plain One Step, in which both partners are facing each other, the gentleman, who should be walking forward, turns the lady so that she is facing in the same direction as himself. It is not necessary to change the step or to stop walking. They then walk forward two steps on the first step of the figure—the gentleman on his left and the lady on her right. Without loosening the hold any more than is necessary, they both turn on the third step, making a revolution toward the inside. After that the arms, which hitherto have been extended straight in front of them, are at the back, and they look over their elbows. Then they

APPENDIX V

walk two more steps, the lady leading with the left foot, the gentleman with the right foot. On the third beat of the music they turn as before, but this time the movement is toward the outside, and again with only an almost imperceptible loosening of the hold. This brings them to the first position of the step, which they may continue any number of times.

To learn this step correctly a little patience is necessary. I advise doing it very slowly at first, so as to get the exact position of the feet and body. Do not let your partner walk away from you, but keep opposite each other as much as possible, and do not turn abruptly. The figure should be danced in a square. If you take the four walls of the room as your guide, you will find the step much easier to learn. The gentleman should keep his right hand very loosely at the lady's back, so that she can turn with ease.

THE SPIN

This is probably the most important step of all, yet there are very few people who do it correctly. One main point you must bear in mind, and that is only to spin on one foot. A peg-top could not spin well if it had two pegs, and it is the same with us. It is absolutely necessary for both lady and gentleman to use the right foot. Now both these feet must be close together. With the left foot you propel yourself round—the gentleman holding his partner closely and bringing her round with a steady pull.

Of course, I need hardly say that you must keep time to the music. As can be seen by the photograph which illustrates this step (and which, by the way, was taken by flash-light in the 160th part of a second, and shows Mrs. Castle and myself whirling at a very great speed), you can either spin on your toe or your heel. It does not matter which. I personally always spin on my heel on a slippery floor and on my toe on a carpet or 'dead' floor.

THE STEP OUT

This is a step which can be done at any time during the One Step. It is simply stepping out at the side of your partner so that instead of walking in front you are walking a little to the side of each other. I will explain in this way:

The gentleman is walking forward and the lady backward, as in the ordinary One Step. Now the gentleman holds the lady a little distance away from him and steps out to his left so that, without changing the direction at all, his right foot is at the side of her right foot instead of being between her feet. You walk several steps this way, and a half turn or spin to the right will bring you to your original position.

A MORE DIFFICULT STEP OUT

Here is another way of doing this step, which is a little more difficult, but much more effective. In this the gentleman is going backward and the lady

APPENDIX V

forward. Now the gentleman holds the lady a little distance away, and turns her so that she takes a half-turn backward, and he takes a half-turn forward, still going in the same direction as they originally started. The fact of your having held the lady away from you during the turn will have caused you both to be walking at the side of each other instead of in the front—and there you are! A careful study of the reproductions of the moving pictures which illustrate their steps, as well as all other steps described, will make them quite clear.

ONE STEP CORTEZ

This step is somewhat on the order of the Step Out, and the position is just the same. The man steps out to the right side of the lady, starting with his left—1 and 2—swishing the lady to his right. That is, he swings the lady to one side as though pushing her out of the way.

He steps back to the side so that he is in front of her—3 and 4. On 4 his right foot is between the lady's feet. This step can be continued as many times as desired and can be finished with a turn. The lady simply walks backwards from side to side.

THE OUTER EDGE

The regular position is assumed, the man going forward and the lady backward. The man steps out to the right side of the lady with his right foot. He then steps to side with his left, draws the right up to it, completing the Draw to the left. The Draw Step is danced in front of the lady. To do this the man steps to the side, one count—that is, when he crosses his foot over his left. Now he brings the lady directly in front of him, continuing the step in that position the three remaining counts. This step can be combined very easily with any of the other steps, as it is simply a walk. The lady starts backward by crossing the left foot in back of the right. She steps out to the right side with the right, draws the left up to it, completing the Draw Step.

ZIG ZAG

The man starts forward by stepping to the right side of the lady with the right foot. He continues two more steps forward on the right side. He then steps to the left side of the lady, crossing the left in front of the right, continuing forward two more steps, thus giving the effect of rolling from side to side. The lady stepping backward left, crossing it in back of the right, etc. To make it more effective the dancers bend on the first step. This is when the man crosses the right over the left and when he crosses the left over the right.

THE POLKA SKIP

We now come to a little step which is quite new, very effective, and very easy. The gentleman, for the sake of argument, we will say, is Castle walking

APPENDIX V

forward and the lady backward. What happens is this: take a little polka skip, one, two, three to one side, and one, two, three to the other; directly after that continue to walk. It is led into by the gentleman, who gives the lady a slight lift, just before doing the step, which he begins with his left foot, like this:

$$\begin{matrix} 1 & 2 & 3 & 1 & 2 & 3 \end{matrix}$$
Left, right, left; and right, left, right.

These steps are naturally taken to Polka time, which is double time to the ordinary walk. And skip the 1, 2, 3. Do not walk it.

THE WIND-UP

This step, while very simple, is hard to explain. The lady backs away from the man a few steps until her right and his left arm are outstretched at arm's-length in front of them. The gentleman 'turns to left' in the same spot while the lady walks around him at the left side until she comes face to face with him again, which winds her right arm around his neck. In describing this step it loses its charm, but if it is properly done it looks very pretty. As soon as the partners are face to face again they let their hands go and take the same position, with the arms as in the start of the dance.

Appendix VI

BY 1913 the Tango had swept through the U.S.A., Britain and the continent of Europe. Tango teas became a prominent feature of many strata of social life. The following extract from *The Tango and How to Dance it* by Gladys Beattie Crozier and published at the end of 1913 provides an insight into this form of *Thé Dansant*.

CHAPTER X

How to arrange an Informal Tango Tea.
Tango Teas a Delightful Form of Informal Hospitality.
Avoidance of Trouble and Expense entailed by an Evening Dance.
Dancing the Tango in a Small Room.
How to Serve Tea at an Afternoon Dance.
Decorations for a Tango Tea.

The informal 'Tango Tea' comes as a delightful resource alike to the wealthy hostess on the look-out for some new and up-to-date form of entertainment, and to the many hospitable people of smaller means, who have been hitherto prevented from giving any sort of dance owing to the unavoidable cost of a ball supper, with the additional expenditure necessary for wines and extra attendance, besides programmes—for a country dance, where the custom of having them still prevails—and music.

Then an evening dance so often entails much general disturbance created by the clearing out of the dancing room and the supper room, and the vexation caused to the master of the house is great on finding that the hall has been unrecognizably transformed into a series of 'delightful sitting-out places' by his energetic young daughters and their friends, adorned with drawing-room chairs, and cushions placed in twos, while the old oak chest in which he keeps his hat, to say nothing of the umbrella stand, have completely disappeared:

'Never again!' is apt to be the parental decree, when, after weeks of persuasion, he has been at last reluctantly persuaded to let such an entertainment take place—a decision to which he may adhere for years, despite all entreaties.

With the introduction of the 'Thé Dansant' the entertaining difficulty

APPENDIX VI

disappears, for a delightful informal 'dancing tea' can be arranged at a few days notice with little more trouble than that occasioned by an ordinary tea party.

For a 'Thé Dansant' it is not in the least necessary to ask everyone one knows to come on the same day. For a small room, ask only six or eight couples who are 'keen about the Tango', inviting them to come from half-past three or four to half-past six or seven, on the first free Saturday afternoon, in order to get an equal number of men and girls, for, although girls can practise the Tango together, for a party it would not be thought amusing to be forced to do so; and most of the younger men are just now so keen about the Tango that they jump at any invitation bringing a chance to dance it as eagerly as though it were one for golf:

As I have already said, in another chapter, quite a small space can be employed for dancing the Tango, and any ordinary-sized drawing-room if the lighter furniture be removed, and the heavier pieces placed against the wall, will provide ample space for a few couples at least to perform together.

In a small house it is often a good plan to clear out the dining-room, and let the dancing take place there, while tea is served in the drawing-room in the ordinary way. If the dining-room side-table or sideboard is too heavy to be easily lifted out, it may be spread with lemonade and claret cup, and tiny tumblers, and a vase or two of flowers, and so made both useful and ornamental.

A large, old-fashioned square hall, with an oak floor, covered merely with rugs, such as is often found in an old country house or rectory, makes a splendid setting for a Tango tea, the bare floor needing merely to be well wiped over with a damp cloth, and then rubbed over with turpentine, to prevent it from being too slippery. This is the very latest plan for Tango dancing, and it certainly makes it much easier for the dancers to keep their balance when performing the more intricate steps and figures.

Tangos can quite well be danced on a smooth carpet, or a not too slippery drugget, though a parquet or other wooden floor is best.

For a Tango tea, where space allows, the tea should be served at small tables arranged round the dancing floor—bridge tables covered with small white cloths answer the purpose admirably—while small gilt chairs which take up very little room, can be easily hired. If the dancing room is too small to allow of this, however, the tables may be arranged in any annex to the dancing room—a back drawing-room or dining room—where the guests at the foremost row of tea tables can watch the dancers, and all the guests are at least within sound of the music, and can enjoy the general air of gaiety which prevails.

Elaborate floral decorations are not necessary at a Tango tea, as they are for an ordinary evening dance. A few vases of flowers upon the mantelpiece, and a 'trophy' of leaves and berries, or a huge jar of tawny chrysanthemums on the piano, give just the right note of colour, and are all that are required.

Index

Aere, 50
Aerel, 49, 52
Allemande, 32, 63, 74, 121
Ambrosius, Giovanni, 33
Arbeau (Jehan Tabouret), *Orchesography*, 57–59, 61–62, 71–73, 76, 78, 83, 96, 99
Art et instruction de bien danser, L', 34
Assembly room balls, 126–7, 153–4

Bacchus, *see* Dionysus
Bach, J. S., 62, 63, 74, 79, 149
Bal des Ardents, Le, 39
Balet Comique de la Reine, 68–70, 72
Ballet, development of, 19–20, 27, 29, 68–72, 93, 98, 104 *et seq.*
  dress, 105–6
  in opera, 112
  Mazurka, 152
  Polka, 135–6
  Polonaise, 150
  Russian, 114
  Waltzes, 131
  see also under name of individual ballets
Balli, definition of, 29
Ballroom Dance Magazine, 157
Ballroom dancing, 50, 52, 75, 139, 161 *et seq.*
Balls, *see* Assembly room balls; Chelsea Arts Ball; Civic Balls; County Balls; Court dancing; Fancy dress balls; Shakespeare Ball; Social dancing; State Balls; Waterloo Ball

Barn Dance, 172, 190
Bassa Danse (Danza), 28–29, 33, 35–37, 44, 51–52, 54, 58–59
Bathyllus, 14
B.B.C., television of ballroom dancing, 192–3
Beauchamps, Charles, 105–6
Beggar's Opera, 114
Bellincioni, writes on court dancing in Italy, 39–40
Boston, *see* Two Step
Botticelli, 45–46
Bourrée, 85–87, 106, 121
Brahms, J., 131
Branle, 51, 59–60, 70, 73, 76, 78
British Association of Teachers of Dancing, 171
Byron, Lord, writes on the *waltz*, 129, 189

Caledonians, 144, 192
Camargo, Marie, 104, 114
Can Can, 134
Canaries, 63
Candombe, 179
Caroso, Fabritio, *El Ballerino*, 71, 96
Castle, Irene and Vernon, *Modern Dancing*, 164, 175–7, 220–4
Caverly, Thomas, 107
Cellarius, 136–7
Cerrito, Fanny, 136
Cha Cha Cha, 189, 194
Chaconne, 87–88, 106
Chadimova, Anna, 134–5
Chain dance form, 44–45

INDEX

Chelsea Arts ball, 173–4
Chopin, F., 131, 138, 149–50, 152
Choral dance, 88
Church views on dancing, 16–18
Civic ball, Milwaukee, 172–3
Clochette, 70
Closson, Ernest, facsimile edition of the 'Golden' Manuscript
Commedia dell 'Arte, growth, 12, 14
Competition dancing, 186–7, 192, 195
Comus, 92–93
Contredanse, 110–11, 125, 127, 140, 145
Copelande, Robert, *Manner of dancynge of bace daunces after the use of Fraunce*, 35, 59
Coppelia, 46, 150, 152
Coralli, Eugene, 135–6
Cornazano, Antonio, 33, 35, 47, 49–51
Cotillon, 88–89, 110, 113, 127, 145–146, 161, 171
Country dancing, 110, 113, 117, 121, 125, 127, 138, 140
Courante, 61–63, 74, 78
Court dancing, 21–22, 32, 37–40, 53 *et seq.*, 112, 138
  see also Elizabethan Court; Social dancing
County balls, 161
Couperin, François, 62
Cretan civilization, dancing in, 5–6
Crozier, Gladys Beattie, *The Tango and How to Dance It*, 179–81, 225–6
Czechoslovakia, origin of the *Polka*, 134–5

d'Albert, Charles, 145
d'Egville, Louis, 126
da Vinci, Leonardo, 41–42, 44
Dance of Savages, 24, 39, 201–4

Dances, *see* Palais de danse; Private dances; Subscription dances; Tea dances *and* under individual names and countries
Dancing, art of, 48
  as a profession, 104
  attacks on, 21, 65, 115, 154–6
  clubs, 181
  competitions, 186–7, 192, 195
  education, 6, *see also* Dancing teachers
  Egyptian, 4–5
  formation, 70, 193
  Greek, 3, 5–11
  history of, 1 *et seq.*
  literature of, 33 *et seq.*
  military, 7
  morals of, 101–2
  Morris, 46
  music for, 36–37, 53, 61–62, 67, 74, 166 *et seq.*
  notation, 17, 27–28, 104 *et seq.*
  old time, 191–2
  Peasant, 30–31
  primitive, 2, 3, 20
  profane, 7–11
  professional, 75
  rhythm of, 3–4, 76
  ritual, 6
  Roman, 11–16
  sacred, 7
  sequences, 37
  suppression of, 16
  views of the Church on, 16–18
  village, 21
  see also Ballet; Ballroom dancing; Balls; Country dancing; Court dancing; Masque; Mime; Social dancing *and* under individual dances and countries
Dancing teachers, development of, 30, 33, 48, 54, 103 *et seq.*, 161–2
  professional associations of, 171 *et seq.*

INDEX

Dancing Times, The, 162, 169, 182
Danze de la Muerte, La, 35
Davies, Sir John, *Orchestra*, 61, 92
de Arena, Antonius, 59
  Ad Compagnonies qui sunt de persona friantes bassas dansa et branles practicantes, 71
de Beaujoyeux, Baltazar (Baldassarino da Belgiojoso), 67–68
de Lauze, F., *Apologie de la Danse*, 96–100
de Medici, Catherine, revives court balls in Italy, 39–40, 59
  sponsors court entertainment, 67–69
de Moroda, Derra, 33
de Saint-Mery, Moreau, *American Journey*, 118
de Sévigné, Madame, 86
Delibes, L., 150
di Piacenza, Domenico, 28–29, 33, 50
Dickens, Charles, *Bleak House*, 120–1
Dictionnaire de Trevour, 55
Dionysus, dances concerned with, 9–10
Dodworth, Allen, *Dancing and Its Relation to Education and Social Life*, 156–7
Dolmetsch, Mabel, 46, 62
  Dances of England and France: 1450–1600, 58–59
Domenico di Piacenza, *see* di Piacenza, Domenico
Dorian, civilization, importance of the dance, 6–7
Double, 52
Douce manière, 73, 110
Drehtanz, 128
Dress, change in style of, 104–5, 124–5
  retention of hats by men in ballroom dancing, 52
Dufort, *Trattato de Ballo Nobile*, 110
Duryea, Oscar, 183–4

Ebreo, Guglielmo (William the Jew), 33
  Fundamentals of the dance, 47–51
Ecossaise, 125
Education for dancing, *see* Dancing teachers
Egypt, dancing in ancient, 4–5
Elizabethan Court, dancing, 57, 63, 111
  spectacles, 24–25
  see also Court dancing; England; Social dancing
Emmeleia, 7
Encyclopaedia Britannica, 165
Endymatia, 8
England, country dancing in, 111
  development of dancing in, 23–26, 47, 54 *et seq.*
  modern style ballroom dancing in, 164 *et seq.*
  Morris dancing in, 46
  quadrille first danced in, 140 *et seq*
  waltz first danced in, 128
Entrée, 106
Essex, J., 108
Evans, Edwin, 138–139

Fancy dress balls, 173–4
Farandole, 13
Fashion, *see* Dress
Feuillet, Raoul Auger, *Choregraphie*, 106
Fokine, Michel, 131, 152
Formation dancing, 70, 193
Fowler, H. W. & F. G., *Of Pantomime*, 8
Fox, Harry, 183–4
Foxtrot, 74, 166, 168, 183–4
France, dancing in, 26–27, 35, 37–39, 51–52, 54 *et sea.*, 112
  influence of, 75
  quadrille in, 142 *et seq.*
  tango, in, 186
  waltz in, 128

Q 229

INDEX

French Revolution, 77, 80, 105, 113, 122, 124-5, 130, 133

Galliard, 55-56, 73, 76
Galop, 134, 147, 161
Gautier, Theophile, 150-1
Gavotte, 70, 76-78, 86, 121-2, 126
Germany, dancing in, 31-32, 64 et seq.
   development of the *waltz*, 128
Gigue, 63-64, 74, 79, 89, 106
Ginner, Ruby, *Gateway to the Dance*, 7, 10-11
Giselle, 135, 136
Golden manuscript, *see Manuscrit des basses danses de la Bibliothèque de Bourgogne, le*
Greek civilization and the dance, 3, 5-11
Grisi, Carlotta, 136
Guest, Ivor, *Victorian Ballet Girl*, 136
Gymnopoedia, 8

Handel, G. F., 74, 79, 149
Hart, Joseph, 143
Helpmann, Robert, 108
Hofer, Mari Ruef, *Polite and Social Dances*, 77, 79
Homer, refers to Pyrrhic dances, 8
   refers to Roman dancing, 13-14
Hornpipe, 83
Horst, Louis, *Pre-Classic Dance Forms*, 79, 83, 87
Humphrey, Walter, 169
Hyporchema, 8

Imperial Society of Teachers of Dancing, 171, 183
International Council of Ballroom Dancing, 188, 195
Italy, court dancing in, 39-46
   development of the dance in, 28-29, 31, 35, 56 et seq.

Jazz, 166 et seq.
Jig, *see Gigue*
Jitterbug, 155, 189
Jive, 189, 194
Jones, Inigo, 92, 94
Jonson, Ben, masques devised by, 94
Jota, 63
Jullien, Louis Antoine, 143

Karsavina, T., 131, 139
Kinkeldy, Dr. Otto, *A Jewish Dancing Master of the Renaissance*, 33, 49, 51
Kirstein, Lincoln, *Dance: a short history of classical theatrical dancing*, 15, 20, 109

Laborde, Monsieur, 145-6
Lancers, 143-5, 157, 161, 172, 190, 192
Landler, 64-65, 128
Lannar, Joseph, 131
Lawes, Henry, 92
Legat, Nicholas, 150
Lehar, Franz, 132
Lenau, Nicholas, *Der Steyrertanz*, 65
Lifar, Serge, 75
Liszt, F., 151
Lucian, writes on the dance, 8, 13
Lully, J. B., 105, 112, 126
Lycurgus, on dancing and education, 3

Maniera, 49
Manuscrit des basses danses de la Bibliothèque de Bourgogne, Le ('Golden' Manuscript), 33, 36-37
Maria, Mlle., 136
Marks, Joseph, E. III., *America Learns to Dance*, 117, 155
Masque, 23, 67, 92-95
   see also Comus
Mattheson, *The Perfect Conductor*, 77, 86, 89
Maxixe (*Maxina*), 175-6, 181-2

INDEX

Mazurka, 147, 151–3
Memoria, 49
Memphitic dance, 9
Mercantina, La, 29
Mersenne, Father, 77, 96
Michel, Arthur, *Dance Magazine of America*, 135
Military dances, 8
Military two step *see* Two step
Milton, John, 75
   Comus, 92–93
Mime, 14, 20, 29
   development in court entertainment, 60
   panto—, 114
Minuet, 61, 63, 78–81, 106, 110, 113, 117, 121–2, 125–7
Miracle plays, 22
Misura, 49
Moresque, 46
Morley, Thomas, describes the *courante*, 61
Morris dancing, 46
Mosheim, *Ecclesiastical History*, 19
Movement and art, 26–27
Movemento Corporeo, 50
Musetta, 77
Music, development for dancing, 36–37, 61–62, 74
   jazz development, 166 *et seq.*
   printing of, 53
   symphonic, 67
Musical Quarterly, 29

Negri, Cesare, 57–58
   Le Gratie d'Amore (revised and called *Nuovi inventioni di Ballo*), 71–72
Negro dancing, 119, 178–9
Neruda, Jesep, 135
Nettl, Paul, *The Story of Dance Music*, 89–90, 135, 144
Nijinsky, V., 131
Nizzarda, La, 57

Noverre, Jean Georges, 107, 114
   Les Lettres sur la Danse et sur le Ballet, 71

Official Board of Ballroom Dancing, 188, 191–2
Old time dancing, 191–2
One Step, The, 165, 175–8, 183, 220–4
Opera ballet, 112
Orchestras, development of, 30

Pageant, 23–24
   see also Masque; Miracle plays; Tournament
Palais de danse, 154, 187
Pantomime, *see* Mime
Paradiso, Il, 41–42, 44
Partire del terreno, 49
Paspe *see* Passepied
Passacaglia, 88, 106
Passepied, 83–85, 121
Pavane, 54–55, 59, 63, 81, 122, 126
Peasant dancing, 30–31
Pemberton, *An Essay for the Further Improvement of Dancing*, 122
Perrot, Jules, 136
Perugini, Mark E., *Pageant of the Dance and Ballet*, 108
Petipa, Lucien, 135
   Marius, 135
Piva, 28, 32, 47
Plato, interpretation of Egyptian dance movements, 5
   on the pursuit of the dance, 3, 7
Playford, 88, 95
   The Dancing Master, 84–85, 110, 117
Plutarch, writes on military dances, 8
Poland, introduction of the *Polonaise*, 149
Polka, 133–9, 157–8, 161, 172, 205–7
Polka Enseignée San Maître, La, 136
Polonaise, 89–90, 147, 149–152

231

INDEX

Ponsonby, Loelia (Duchess of Westminster), *Grace and Favour*, 185
Porter, Evelyn, *Music through the Dance*, 90
Primitive dancing, 2–3, 20
Printing, development of and its effect on music, 53
Private dances, 161
Profane dances, 7–11
Professional dancing, 75
Professional partners, 137
Public dance halls, 161–2
  see also Palais de danse
Punch, cartoon on the *Boston*, 170
  satirizes the *Polka*, 138
Purcell, Henry, 79
Puritans, their effect on dancing, 95–96
Pylades, 14
Pyrrhic dances, 8, 144

Quadernaria, 28
Quadrille, 89, 138, 140–147, 161, 171
Quickstep, 168–9
Quirey, Belinda, 51, 80

Ragtime, 166
Rameau, Jean Philipe, 62, 112
  Pierre, 118; *Le Maître à Danser*, 107–9
Reels, Scotch, 125
Religious dancing *see* Sacred dancing
Reprise, 52
Révérence, 51
Rhythm, 3–4, 76
Rich, John, 108, 113–14
Richardson, P. J. S., 34, 143, 152–3, 164
  The History of English Ballroom Dancing, 184
  The Social Dances of the Nineteenth Century, 127, 133, 165–6
Richepin, Jean, 178
Rigaudon, 82–83, 86, 121

Ritual dancing, 6
Roman dancing, 11–16
Russia, dancing in, 114, 128, 152

Sachs, Curt, *World History of the Dance*, 36, 44, 46, 55, 73, 83, 132–3, 164
Sacred dancing, 7
Sacred music, 21
Sailors' Hornpipe, 83
St. Augustine, on the dance, 17–18
St. Chrysostom, on the dance, 18
Saint-Leon, Arthur, 136
Salian dances of ancient Rome, 11
Salomo, Hacen be, 27
Saltarello, 28–29, 36–37
Sarabande, 74, 79, 81–82, 106
Scholes, Percy, *Oxford Companion to Music*, 132, 153, 179
Schuhplatter, 63
Schumann, R., 131
Scott, Edward, 148–9, 170
  Dancing as an Art and Pastime, 140–143, 144–5
Scottish music and dancing, 125
Seises, Les, 47
Set dances, *see Quadrille*
Shakespeare ball, 173–5
Sharpe, Cecil and Oppe, A. P., *The Dance*, 125
Silvester, Victor, 187–8, 192–3
Simple, 52
Siri, Eros Nicola, 178
Sleeping Beauty, The, 150
Smetana, B., 138
Social dancing, 14–15, 20, 23, 53 et seq., 208–19
  as professional entertainment, 75
  breakdown in formality of, 112
  development in twentieth century of, 163 et seq.
  literature of, 34
  organisation of, 117
  see also Court dancing

232

INDEX

Socrates, opinion of the dance, 3
Spain, dancing in, 32, 55 et seq.
   literature of dancing, 35
   Moresca, 46
   Pavane, 55
Spectator, The, attack on the dance, 101
Spectre de la Rose, Le, 131
State balls, 161, 174
Strauss, Johann, 131
Stravinsky, Igor, 76
Subscription dances, 170–1
Swan Lake, 150, 152
Sylphides, Les, 131, 152

Taglioni, Marie, 113
Tango, 168, 178–81, 185–6, 225–6
Taylor, Cecil H., 171
Tchaikovsky, P., 150
Tea dances, 180–1
Teaching of dancing, *see* Dancing teachers
Television, 70, 192–3
Times, The, attacks the *waltz*, 129
Tourdion, see *Saltarello*
Tournaments, 22
Trihory, see *Passepied*
Triomphe de L'Amour, Le, 105
Twist, The, 155, 189
Two Step, 161, 165, 171
   Boston, 164–5, 169–70, 172, 175, 181
   Military, 175, 190, 192

U.S.A., attacks on morality of dancing, 154–6
   ballroom dancing in, 164 *et seq.*
   development of dancing, 114–16
   jazz in, 167 *et seq.*

Veleta, 171–2, 175, 190, 192
Verspuy, Marius, of Auvergat, 87
Viennese waltz, 131
   see also *Waltz*
Village dancing, 21
Volta, La, 56–58, 66, 73, 128, 130

Waltz, 64, 80, 127–34, 138–9, 141, 147, 156–7, 161, 163, 165, 169, 171, 172, 184, 189, 190, 192
Weaver, John, 108–9, 113, 118
   Anatomical and Mechanical Lectures, 107
   Essay towards an history of Dancing, 107
Weber, Carl Maria, *The Invitation to the Dance*, 130–1
Welsford, Enid, *The Court Masque*, 93
Whiteman, Paul, 167
Wickham, Glynne, *Early English Stages 1300 to 1660*, 24
Wildeblood, Joan, 51, 96
Wood, Melusine, 46, 51